The Ultimate Beatles Quiz Book

The Ultimate Beatles Quiz Book

Michael J. Hockinson

St. Martin's Press
New York

Library of Congress Cataloging-in-Publication Data

Hockinson, Michael J.
    The ultimate Beatles quiz book / Michael J. Hockinson.
        p.   cm.
    ISBN 0-312-07104-3
    1. Beatles—Miscellanea.   2. Rock musicians—England—
Biography.
    I. Title.
    ML421.B4H6   1992
    782.42166'092—dc20   91-33833
                                                                   CIP

The inclusion of photographs of bootleg or counterfeit recordings and/or the associated jackets of such recordings in this volume should not be construed or interpreted as an endorsement of the practice of record piracy on the part of the author or the publisher.

First published in the United States of America under the title *Nothing is Beatleproof* by Popular Culture, Ink.

First U.S. Paperback Edition: January 1992
10 9 8 7 6 5 4 3 2 1

To Beve

For putting up with index cards all over the kitchen table,
Late night typing and expletives deleted,
The emotional ups and downs of writing a book.

For your ceaseless encouragement and suggestions -
For all the calls above and beyond,
This book is for you.

(B. I. L.Y.)

THANK U VERY MUCH

Ann Adams, George Anisowicz, Barbara Beden, Richard Brautigan, Jovi Carlyle, Paul DiTomasso, Ken Doop, Archer Dusablon, Erik Engelke, Stan Foreman at "Capitol," Sylvia Giustina, Dianne Hollen, Connerton Kiggins, Bill King, Jeffery Lanners, Randy Lauer, Mark Lewisohn, Dalana Lyn, Lowell MacGregor, Maurina Manning, James Marks, Roxie and Heather Martin, Patti Mecham, Tim Mertz, Karen Pederson, Wally Podrazik, Tracy Price, Elizabeth Racy, Janet Ragsdale, Jewelie Randall, Joyce Sanderson, Tom Schultheiss, Tim Simmons, Mitzi (Tilbrook) Thomas, Kimo Tichgelaar, and Jon & Liz Trietsch.

THE GEORGE S. PATTON AWARD (SPECIAL TANKS)

To Mother Mary - speaking words of wisdom. To Donald, me No.1 Dad and Pat (Homeboy!), me bro. To my grandmother, Helen Kiggins McAleer.

To Maria Larson - thank you for sharing many things with me, including my first Beatlefest, Chicago, 20-22 August 1982.

The Wheel Watcher. The Bluebird. The Quiet Fab. The Greatest.

PREFACE

Carol D. Terry's exhaustive Beatles bibliography, *Here, There & Everywhere* (another Popular Culture, Ink. title, originally published by Pierian Press, 1985) lists six different trivia tomes (five books and one board game) published between 1964 and 1984. A playing card format trivia game published since Terry's book brings the total to seven. So, why would I go to all the trouble (over five year's worth) to prepare an eighth entry in the Beatles trivia sweepstakes, one that the esteemed folks at Popular Culture have christened the maiden entry in their new Trivia Series?

When I decided that the first book I wanted to write should be a Beatles book, I gave a lot of thought to selecting the area relating to the group to which I felt I could bring a fresh approach. As Hunter Davies, Nicholas Schaffner, and Philip Norman seemed to have the biographical angle covered (though that's not stopped anyone yet), and Harry Castleman and Wally Podrazik have the discographical aspect under wraps (with three fine titles published by Popular Culture), I decided to take a look at Beatles trivia, an area that has challenged and perplexed me since I won my first Beatlefest trivia quiz in Chicago in 1983.

I felt that the Beatles trivia quiz books in print at the time were either too easy to be a real challenge to the hardcore fan, or were too sterile in their presentation of Beatle facts. Most appeared to be written more with "the quick buck" in mind rather than out of any real love for the group and their music.

Fate had a big part to play in the writing and publishing of this book. As each draft was typed, submitted, reviewed and revised, events conspired to make information available to me at the time I most needed it.

The best example of this is the access I had to Mark Lewisohn's superb Beatle "bibles," *The Beatles Live!* and *The Beatles: Recording Sessions*, both published during the final months spent revising the final draft of this book. *The Ultimate Beatles Quiz Book* reflects all the new facts and correct dates introduced to Beatles history because of the diligent efforts of Mr. Lewisohn. I am pleased to be one of the first authors to benefit from his research; I owe him a great debt of thanks.

The results of my labors are before you now—a challenging series of questions with answers that offer a little bit extra in the way of Beatles lore. *The Ultimate Beatles Quiz Book* was written by a Beatle fan for Beatle fans. It is my hope that the facts presented here are of some interest and substance; long after you have met the book's initial challenge, you may find it a useful reference tool (one reason St. Martin's Press has included four great indexes in the back).

Every effort has been made to create a book that's the "Toppermost of the Poppermost." Should you come across what you think is an error, I'd welcome your correspondence, sent to my attention care of St. Martin's Press. Please include any relevant documentation, if possible.

We hope you will enjoy the show.

M.J.H.

FOREWORD

Greetings Fab Four fanciers! Welcome to another tremendous tome from Beatles Book HQ, Ann Arbor! Glad we could entice you to take the trivia challenge!

After being offered many different Beatles trivia manuscripts for possible publication over the past fifteen years, *The Ultimate Beatles Quiz Book* is the one we chose to start off our new Trivia Series with a Bang! We hope it makes the same impression on you that it made on us, and that you'll welcome it as a new and valued addition to your Beatles library.

Old habits die hard, so we've given up trying to change and have instead just worked a series of four reference features—indexes, yes, I'll just go ahead and say the word—into our first (gulp!) "trivia" book. We just couldn't help ourselves. Yup, it's true we already have a separate "Reference Series," so why are we being soooo serious about a pop culture fad format like "trivia"?! Well, why would any publisher in the world (us!)) enjoy the singular distinction of having published twenty-one books on the Beatles (with more Fab Four titles on the way)?! Think about it.

The reason is because both the trip and arrival at the end are great fun, formal trappings aside, and *The Ultimate Beatles Quiz Book* is nothing if not fun right down to its (Apple) core. Indexes? Well, why not. Think of them as the place where you can go and do a quick scan for an answer...er, search for clues that will help you formulate an answer...without feeling guilty about actually looking up the answer! There you go.

After a brief preface by the author, it will be time to get into the spirit of things. As you'll notice, Mike sure does, so just follow his lead! Break out that Blue Meanie Halloween costume, synchronize your "Yellow Submarine" watch, fill up your Beatles lunch box and thermos, set aside about...oh, four or five days, and get ready for a non-stop whirl through backwoods Beatledom.

(Oh, yeah, if you happen to finish before the rest of us, there are even more questions to keep you busy! Pick any date in the Date Index and see if you can remember what of Beatles note happened on that day! Then just follow the page reference back to the answer. Say, why do you think we printed all those dates the way we did throughout the book?! Hard not to notice, huh!)

Tom Schultheiss

CONTENTS

LIST OF ILLUSTRATIONS

Advertisements & Posters

Books & Booklets

Recording Sleeves

Miscellaneous

CHAPTER 1

A Love That Lasts Forever

Welcome to Beatles Trivia 102! I'm glad you've all elected to take the class. Now, I'm going to assume you're already aware of who the Beatles' drummer was before Ringo, that "Scrambled Eggs" was the working title for "Yesterday," and that the last album the Fabs recorded was called **Abbey Road**, so we'll dispense with those questions straight away. This book will be a bit harder than trivia texts you've read in the past; there will be no fill-in-the-blank responses, no multiple choice quizzes, and you can slap my wrists if you see even one true/false question in any of the next fifty chapters. I've gathered my questions and answers from literally hundreds of different and ofttimes obscure sources; I'm hoping that by the time you're done working your way through this book even some of you hardcore fans will have learned something about the Beatles that you didn't already know.

Let's start off with a quiz on Beatles songs and composers.

1. List the titles of the songs on the Beatles' Decca audition tape penned by Lennon and McCartney.

2. Issued nearly twenty years apart, which U.S. Beatles singles feature "I'm Happy Just To Dance With You" as their B-sides?

3. For a short time in early 1966, four Beatles songs - "What Goes On," "Nowhere Man," "If I Needed Someone," and "Drive My Car" - were restricted from radio airplay in the U.S. even though "The Beeb" was allowed to play the songs in England. Why was that?

4. Name five songs and/or melodies excerpted within the Beatles' summer of love anthem, "All You Need Is Love."

5. In December of 1969, John had planned to release "You Know My Name (Look Up The Number)" (eventually tagged for the backside of "Let It Be"), as the A-side of a Plastic Ono Band single. What would have been that single's flipside?

6. Which song was included on "The White Album" because Pattie Harrison liked it?

7. During filming for "Let It Be," what song by the Animals did the Beatles ruthlessly parody?

**The Beatles' Minneapolis, Minnesota, press
conference, 21 August 1965.
Previously unpublished photo by Dalana Lyn.**

8.   According to dialogue on the "Let It Be" movie soundtrack, who is the composer of "(Can You) Dig It" [sic]?

9.   Which songs on the "Let It Be" movie soundtrack have never been released on record except on bootlegs?

10.   Name three songs from the unreleased **Get Back** LP that were not issued, in any form, on the **Let It Be** album.

11.   Name the songs recorded during the Beatles' 30 January 1969 session atop the roof of 3 Savile Row to make it onto the **Let It Be** album.

12.   According to dialogue on the **Let It Be** LP, which song does John announce will be the Beatles' next, following his improvisational song, "Dig It"?

13.   Which Beatles song borrowed lyrics from the Merseys' hit, "Sorrow"?

14.   What was the first Beatles song to be recorded at Abbey Road studios on a four-track machine?

15.   What were the titles of the songs on the first Beatles single issued in France?

16.   List (in order) the songs comprising "The Beatles' Movie Medley."

17.   What is on the B-side of promotional copies of "The Beatles' Movie Medley"?

18.   Name two songs the Beatles recorded and released that are in the public domain (P.D.).

19.   How many songs released by the Beatles have been credited as having been written by all four members? Please list their titles.

20.   Name the song(s) the Beatles have released that feature reprises later in their respective album(s).

21.   What is the title of the first song Geoff Emerick engineered for George Martin and the Beatles?

22.   List all the instrumental tracks that the Beatles have released.

23.   John, Yoko, and George have all been sued at various times in their careers for copyright infringement. Name the song each wrote and the song it allegedly infringed upon.

24.   John and Paul have both written completely different songs using the same title. What is that title?

25.   Which Beatle released a solo album containing songs whose publishing rights are assigned under the company name "Wobble Music, Ltd."? What is the title of the album these songs are on?

**A LOVE THAT LASTS FOREVER
(ANSWERS)**

---

1.   Lennon and McCartney songs from the Decca audition tapes of 1 January 1962 include "Hello Little Girl," "Love Of The Loved," and "Like Dreamers Do."

2.   "I'm Happy Just To Dance With You" is the B-side of "I'll Cry Instead" (1964) and "The Beatles' Movie Medley" (1982).

3.   Though they appeared on the British version of **Rubber Soul**, released 3 December 1965, these songs were left off the U.S. version. Airplay was restricted because they had not yet been officially released in the U.S. All four songs were included on the **"Yesterday"...And Today** LP, released 20 June 1966.

4.   "All You Need Is Love" borrows from the French national anthem, "La Marseillaise," a Bach Two-Part Invention in F, Glenn Miller's "In The Mood," "Greensleeves," and "She Loves You."

5.   "You Know My Name (Look Up The Number)" was once slated for release under John's Plastic Ono Band moniker as the A-side of U.K. Apple single APPLES 1002. Its B-side would have been "What's The New Mary Jane."

Q & A #16

6. A portion of "Wild Honey Pie" was included on "The White Album" because Pattie Harrison liked it.

7. During the filming of "Let It Be," in a segment not included in the final edited version, John and Paul take great pleasure in parodying "House Of The Rising Sun."

8. "(Can You) Dig It" was written by Georgie Wood.

9. "Suzy Parker," "Besame Mucho," "Shake, Rattle And Roll," and a medley of "Kansas City"/"Lawdy Miss Clawdy" are included on the "Let It Be" movie soundtrack, but were left off the official album.
   (Also not released, a rather amnesic rendition of Smokey Robinson's "You Really Got A Hold On Me," and an extended version of "Dig It.")

10. Songs included on the **Get Back** LP, but omitted from the **Let It Be** album include an instrumental link entitled "Rocker"; "Save The Last Dance For Me," and "Teddy Boy."
   ("Teddy Boy" later showed up on Paul's **McCartney** album.)

11. Rooftop renditions of "I've Got A Feeling," "One After 909," and "Dig A Pony" were included on the **Let It Be** album.

12. "Hark, The Herald Angels Come."

13. "It's All Too Much"
   ("With your long blonde hair and your eyes of blue.")

14. The Beatles' first four-track recording was "I Want To Hold Your Hand."

15. The French, rather fond of EPs, got their first Beatles 45 rpm in 1967 when EMI-Odeon released "All You Need Is Love" b/w "Baby You're A Rich Man."

16. The songs comprising "The Beatles' Movie Medley" are "Magical Mystery Tour," "All You Need Is Love," "You've Got To Hide Your Love Away," "I Should Have Known Better," "A Hard Day's Night," "Ticket To Ride," and "Get Back."

17. Paul, George and Ringo talk about their first movie, "A Hard Day's Night," in "Fab Four On Film," the B-side of the Beatles' "Movie Medley" promotional single.

18. Two songs recorded by the Beatles in the public domain are "Maggie Mae" (from **Let It Be**) and "The Saints" (featuring Tony Sheridan on vocals.)

19. All four Beatles are credited as the composers of "Flying" and "Dig It."
   (Though not yet generally released commercially, the song "Christmas Time (Is Here Again)," the basis for the group's 1967 fan club Christmas message, also shares its composer credits among all four Beatles.)

20. "Sgt. Pepper's Lonely Hearts Club Band" is the only song the Beatles released featuring a reprise.

21. The first Beatles song Geoff Emerick engineered was "Tomorrow Never Knows" for the **Revolver** LP, 6 April 1966.

22. The Beatles' instrumental cuts are "Cry For A Shadow" (from the May 1961 Tony Sheridan/Beatles session) and "Flying" (included on **Magical Mystery Tour**).

23. John - "Come Together" /"You Can't Catch Me"
   (John covered the latter song, made famous by his idol, Chuck Berry, on his **Rock 'N' Roll** album.)

   Yoko - "Yes I'm Your Angel"/"Makin' Whoopee"
   ("Makin' Whoopee" was written in 1928 by Gus Kahn and Walter Donaldson; it was covered by Beatles fellow traveler Harry Nilsson on his RCA album **A Little Touch Of Schmilsson In The Night.**)

   George - "My Sweet Lord"/"He's So Fine"
   (The latter song was made famous by the Chiffons.)

24. "Woman"
   (Paul gave Peter and Gordon his "Woman," which they recorded at Abbey Road studios in December 1965. McCartney's composer credit for the resulting single, released in the U.S. the following Janu-

ary, was listed under the pseudonym "Bernard Webb." John's "Woman" was written for his **Double Fantasy** album, released in November 1980.)

25.   Ringo Starr co-wrote several of the songs on his **Old Wave** album under the publishing banner of "Wobble Music, Ltd."
      (Starr formed Wobble Music Ltd. on 26 July 1973.)

CHAPTER 2

HEY MISTER,
CAN WE HAVE OUR BALL BACK!

Ah, the Beatles' first movie, "A Hard Day's Night" - wasn't it the gear? Y'know, the big hammer, smashing! Remember the scene on the train where Paul and Audrey have a tug-of-war over Grandfather while George and John egg them on? You don't? How about the scene where Paul pretends he's bullfighting with an executive's limosine? No? Well, surely you remember Paul's big solo scene where he chats up this young bird...er... actress in the rehearsal room, right?

Don't feel bad if you can't remember these scenes: they were cut from the final script, don't ye know! The following questions, however, were drawn from scenes included in AHDN. Don't be working like a dog answering them, okay?

1. List all of Pattie Boyd's lines in AHDN.

2. Early on in the film, Ringo confides to George that he has an inferiority complex. What activity did he describe as his "active compensatory factor"?

3. Following the Beatles' escape from their fans at London's Paddington Train Station, the screen is briefly filled by the sleeve from this LP which, as the camera pulls back, we see is being inspected by Paul's grandfather (played by Wilfred Brambell). What is the title of this album?

4. Among the fan club mail which Ringo is deluged with when the boys reach their hotel is an invitation to this club's gaming rooms, which Paul's grandfather graciously accepts. What is the name of this "gambling den," as Grandfather called it?

5. How does Shake (played by John Junkin) get past the gambling club's attendant in order to assist the Beatles in retrieving "Lord John McCartney"?

6. Who thought up the shaving scene between George and Shake?

7. Who is Simon Marshal?

8.   When Paul's grandfather first appears through the stage trap door, what scene does he disrupt?

9.   Name the performer with ten (soon to be nine) disappearing doves.

10.   Who are Charley's mates? (Charley is the boy who owns the tire that Ringo collides with while he is out "parading.")

11.   During the pub scene, what games does Ringo play or disrupt?

12.   Where are the Beatles headed in their helicopter as the movie concludes?

13.   What play did the Beatles see Victor Spinetti in that convinced them he should be in AHDN?

14.   How did it happen that Pattie Boyd came to audition for a role in AHDN?

15.   Which song sequence was the first to be filmed?

16.   Who was dubbed the White Rabbit?

17.   On 6 July 1964, the London Pavilion at Piccadilly Circus hosted the Royal World Premiere of "A Hard Day's Night." Attended by Princess Margaret and the Earl of Snowdon, what two charities did monies from this premiere benefit?

18.   "Village Voice" critic Andrew Sarris, in his introduction to J. Philip Di Franco's book of the movie, compared the Beatles' first film to this cinema classic, calling AHDN "...the [blank] of jukebox musicals." What film did Sarris cite?

19.   Why would AHDN producer Walter Shenson have had reason to smile on 31 December 1979?

20.   When "A Hard Day's Night" was re-released with a new Dolby stereo soundtrack, 29 May 1981, for a two-week premiere run at the Century 21 theater in San Jose, California, a new still-photo collage prologue was added to the film. What song is heard over this

the
GEORGE
SHEARING
Quintet and Orchestra

White Satin

new opening?

1.   Playing a girl named Jean, the future Mrs. Harrison's only line in "A Hard Day's Night" is - "Prisoners!"

2.   Ringo's compensatory factor to his inferiority complex is "playing the drums."

3.   Grandfather is holding the sleeve to **White Satin** by the George Shearing Quintet and Orchestra.

4.   Grandfather accepts Ringo's invitation to "Le Circle Club."

5.   Shake gets past the attendant by telling him he's Ringo's sister.

6.   George thought up the shaving scene.
     (It was Walter Shenson's idea to put John in the bathtub.)

7.   Simon Marshal (played by Kenneth Haigh) is the name of the television director who mistook George for the actor he was expecting for a commercial Marshal was planning for a collection of shirts.

8.   Grandfather's sudden onstage cameo interrupts a toast scene from the Strauss operetta, "Die Fledermaus" ("The Bat").

9.   Leslie Jackson.

10.   Charley's mates are Ginger, Eddy Fallon, and Ding Dong.

11.   Shove-halfpenny, bar skittles, and darts.

12.   The helicopter the Beatles boarded was taking them to their next gig, a midnight matinee in Wolverhampton.

13.   Spinetti's performance in "Oh What A Lovely War" convinced the Beatles that he should be in "A Hard Day's Night."

(Spinetti's drill sergeant role in "Lovely War" was briefly reprised when he appeared as the Recruiting Sergeant in "Magical Mystery Tour.")

14. Dick Lester had previously directed Pattie in a Smith's Crisps TV commercial.

15. "I Should Have Known Better."

16. The White Rabbit (as she was called during the editing of AHDN) was a blonde-haired girl in the La Scala Theatre audience present during the final TV theatre auditorium scene.

(Constantly in tears, she is seen a total of four times beginning with the audience applause just prior to the Beatles' final number, "She Loves You." For those adept at reading lips, The White Rabbit's favourite Beatle was George.)

17. Monies from the premiere of AHDN benefitted the Docklands Settlements and the Variety Club Heart Fund.

18. Andrew Sarris called "A Hard Day's Night" "the 'Citizen Kane' of jukebox musicals."

19. A clause in Walter Shenson's contract with United Artists stipulated that on 31 December 1979, the film rights to "A Hard Day's Night," after having previously been held by UA for fifteen years, would revert back to Shenson.

(Shenson's contract clause also applied to "Help!". Consequently, a year later on 31 December 1980, the rights to this film became his as well.)

20. Featuring many of Robert Freeman's still photographs, the new photo collage prologue is set to "I'll Cry Instead."

(Billed as "The Greatest Rock & Roll Comedy Adventure," Universal began their national re-release of "A Hard Day's Night," 29 January 1982.)

Q & A #15

CHAPTER 3

REVOLVERS

Phase One, in which Doris gets her oats. (Question: Is Doris related to Drake's Drum?) Beatlooniness aside, here's a great lot of questions on the albums of our boys. (By the way, did you know that if you steam off the jacket of this book you'll find a rejected cover for "The White Album"?)

1. What is the title of the Melvin Records bootleg that parodies the cover of the Vee-Jay album **The Beatles Vs. The Four Seasons?**

2. What is the title of the first song the Beatles recorded for **Revolver?**

3. Excluding "Strawberry Fields Forever" and "Penny Lane," what was the first song recorded for **Sgt. Pepper?** What was the last song?

4. John wanted to include this instrument on "Being For The Benefit Of Mr. Kite," but there wasn't one to be found anywhere in the world that he could play by hand. What instrument was it?

5. Name the people on the cover of **Sgt. Pepper** depicted, courtesy of Madame Tussaud's, in wax.

6. Whose idea was it to segue the reprise of "Sgt. Pepper" into "A Day In The Life"?

7. How much were Peter Blake and Jann Haworth paid to assemble the **Sgt. Pepper** cover?

8. Who was the leader of the forty musicians who played on "A Day In The Life," 10 February 1967?

9. Who did the liner notes for the **Yellow Submarine** album sleeves in the U.S. and the U.K.?

10. When "The White Album" was released in the U.K., who got album #8?

11. What's the easiest way to identify a 1979 reissue of the **Let It Be**

album on Capitol?

12. Among bootleg aficionados, what two names are the outtakes from **Let It Be** commonly referred to as?

13. Contending that David Wiggs' interview album, **The Beatles Tapes**, might be misconstrued as a Beatles album and a reflection of their current views on life, which two Beatles sued unsuccessfully to have the package removed?

14. Which Beatles album did George Martin pen the liner notes for?

15. Why was the cover of Rhino Records' collection of Beatles novelty songs, **Beatlesongs**, pulled and another design substituted?

16. Which Beatles album featured these headlines on its cover: "Facts About Paul's Race Horse," "The Day They Fished From The Hotel Window," and "George Talks About The Paddy [sic] Boyd."

17. In this LP's liner notes, Capitol Records touted this album was "...like spending a very special evening in the company of The Beatles themselves!" Which album were they describing?

18. Which Beatles album did John once call a "Beatles Country and Western L.P."?

19. Which Beatles single was advertised as being "The Beatles as nature intended"?

20. Which album was once lauded as being "...a new phase BEATLES album"?

21. Which Beatles album contains such titles as "Who's A Millionaire," "Victims Of Beatlemania" and "Sneaky Haircuts and More About Paul."

22. What is the title of the first Beatles bootleg LP?

23. What is the title of the pirate compilation that caused Capitol to issue its own anthology collections, **The Beatles: 1962-1966** and **1967-1970?**

24. What is the title of the first Beatles record available on compact disc (CD)?

25. Name the first Beatles LP in the U.K. to feature a foldout cover.

26. Name the first Beatles LP in the U.S. to feature a foldout cover.

27. What is the title of the only Beatles record released in Mobile Fidelity Sound Labs' UHQR series?

28. What is the title of Russia's first official Beatles release? What record label is it on?

29. The Beatles and Spike Milligan both donated tracks to a charity LP issued in 1969. What is the name of this album?

30. Besides **The Beatles At The Hollywood Bowl** album, and discounting bootlegs, where else can one hear the Beatles performing on disc at the Hollywood Bowl?

31. The infamous butcher sleeve photo from **"Yesterday"...And Today** was again rejected by Capitol as the cover for which Beatles compilation album?

32. Which single did Capitol issue in the seventies in a picture sleeve resembling the cover of a Beatles album released in the sixties?

33. On which Beatles album cover can one find a picture of Klaus Voormann?

34. In 1984 magazine ads for their four-track recorders, this electronics company used the cover of a Beatles album. Name the company and the album they used.

35. Three U.S. albums, issued at various times in the life of the Beatles' catalogue, have been packaged in two entirely different cover formats. Discounting the numberous (and ongoing) repackagings of the Tony Sheridan/Beatles and Star Club material, and the Decca audition tape albums (of questionable legality), what are the names of these three albums?

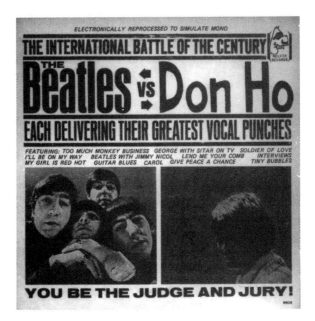

Q & A #1

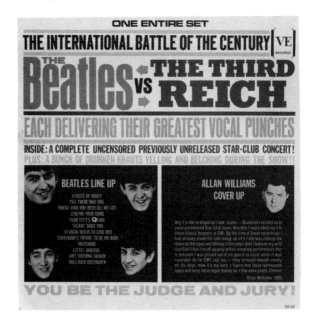

REVOLVERS
(ANSWERS)

1. **The Beatles Vs. Don Ho**
(In 1986, VE Records released **The Beatles Vs. The Third Reich**, a bootleg of the raw, unedited Hamburg Star Club recordings featuring a full-color album sleeve parody of the Vee-Jay album.)

2. The first song the Beatles recorded for **Revolver** was "Mark I," later retitled "Tomorrow Never Knows," on 6 April 1966.
(Neil Aspinall once referred to the song as "The Void.")

3. "When I'm Sixty-Four" was the first song the Beatles recorded for **Sgt. Pepper** beginning on 6 December 1966. The last song recorded was "Within You Without You" completed on 3 April 1967.
("With A Little Help From My Friends," widely cited as the last song, was actually recorded on 29-30 March 1967.)

4. For "Being For The Benefit Of Mr. Kite," George Martin searched in vain for a manually playable calliope.
(John's inspiration for this song was a circus poster, dated February 14, 1843, "liberated" according to Derek Taylor in his 1987 book, *It Was Twenty Years Ago Today*, "from a cafe during the filming of the 'Penny Lane'/ 'Strawberry Fields Forever' clips." Based on the author's careful scrutiny of a photo of this poster in Taylor's book, the poster (in its entirety) appears to read as follows (see next page):

5. Now appearing in wax on the cover of **Sgt. Pepper** are: Diana Dors, Lawrence of Arabia, Sonny Liston, Dr. Livingstone, George Bernard Shaw, and the 1964 Beatles.
(Two additional wax figures of young girls also appear on the cover. The first, a wax hairdresser's dummy, is just below and to the right of Bob Dylan while the second is next to Stuart Sutcliffe. Madame Tussaud's was about to melt down the wax figure of Sonny Liston when it was rescued by Peter Blake for the cover of Pepper. Blake still owns the figure, which is stored in his West London studio.)

6. As recounted in Derek Taylor's book *It Was Twenty Years Ago Today*, it was Neil Aspinall's idea to segue the reprise of "Sgt. Pep-

PABLO FANQUE'S CIRCUS ROYAL, TOWN-MEADOWS, ROCHDALE.

Grandest Night of the Season!
AND POSITIVELY THE
LAST NIGHT BUT THREE!
BEING FOR THE
BENEFIT OF MR. KITE,
(LATE OF WELLS'S CIRCUS) AND
MR. J. HENDERSON,
THE CELEBRATED SOMERSET THROWER!
WIRE DANCER. VAULTER. RIDER. &c.

On TUESDAY Evening, February 14th, 1843

Messrs. KITE & HENDERSON, in announcing the following Entertainments, assure the Public that this Night's Productions will be one of the most
Splendid ever produced in this Town, having been some days in preparation.

MR. KITE will, for this Night only, introduce the
CELEBRATED
HORSE, ZANTHUS!
Well known to be one of the best Broke Horses
IN THE WORLD!!!

Mr. HENDERSON will undertake the arduous Task of
THROWING TWENTY ONE SOMERSETS,
ON THE SOLID GROUND.

Mr. KITE will appear, for the first time this season,
On the Tight Rope,
When Two Gentlemen Amateurs of this Town will
perform with him.

Mr. HENDERSON will, for the first time in Rochdale
Introduce his extraordinary
TRAMPOLINE LEAPS
AND
SOMERSETS!

Over Men & Horses, through Hoops, over
Garters, and lastly, through a Hogshead of
REAL FIRE! In this branch of the profession
Mr. H challenges THE WORLD!

For particulars see Bills of the day.

JONES A. CROSSKILL, PRINTERS AND BOOKSELLERS,
YORKSHIRE STREET, ROCHDALE.

per" into "A Day In The Life."

7.   From the EMI-assigned budget of £1500 paid gallery owner Robert Fraser to coordinate the LP's jacket artwork, Blake and Haworth were only paid £200 (by Fraser) to assemble most of the cover of **Sgt. Pepper.**

8.   The leader of the forty musicians who played on "A Day In The Life" was Erich Gruenberg.

9.   Dan Davis wrote the U.S. liner notes for **Yellow Submarine.** In the U.K., the job fell to Derek Taylor, who wrote the introduction, and Tony Palmer, who penned the main text.

10.   "White Album" #8 went to John's boyhood mate and manager of the ill-fated Apple Boutique, Pete Shotton.

11.   When Capitol reissued **Let It Be** in March 1979, the foldout cover was not retained.
   (The photos once included in this foldout were put on the LP's inner sleeve. The reissued **Let It Be** also includes a poster of the LP's front cover.)

12.   The outtakes from **Let It Be** are most frequently referred to as the "Sweet Apple Trax" or the "Get Back Sessions."

13.   George and Ringo tried without success in 1976 to halt the release of **The Beatles Tapes.**

14.   George Martin wrote the liner notes for **The Beatles At The Hollywood Bowl,** an LP he remixed from the original three-track tapes the songs were recorded on.

15.   On **Beatlesongs'** original cover (drawn by William Stout), a caricature of Mark David Chapman (a copy of *A Catcher In The Rye* at his feet) is seen at a Beatles convention helping to hold a "We Love You Beatles" banner. The substituted cover features a photograph of Beatles memorabilia.

16.   These and other startling questions are posed to one who owns a copy of **Hear The Beatles Tell All** (Vee-Jay).

17. Capitol would like you to spend a very special evening in the company of the Beatles by purchasing their double LP documentary album, **The Beatles' Story.**

18. The Beatles' C&W LP, in John's estimation, was **Beatles For Sale.**
    (See "The Beatles Monthly Book" No. 17.)

19. "The Beatles as nature intended" was a description of their single, "Get Back" b/w "Don't Let Me Down."

20. The Beatles' new phase album was **Let It Be.**

21. The aforementioned tracks are included on **The Beatles' Story.**

22. The first Beatles bootleg (in strictest terms, a pirate disc) was **The Original Greatest Hits** (GRC-1001) issued by Greatest Records.

23. **Beatles Alpha Omega Vol.1** (Audio Tape)

24. The first Beatles album issued on CD was a Japanese pressing of **Abbey Road** (now deleted).
    (The year 1987 saw EMI/Capitol release all the Beatles' original British titles on compact disc. **Please Please Me, With The Beatles, A Hard Day's Night** and **Beatles For Sale** were released first on 26 February, with **Help!, Rubber Soul,** and **Revolver** up next on 30 April. The **Sgt. Pepper** CD was released June 1st to coincide with the twentieth anniversary of the LP's original release in the U.K., although officially "Pepper" debuted in the Beatles' homeland on 26 May 1967.)

25. The first U.K. Beatles foldout album was **Beatles For Sale.**

26. The first U.S. Beatles foldout album was the Vee-Jay double-LP, **The Beatles Vs. The Four Seasons,** issued 1 October 1964.
    (The second foldout album, also on Vee-Jay, was issued less than two weeks later on 12 October 1964: **Songs, Pictures And Stories Of The Fabulous Beatles.** Capitol followed suit on 23 November 1964 with its first foldout, **The Beatles' Story.**)

27. Mobile Fidelity's only UHQR (Ultra High Quality Record) Beatles album was one issued in 1982 for **Sgt. Pepper.**

4-TRACK MASTERPIECES

While the Beatles were teaching Sgt. Pepper and the Band to play, twenty years ago, George Martin was getting everything down on a 4-track tape recorder. Even by today's standards it's a masterful feat of technology.

So is the X-15, in its own way. It's the ultimate evolution of 4-track recording, designed by the engineers who invented the format of a multitrack cassette recorder/mixer.

This is the one that's really portable, easy to use and costs less than $500, retail. Plus, there's a companion mixer/compressor, microphones, headphones, self-powered speakers, the works.

It's all together, all affordable. So if you have a little masterpiece of your own in mind, see your Fostex Dealer today.

FOSTEX®
MULTITRACK DIVISION

FOSTEX CORPORATION OF AMERICA, 15431 Blackburn Ave., Norwalk, CA 90650 (213) 921-1112

Q & A #34

28. The first official Russian Beatles record was a **Let It Be** EP, released in 1972 on the Melodia label.

(One of the first rock albums ever released in Russia was **Band On The Run**. In March of 1986, Russia released its first official Beatles albums. Titled **A Hard Day's Night** and **A Taste Of Honey** (!), the first pressings of these albums sold out almost immediately.)

29. The Beatles and Spike Milligan both contributed cuts to the 1969 EMI/Starline charity LP, **No One's Gonna Change Our World**. The album's title is derived from the Beatles' song donation, their first version of "Across The Universe."

(Spike Milligan, in addition to writing the album's liner notes with Prince Philip, contributed the cut "Ning Nang Nong/The Python.")

30. A snippet of "Twist And Shout," from the Beatles' 23 August 1964 Hollywood Bowl concert, opens side one of **The Beatles' Story**.

31. Suggested by Randall Davis, Capitol's director of merchandising and advertising, the butcher sleeve photo was rejected as the cover art for the U.S. **Rarities** album.

32. The picture sleeve for "Ob La Di, Ob La Da" b/w "Julia" resembles the cover of "The White Album," down to the inclusion of a serial number in the lower right-hand corner.

33. Klaus Voormann can be seen just below the caricature of John's lips on the cover of **Revolver**.

(Voormann came up with about fifteen different alternative designs for the **Revolver** cover, including the one from which the final cover drawing was based, a tiny sketch of the four Beatles heads and their hair.)

34. Foster Multitrack Division used the cover for **Sgt. Pepper** in print ads for its four-track recorder.

35. The three U.S. Beatles albums presented in two entirely different cover formats include: **Jolly What! The Beatles And Frank Ifield On Stage** (Vee-Jay,1964); **"Yesterday"...And Today** (Capitol, 1966); **Rock 'N' Roll Music** (Capitol, 1976, revised, 1980).

CHAPTER 4

A LEGEND
THAT WILL LAST A LUNCHTIME

Could John, Paul, George, and Ringo become, respectively, Ron, Dirk, Stig and Barry, that cuddly Prefab Four better known as The Rutles? What better foil for a bit of "mickey-taking," as John liked to call it, than the Beatles' legendary rise to fame? What better loonies to dream it up than Monty Pythoner Eric Idle and former Bonzo Dog, Neil Innes. In his autobiography, *I Me Mine*, George called the Rutles, "...the tribute beyond all other tributes to the Beatles' story."

Once you've answered these Rutle questions, try your hand at another Beatles tribulation...uh...tribute from Robert Stigwood, the Bee Gees, and Peter Frampton.

1.   What were the names of the original members of the Rutles?

2.   Who played Brian Thigh, the man who turned down the Rutles?

3.   A parody on the title of Brian Epstein's autobiography, what was the name of Rutles manager Leggy Mountbatten's first book?

4.   What was the title of the book written by John's Rutles counterpart, Ron Nasty?

5.   Name the men who were, respectively, the Rutles' producer and music publisher.

6.   Who directed the Rutles' two film classics, "A Hard Day's Rut" and "Ouch!"?

7.   While Bob Dylan reportedly introduced the Beatles to marijuana in 1965, what substance did he introduce the Rutles to?

8.   On what song does Ron supposedly sing "I buried Stig," purportedly a clue in the "Stig Is Dead" rumor?

9.   When Basil Pao designed his parody of the **Sgt. Pepper** album cover, **Sgt. Rutter's Only Darts Club Band**, for the cover of **The Rutles** LP, whose likenesses were removed from the **Pepper** cover to

Cover of the booklet included with the LP The Rutles.

accomodate **Rutter**?

10. While the Beatles took a Magical Mystery Tour, what did the Rutles take?

11. What is the title of the Rutles' animated feature film?

12. What happened to the Rutles' boutique?

13. While the Beatles' record label featured a green Granny Smith apple, what fruit did Rutle Corp. use?

14. What was the title of the final album the Rutles released?

15. "You Need Feet" was the soundtrack to what film by Ron and wife Chastity?

16. In addition to "You Need Feet," four other songs were included in the home video release of "The Rutles" that were not included on the 1978 album. Name the songs.

17. Why would the following artists and/or groups be of interest to Rutles fans: I. J. Waxley, The Punk Floyd, Arther Hodgeson and the Kneecaps, and the Bigamy Sisters?

18. At the time of its release, who was in charge of promoting **The Rutles** soundtrack album at Warner Bros.?

19. What connection do the Rutles share with a Beatles bootleg titled **Indian Ropetrick**?

20. What is former Monkee Mike Nesmith's connection with the Rutles?

21. Before the Rutles, Neil Innes worked with Paul's brother, Mike McGear, in a musical/comedy group. What was their name?

There are some who would call Robert Stigwood's 1978 film, "Sgt. Pepper's Lonely Heart's Club Band," a vinyl and celluloid blasphemy. (Mind you, its soundtrack was arranged and produced by no less than George Martin!) Nevertheless, some of you must've taken it on the chin and seen this movie, maybe even in a paying theater. While you have my condolences if

you did, it might help you in answering the next nine questions:

22. What was the full name of Old Sgt. Pepper (played by Woodrow Chambliss)?

23. What is the name of Sgt. Pepper's hometown?

24. When Sgt. Pepper died, 16 August 1956, what did he leave to his grandson, Billy Shears?

25. What is the name of the record company whose chairman tricks the new "Lonely Hearts Club Band" into signing a contract with them?

26. When that demented ex-real estate agent, Mean Mr. Mustard (played by Frankie Howerd) steals Sgt. Pepper's instruments, who is he instructed to deliver them to for safekeeping?

27. "Sgt. Pepper's" screenwriter, Henry Edwards, has also distinguished himself in another Beatle-related project. What was that project?

28. Stigwood's "Sgt. Pepper" and the Beatles' movie, "Let It Be," amazingly enough, have this musician in common. Who is he?

29. When "Sgt. Pepper's Lonely Hearts Club Band" and the accompanying RSO Records soundtrack were released in 1978, Capitol placed cartoon balloon stickers on their current pressings of Beatle "Peppers." What did these balloons declare?

30. In a 1986 interview published in "Rolling Stone," Peter Frampton (who played Billy Shears) admitted that doing "Sgt. Pepper" was a mistake. Frampton tried to justify his participation in the film by reminding himself that this person was going to be in it. Who was it?

**A LEGEND
THAT WILL LAST A LUNCHTIME
(ANSWERS)**

---

1. When the Rutles first appeared in Britain on Eric Idle's 1976 series, "Rutland Weekend Television," the line-up of the Prefab Four

was Dirk, Stig, Nasty and Kevin. Kevin, of course, was later replaced by Barry on drums.

2. Brian Thigh was played by Dan Aykroyd.

3. Leggy Mountbatten's book was titled *A Cellar Full Of Goys*.

4. Ron Nasty's first book was titled *Out Of Me Head*.

5. The Rutles' producer was Archie Macaw; their music publisher was Dick Jaws.

6. "A Hard Day's Rut" and "Ouch!" were directed by noted Rutland director Dick Leicestershire.

7. Dylan introduced the Prefabs to tea.

8. Ron supposedly sang "I buried Stig" on "I Am The Waitress," a song from the Rutles' **Tragical History Tour** soundtrack LP.

9. Heads removed from **Sgt. Pepper** for **Sgt. Rutter** include the Beatles, circa 1964 (in wax), the Beatles of 1967, and all traces of Liverpool footballer Albert Stubbins.

10. Playing four Oxford history professors on a walking tour of English tea shops, the Rutles took a "Tragical History Tour."

11. "Yellow Submarine Sandwich"

12. Three weeks after it opened, the Rutles' boutique was blown up by Ron Nasty.

13. The logo fruit of Rutle Corp was a banana.
        (**The Rutles**, a four-song 12-inch promotional EP on yellow vinyl, was issued by Warner Bros. in 1978 with a banana label.)

14. **Let It Rot** was the Rutles' last album release.
        (While **Rot** was the last Rutle album released, every loyal Rutles fan knows that **Shabby Road** was their last recorded album.)

15. "You Need Feet" was the soundtrack to Ron and Chastity's *cinema verite*, "A Thousand Feet Of Film."

16. Four songs not included on **The Rutles** soundtrack album were "Goosestep Mama," "It's Looking Good," "Get Up And Go" (a sendup of "Get Back"), and "Between Us."

(Rutle-era demos exist for the following songs that have yet to be commercially released: "Wendy Wetlips' Ready-mades," "What Do You Do?" and "Montana Cafe Forever.")

17. All these artists released (fictional) albums on the Rutle label. (From the inner sleeve of **The Rutles** album: Waxley, **Forever Waxley**; Floyd, **White Dopes On Punk**; Hodgeson, **Knees Up**; Bigamy Sisters, **Nobody Does It Wetter.**)

18. Serving at the time as Warner Bros.' Vice President and Director of Creative Services, Derek Taylor personally handled the promotion of **The Rutles** LP.

19. The bootleggers responsible for compiling **Indian Ropetrick** (also issued as **Spiritual Regeneration**) included the Rutles song "Cheese And Onions," which they attempted to pass off in the liner notes as a Lennon outtake.

20. Nesmith owns Pacific Arts Video Records, which released "The Rutles" to the home video market.

21. Neil Innes and Mike McGear were both members of "GRIMMS."

G = (John) Gorman
R = (Andy) Roberts
I = (Neil) Innes
M = (Roger) McGough
M = (Mike) McGear
S = (Viv) Stanshall

("GRIMMS" also counted Gerry Conway and Zoot Money among its members.)

22. Old Sgt. Pepper's full name was Sgt. Phineas Patrick Paul Pepper.

23. Sgt. Pepper's hometown is Heartland, U.S.A.

24.   Sgt. Pepper left his grandson, Billy, his war medal, the Golden Eagle.

25.   The chairman of Big Deal Records, B.D. Brockhurst (played by Donald Pleasence) tricked the boys of the new "Lonely Hearts Club Band" into signing a contract.

26.   Keeping the bass drum for himself, Mean Mr. Mustard delivered Sgt. Pepper's silver cornet to Dr. Maxwell Edison (Steve Martin), his tuba to Father Sun (Alice Cooper), and the trumpet to the Future Villain Band (Aerosmith).
      (Aerosmith performed "Come Together" on the "Pepper" sound-track, but it wouldn't be their last visit to the Lennon/McCartney songbook. Steve Tyler lent his vocals to the group's cover of "I'm Down" on their 1987 Geffen LP, **Permanent Vacation**.)

27.   Henry Edwards co-wrote the book *Loving John* with May Pang.

28.   Billy Preston, really puttin' it to the keys in "Let It Be," plays the Sgt. Pepper who emerges from the weathervane to rescue Billy Shears and bring his beloved Strawberry Fields (Sandy Farina) back to life.

29.   Capitol's "Pepper" sticker reads "The Original Classic."

30.   "That was my credibility for doing ["Sgt. Pepper"], that Paul would be in it. But in the end, his part was played by Billy Preston. That's as close to a Beatle as we got." - Peter Frampton, from "Rolling Stone" No. 477, 3 July 1986.

CHAPTER 5

LISTEN TO THE COLOR

OF THEIR DREAMS

While music scholars and the Beatles themselves have always contended that the group's chemistry was made up of four equal parts (John, Paul, George, and Ringo), the split of the group at the dawn of the seventies illustrated that some parts of that formula were perhaps more equal than others. As the eighties came to a close, most of John and Paul's solo LP's were still in print and making the transition to CD immortality. Alas, many of the solo outings George and Ringo released are now out of print. For you newer fans, it may take some scouring of the cutout bins and used record shops to score a complete collection of these. Really, it's worth it though. How else do you expect to get through this next quiz?

1. What will I be "if I grow up"?

2. What can you do "without going out of your door"?

3. What will you find "when you've seen beyond yourself"?

4. What really "blows down those blues"?

5. What is "a little dark and out of key"?

6. If your mind is this, "try thinking more (if just for your own sake)."

7. Where do the Beatles sing about "them old twelve-bar blues"?

8. What are the lyrics to "The Inner Light" based upon?

9. Who contributed a line to the Harrison/Clapton composition "Badge"?

10. George has said that if he were to rewrite the bridge lyrics to "I Want To Tell You," two lines would be revised. What are those two lines and how would he have amended them?

In the next three questions, identify the Beatles song that contained these lines in an early working draft later omitted from the final recorded version:

11. "When I see you at the door/I know your [sic] worth waiting for/ For the moment that you speak/I know I'd wait here all week."

12. "You may work hard trying to get some bread/You won't make out before your [sic] dead."

13. "You know I love that woman of mine/And I need her all of the time/And you know what I'm telling you/That woman, that woman don't make me blue."

14. According to this "Harrisong," what is the "only thing" the Pope is "qualified to quote us"?

15. In which of George's songs can you hear of someone swimming like Richard III?

16. Why have "We Gotta Save The World"?

17. During the Beatles' recording of this song, a bottle of "Blue Nun" wine could be heard vibrating from atop a Leslie speaker cabinet. What is this song's title?

18. George hopes "to get out of this place by..." whose grace?

19. Which of George's songs does he preface with the announcement, "....we've got a B-side to make, ladies and gentlemen. We haven't got much time now, so we better get right on with it."

20. George's working title for this song, which Ringo later recorded, was "Whenever." "Whenever" has been recorded under two different titles. What are they?

21. In this Beatles song, "I met you in the morning waiting" for something. What was I waiting for?

22. "It would be nice, a paradise," was a line from an early working version of which Starkey composition?

23. In this "Sta*rtling Music" song, Ringo will "play the piano if

it's..." what?

24. What is the title of this U.S. Top Ten for Mr. Starkey that fades with Ringo saying "Put mine in a boot."

25. "Please believe me," sings Ringo, "I wish this song was yours instead of mine." Which song is he referring to?

26. John mentioned Sexy Sadie in the song of the same name. In which song does Ringo mention her?

27. "Pigs will fly and the earth will fry" when what happens?

28. Ringo: "My dog doesn't eat meat."
("Why doesn't your dog eat meat?")
Ringo: "We don't give it any."
("Why don't you give your dog meat?")
Ringo: "He's been dead two years now."

The preceding awful joke was told by Ringo during the middle eight break of what song?

29. "Wave to a man in a Rolls 'cause he knows how to live." In what song does Ringo offer this advice?

30. In Ringo's 1981 remake of "Back Off Boogaloo," Harry Nilsson can be heard in the background singing a disjointed medley of five Beatles songs. What are the titles of those songs?

**LISTEN TO THE
COLOR OF THEIR DREAMS
(ANSWERS)**

---

1. "I'll be a singer, wearing rings on every finger"
("Old Brown Shoe")

2. "Know all things on earth"
("The Inner Light")

3. "Peace of mind"

(From "Within You Without You." George's former sister-in-law, Jenny Boyd, recalls relaying to George the line "Life goes on within you and without you" from a book she was reading at the time, *Karma and Rebirth* by the Buddhist scholar, Christmas Humphreys.)

4. "Coconut fudge"
  ("Savoy Truffle")

5. "The harmony"
  ("Only A Northern Song")

6. "Opaque"
  ("Think For Yourself")

7. "For You Blue"

8. "The Inner Light" is taken from the book *Lamps Of Fire*, a translation of the *Tao Te Ching*.

9. For the second verse of "Badge," Ringo contributed to the line: "I told you not to drive in the dark, I told you *about the swans that live in the park*."

10. The lines appear in the third verse of "I Want To Tell You": "But if I seem to act unkind/It's only me, it's not my mind..." would now be corrected by George to read "Although I seem to act unkind/ It isn't me, it is my mind..."

11. "Blue Jay Way"

12. These unrecorded lines were once considered for "Taxman."

13. This verse was not included in the final recorded version of "Something."

14. "While the Pope owns 51% of General Motors," sings George in the third verse of "Awaiting On You All," "...the Stock Exchange is the only thing he's qualified to quote us."

15. An inhabitant of the song "Soft Hearted Hana" swims like Richard III.

Q & A #28

16. "We Gotta Save The World" because "Somebody else may want to use it" and "Somebody's children they may need it."

17. At the close of "Long Long Long," a certain note Paul played on the organ caused the wine bottle to rattle.

18. "The LORD SRI KRSNA'S GRACE"
    ("Living In The Material World")

19. George's very hoarse (and slightly sarcastic) spoken intro precedes "I Don't Care Anymore," the B-side of the "Dark Horse" single released in the U.S.

20. When George gave "Whenever" to Cilla Black to record in the fall of 1972, it was titled "When Every Song Is Sung" (Cilla's version has yet to be released). When Ringo recorded the song for his **Roto-gravure** album in 1976, it was retitled "I'll Still Love You."

21. "The tides of time"
    ("What Goes On?")

22. These lines were omitted from "Octopus's Garden."
    (Ringo sings his early version of this song in the movie "Let It Be.")

23. Ringo will "play the piano if it's in C."
    ("Early 1970")

24. "Put mine in a boot" can be heard at the fade of "No No Song."

25. Ringo wishes "Step Lightly" (from the **Ringo** album) was your song.

26. Sexy Sadie makes a cameo appearance in "Devil Woman."
    ("Sexy Sadie, you look like the devil to me.")

27. "When they get me doing honest hours"
    ("Snookeroo," from the LP, **Goodnight Vienna**.)

28. Keith Moon acts as straight man for Ringo's joke on "Together," a song from Keith's only solo album, **Two Sides Of The Moon** (Track/MCA).

29. Ringo advises you to wave at Rolls owners in "Stop And Take The Time To Smell The Roses," from his 1981 Boardwalk LP, **Stop And Smell The Roses**.

30. During Ringo's remake of "Back Off Boogaloo" (included on **Stop And Smell The Roses**), Harry Nilsson sings lines from "With A Little Help From My Friends," "Help!," "Lady Madonna," "Good Day Sunshine," and "Baby You're A Rich Man."

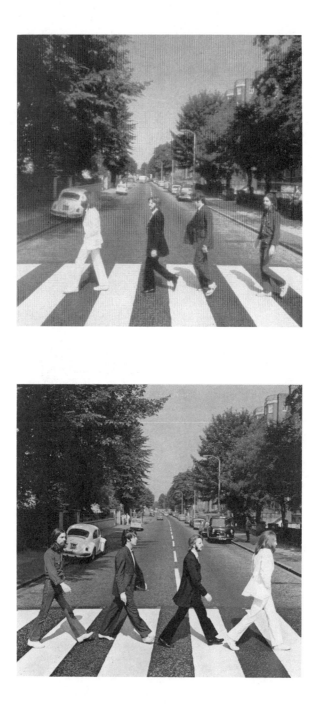

CHAPTER 6

Q. WHY DID THE BEATLES CROSS ABBEY ROAD? A. TO MAKE GOOD MUSIC!

It meant some days in preparation, but a splendid time was guaranteed for all the day a new Beatles album hit the streets. As a second generation fan, I'm sometimes as green as a Granny Smith apple over you first generation fans (you know who you are), living through the Beatles sixties as you did. For you especially, these song titles are intended to test your recall of the names of the first Beatles LPs they appeared on in both the U.S. and the U.K.

1. "Cry For A Shadow"

2. "Love Me Do" (version two)

3. "Komm, Gib Mir Deine Hand"

4. "Bad Boy"

5. "I've Just Seen A Face"

6. "What Goes On?"

7. "I'm Only Sleeping"

8. "Strawberry Fields Forever"

9. "Across The Universe" (version one)

10. "Old Brown Shoe"

Q & A #2

1. "Cry For A Shadow"
The Beatles With Tony Sheridan And Their Guests (U.S. - MGM, 3 February 1964)
Let's Do The Twist, Hully Gully, Slop, Surf, Locomotion, Monkey (U.K. - Polydor, 8 May 1964)

2. "Love Me Do" (version two)
Introducing The Beatles (U.S. - Vee-Jay, 22 July 1963)
Please Please Me (U.K. - Parlophone, 22 March 1963)
(Version two of "Love Me Do" features Ringo on tambourine and session man Andy White on drums.)

3. "Komm, Gib Mir Deine Hand"
Something New (U.S. - Capitol, 20 July 1964)
Rarities (U.K. - Parlophone, 10 November 1978, as a bonus disc in **The Beatles Collection** boxed set. **Rarities** was issued in the U.K. separately on 19 October 1979.)

4. "Bad Boy"
Beatles VI (U.S. - Capitol, 14 June 1965)
A Collection Of Beatles Oldies (But Goldies) (U.K. - Parlophone, 10 December 1966)

5. "I've Just Seen A Face"
Rubber Soul (U.S. - Capitol, 6 December 1965)
Help! (U.K. - Parlophone, 6 August 1965)

6. "What Goes On?"
"Yesterday"...And Today (U.S. - Capitol, 20 June 1966)
Rubber Soul (U.K. - Parlophone, 3 December 1965)

7. "I'm Only Sleeping"
"Yesterday"...And Today (U.S. - Capitol, 20 June 1966)
Revolver (U.K. - Parlophone, 5 August 1966)

8.   "Strawberry Fields Forever"
Magical Mystery Tour (U.S. - Capitol, 27 November 1967)
The Beatles 1967-1970 (U.K. - Apple, 20 April 1973)
(Before "The Blue Album," this song was available in the U.K. in single and EP form only; Parlophone did not issue "Strawberry Fields Forever" on a **Magical Mystery Tour** album until 19 November 1976.)

9.   "Across The Universe"
Rarities (U.S. - Capitol, 1 December 1978 as a bonus disc in **The Beatles Collection** boxed set. A revised **Rarities** LP including this song was issued by Capitol, 24 March 1980.)
No One's Gonna Change Our World (U.K. - World Wildlife Charity LP, EMI Starline, 12 December 1969)
(Although versions one and two of "Across The Universe" use the same take of the song (take 8, recorded 4 February 1968), version one features a mix that includes a sound effects intro of birds chirping and flapping their wings, children at play in a playground, as well as the falsetto harmonies of 16-year-old Lizzie Bravo and 17-year-old Gayleen Pease.)

10. "Old Brown Shoe"
Hey Jude (or **The Beatles Again**) (U.S. - Apple, 26 February 1970)
The Beatles 1967-1970 (U.K. - Apple, 20 April 1973)
(Before "The Blue Album," this song was only available in the U.K. as the B-side of "The Ballad Of John And Yoko" single; Parlophone did not issue a **Hey Jude** LP in the U.K. until 11 May 1979.)

CHAPTER 7

WORDS ARE FLYING OUT

The Beatles have had a lot to say over the years. Their words have influenced the thinking of millions, often unintentionally! There were times when the things they said got them into trouble. Other times, their quotations have been dissected beyond recognition for hidden meanings and secret messages. (Say the word and you'll be free indeed!) In this quiz, some of their words, along with those spoken by others about them, have been rescued from the restless wind inside the letter box. Can you remember whence they came?

1.   "It'll be the usual rubbish, but it won't cost much." What was John referring to?

2.   What did John once call "...as relevant as Vietnam"?

3.   Of Jesus Christ, John said he was "all right." How did Mr. Lennon describe Jesus' disciples?

4.   When John and Yoko attended the premiere of "The Magic Christian" (11 December 1969), they arrived in a Rolls Royce covered in posters declaring something. What did those posters say?

5.   "I wrote it for breakfast, recorded it for lunch and we're putting it out for dinner." John said this about which one of his songs?

6.   Marshall McLuhan once asked John, "Can you recall the occasion or the immediate reasons for your getting involved in music?" John's answer was that he had heard somebody. Who had John heard?

7.   Which album did John describe as "John Lennon and Harry Nilsson having a fit in L.A."?

8.   Once, John publicly referred to this person as "....an old estranged fiancee of mine." Who?

9.   Where does Dr. Winston O'Boogie declare that "A conspiracy of silence speaks louder than words"?

10.   Paul once wrote, "P.S. I like the drawings too," as the conclud-

ing statement to his introduction of what book?

11. In "A Hard Day's Night," a reporter asks Paul, "Do you often see your father?" What was Paul's reply?

12. At the conclusion of the final runthrough of "Get Back" from the film "Let It Be," Paul says "Thanks, Mo." Who was he thanking?

13. "Linda and I are the only two who will be sick of it by the release date." What was Paul talking about?

14. When Don Novello (a.k.a. Father Guido Sarducci) asked Paul what animal he'd like to be, what was Paul's reply?

15. Following the release of **Valotte**, Paul sent Julian Lennon a telegram. What did it say?

16. "There was nothing the matter with him that a little extra love wouldn't have cured." Who was George referring to?

17. Which of George's songs was once described by him as "...one of them repetitious numbers which is gonna have twenty million people with the Phil Spector nymphomaniacs all doing backing vocals..."

18. In "A Hard Day's Night," what was Ringo's reply to a reporter who asked him, "Are you a mod or a rocker?"

19. What did Ringo once tell David Wigg he wanted to be reincarnated as?

20. In 1981, Bruce Springsteen's drummer, Max Weinberg, asked Ringo if he had any unfulfilled ambitions. What was Ringo's reply?

21. Who said, "Today's Beatles fan is tomorrow's baseball fan"?

22. Who once said of the Beatles, "They are Britain's secret weapon"?

23. Who once told Ed Sullivan, "The Beatles are the healthiest thing to happen to show business since the discovery of penicillin."

24. Which Beatles song did William Mann, music critic for the "London Times," describe as having "...chains of pandiatonic clusters"?

25. "There is little or nothing on the album which cannot be reproduced on stage, which is, as students and critics of popular music know, not always the case." Who wrote this rather ironic statement, considering the direction the group was headed in, and what Beatles album was he describing?

26. Who once compared the songs of the Beatles to "...the silence of flooded houses"?

27. On 19 June 1967, Paul was interviewed for Independent Television News. During the course of the interview, Paul told the reporter: "You're asking me the question and if you want me to be honest, I'll be honest. You've got the responsibility not to spread this now." What did Paul feel the ITN had the responsibility not to spread?

28. Where can Beatle fans find a reference to "Agnes - the inquisitive baby sitter next door in California"?

29. What is the significance of the phrase "Don't Drop Out" to a Beatles fan?

30. "Where's the bus?"

31. Where could you have read this statement previously: "Don't think they didn't know about Hitler."

32. What quotation is attributed to Eric Clapton on the back cover of the **Live Peace In Toronto** album?

33. Where did sharp-eyed Beatle people first read this phrase: "Ono news that's fit to print."

34. What is the significance of the following statement: "John Lennon, June 1952, Age 11."

35. Where can Beatle fans read the phrase, "Duit On Mon Dei"?

36. Which Beatle's solo album contains the words, "You don't have to be first, but make sure you're not last - a local Gynecologist."

37. Which Beatle's solo album contains the quotation, "Rock on

lovers everywhere, because that's basically it."

38. Who once said, "Being born in Scotland carries with it certain responsibilities." On which Beatle's solo album can one find this quotation?

39. What was George Martin's two-word comment on **Unfinished Music No. 2: Life With The Lions**?

40. During a New York radio appearance in 1974, John referred to the Yardbirds as "Son of Stones." During that same program, what group did Lennon identify as "Son of Beatles"?

41. "We try to put more sunshine into our songs than the Beatles and more rock than the Beach Boys." Who is quoted as saying this and what group was he with when he said it?

42. Who are the self-proclaimed "Keepers of the wishing well"?

43. On whose solo album is one reminded to "Buy a Terry Southern book"? Also, which Beatle's solo album offered "Thanks to Kilgore Trout and all the Beavers"?

44. "In this wrapper is the music they made. Can you dig it?" What album did Clint Harrigan say you should attempt to dig?

45. "When two great saints meet, it is a humbling experience. The long battles to prove he was a Saint." Who is quoted as saying this and on which Beatle's solo album is the attribution made?

**WORDS ARE FLYING OUT
(ANSWERS)**

---

1. John, speaking on the Beatles' 1964 Christmas message, was talking about his upcoming book *A Spaniard In The Works*.

2. John was referring to Roger Whitaker's butcher sleeve photo for **"Yesterday"...And Today**.

3. In his interview with Maureen Cleave, first published 4 March

1966 in London's "Evening Standard," John called Jesus' disciples "thick and ordinary."

4.   "Britain Murdered Hanratty"
   (Many people believe James Hanratty was innocent of the 1961 murder of Michael Gregson on the A6 highway, for which Hanratty was hanged in April 1963.)

5.   According to print ads for the "Instant Karma" single, the song was "Ritten, Recorded, Remixed 27th Jan. 1970."

6.   John told Marshall McLuhan he had heard Elvis Presley.

7.   John and Harry having a fit in L.A. is Lennon's description of the recording of Nilsson's **Pussycats** album.
   (Among the people thanked on the back of the **Pussycats** sleeve is comedienne Dianne Hollen. In 1974, Dianne worked as an administrative assistant for the recently opened Burbank Studios, located on the old Warner Bros. lot in Los Angeles, where the basic tracks for the album were recorded. Interviewed by the author in 1987, Dianne most clearly recalls the sessions for "Rock Around The Clock" :

   "It seems like they did it eight million times and they played it really great," remembers Dianne, "everybody was really excited about it. They had three drummers set up there at the same time, Ringo, Jim Keltner, and Keith Moon and that was pretty incredible. Moon was just a maniac. Nilsson was real nice; I don't remember him being sober the whole time I was there - he was really drunk. I got really weird vibes from Ringo. Everybody else was dressed in the "hippie" clothes of the time, and basically Ringo - all he wore through the whole session was a three-piece white suit. Lennon seemed to be kind of distant. He was very polite, very soft-spoken, but he just seemed totally dominated by May Pang; she just took care of everything.")

8.   John's "estranged fiancee" was Paul.
   (John made this statement during his announcement prior to performing his last song before a concert audience, "I Saw Her Standing There," at Elton John's 28 November 1974 show at Madison Square Garden.)

9.   Dr. Winston O'Boogie's words of wisdom are on the back of the **Shaved Fish** album sleeve.

10. Paul's concluding statement was part of his introduction to John's book, *In His Own Write*.

11. Paul's reply: "No, actually we're just good friends."

12. Paul was thanking Ringo's wife, Maureen, who was clapping the loudest.

13. Paul was referring to his first solo album **McCartney**. Until a few weeks before its release, only the immediate McCartney family and a handful of engineers had heard the album, making it, in Nicholas Schaffner's words, "...one of the best kept secrets in rock."

14. Paul told Father Guido (on the 17 May 1980 telecast of "Saturday Night Live") that he would like to be a koala bear.

15. Paul's telegram to Julian read, "Good luck, old fruit."

16. George was referring to Brian Jones, founder of the Rolling Stones, on the occasion of Jones's death, 3 July 1969.

17. "Ding Dong, Ding Dong"

18. Ringo's reply was, "No, I'm a mocker."

19. Ringo wanted to come back as one of his cats.

20. "To have been in the audience when the Beatles played."
      (From Weinburg's book *The Big Beat - Conversations With Rock's Great Drummers*. While he was probably referring to his desire to have been in the audience during a show at the height of Beatlemania, technically, Ringo had been in the audience during a Beatles performance on at least one occasion. According to *The Beatles Live!*, Mark Lewisohn's indispensable chronology of the group's stage shows, Ringo, while still the drummer for Rory Storm and the Hurricanes, was in the audience with fellow band member Johnny Guitar the night the Beatles played at Litherland Town Hall, 5 January 1961.)

21. This quotation is attributed to Charles O. Finley, owner of the Kansas City Athletics.
      (Finley paid Brian Epstein $150,000 for one unscheduled per-

formance by the Beatles at the city's Municipal Stadium, 17 September 1964.)

22. Britain's Prime Minister, Sir Alec Douglas-Home.

23. Richard Rodgers.

24. "This Boy"

25. This quotation was taken from Derek Taylor's liner notes for the U.K. LP, **Beatles For Sale.**

26. Richard Brautigan, in his introduction for the book *The Beatles Lyrics Illustrated*, compared the songs of the group to "the silence of flooded houses."

27. Paul felt that the ITN had a responsibility not to spread the news of McCartney's admission in the 16 June 1967 issue of "Life" magazine that he had taken LSD.

28. Agnes is mentioned in the liner notes for the U.S. edition of the **Yellow Submarine** album.

29. Swan Records placed the phrase "Don't Drop Out" on the labels of their Beatles singles "She Loves You," "Sie Liebt Dich" (both backed with "I'll Get You"), and on the one-sided promo single "I'll Get You," presumably as an encouragement to young record buyers to stay in school.

30. The bus is "ten miles north on the Dewsbury Road. (And they're having a lovely time!")
      (Dialogue is from the "Magical Mystery Tour" television special.)

31. This statement is on the back cover of John and Yoko's **Some Time In New York City** album.

32. "Hare Krishna"

33. This quotation is from the front cover of **Some Time In New York City.**

34. This statement was written by John at the top of a drawing he'd made of a football (rugby) match, a drawing later included as part of the artwork for his **Walls And Bridges** LP.

(The artwork for **Walls And Bridges** was originally intended for the **Rock 'N' Roll** album sleeve.)

35. This statement is on the cover of the **Ringo** album and on the cover of Harry Nilsson's RCA album **Duit On Mon Dei.**

36. This statement is on the back cover of Ringo's **Blast From Your Past** album.

37. This phrase appears among the liner notes on the back of the **Venus And Mars** album sleeve.

38. Derek Taylor is quoted as saying this on the back of the **Live Peace In Toronto** album sleeve.

39. "No Comment"

40. While guest deejaying on New York's WNEW-FM, the afternoon of 28 September 1974, John prefaced his playing of Electric Light Orchestra's "Showdown" by referring to them as "Son of Beatles."

41. This quotation is attributed to Eric Carmen while he was a member of the Raspberries.

42. The keepers of the wishing well are Yoko and Sean.

(Statement is from the back of Yoko's Polydor album, **It's Alright.**)

43. Ringo's **Goodnight Vienna** album plugs the books of Terry Southern (*Magic Christian, Candy*), while the booklet from the **Ringo** album offers thanks to Kilgore Trout *and all the Beavers.*

44. If you're able, Clint Harrigan would like you to dig Wings' 1971 LP, **Wild Life.**

45. This quotation, from the front cover of **Unfinished Music No.1: Two Virgins**, is attributed to Paul.

CHAPTER 8

WE HOPE YOU
WILL ENJOY THE SHOW

Did you ever see the Beatles in concert? I surely wish I could have! What would you have given to be walking past the Indra in Hamburg one hot night in late August 1960? How about queuing up all night in front of the Cavern with the original Beatlettes just to see you-know-who the following night? Would a front-row vantage point for the group's Apple rooftop concert of 30 January 1969 be more to your liking? Tell you what, while you're doing this quiz on Beatles/Beatle-related concerts over the years, will somebody be so kind as to pass me the nearest time machine?

1.   The McCartney Brothers (Paul and Mike) performed only once in their brief career as a duo. What songs did they sing and where?

2.   When the Silver Beetles [sic] auditioned for Larry Parnes at the Wyvern Social Club, 10 May 1960, who were they hoping to back on a tour, had they "passed the audition"?

3.   From 20-28 May 1960, the Silver Beetles toured Scotland backing whom?

4.   When the leader of this Liverpool group turned down Allan Williams's offer of a booking at Bruno Koschmider's Indra Club (beginning 17 August 1960), it afforded the Silver Beetles [sic] their first trip to Hamburg. Name this group and their leader.

5.   When the Beatles (with Pete Best) made their first appearance at Hamburg's Star Club (13 April through 31 May, 1962), who were the supporting bands?

6.   Following the Beatles' first concert appearance at London's Royal Albert Hall, 18 April 1963, one member of the Rolling Stones was mistaken for a Beatle while helping them carry their guitars and amplifiers to the stage door. Which Stone was it?

7.   Ringo played his Ludwig Super Classic PC "Beatles"-logo drums for the first time in public on what show?

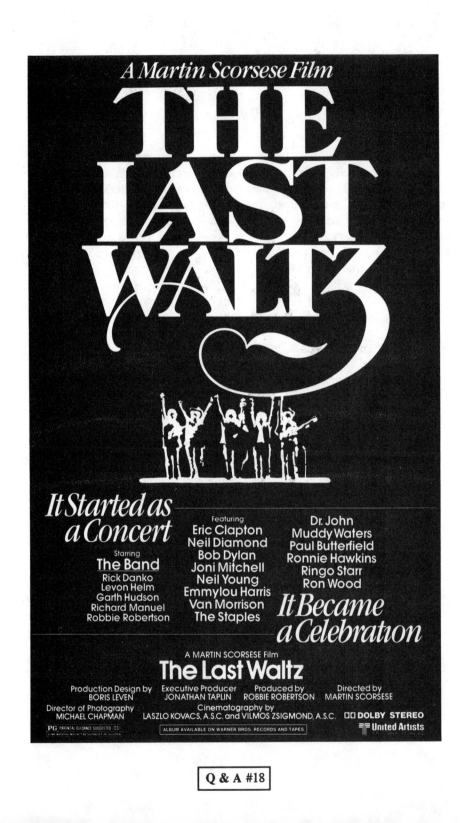

Q & A #18

8. After selling out both of his Carnegie Hall Beatles shows (12 February 1964), at what venue did Sid Bernstein want to promote a follow-up Beatles concert?

9. When the Beatles arrived in Cincinnati (27 August 1964) to play at the Cincinnati Gardens that evening, what song did they serenade the airport crowd with?

10. What did John do for the first time in public at the Beatles' first Shea Stadium concert, 15 August 1965?

11. Did the Beatles ever perform in their Sgt. Pepper suits? If you said yes, please specify where.

12. Why didn't John perform at George's Bangla Desh concert, held in Madison Square Garden, 1 August 1971?

13. What was Paul's condition (ultimately rejected) to George before he would agree to play the Concert for Bangla Desh?

14. To the nearest million, how much money did the Bangla Desh concert raise?

15. Name two occasions upon which John and Stevie Wonder appeared on the same bill.

16. John Lennon's three songs at Elton John's 28 November 1974 concert at Madison Square Garden, "Whatever Gets You Through The Night," "Lucy In The Sky With Diamonds," and "I Saw Her Standing There," were all released on an EP in 1981, but a complement of Elton's songs from this show appeared first on what album?

17. Why was there a delay of several weeks between Wings' last European tour date (Paris, 26 March 1976) and the start of their American tour (in Fort Worth, Texas, 3 May 1976)?

18. In Martin Scorsese's 1977 film of the Band's farewell concert, "The Last Waltz," what song does Ringo play drums on?

19. Had Paul's marijuana gone unnoticed when he arrived at Tokyo airport 16 January 1980, he would have played the Nippon Budokan Hall seven times. The programs from this appearance (now worth as

much as $50) featured a picture of Paul Newman. Why was it included?

20. Who played the music in the Great Throne Room at Buckingham Palace as the Beatles received their MBE's from Queen Elizabeth, 26 October 1965? What selections did they perform?

21. Shortly before his death, Brian Epstein offered to set up an international tour of Europe for this New York-based band. Earlier, Brian wanted the same band's publishing company, "Three Prong Music," to merge with Nemperor. What was the name of this band?

22. When Led Zeppelin played the L.A. Forum in September of 1970, their set included a medley of "Communication Breakdown," "Good Times, Bad Times," the Buffalo Springfield's "For What It's Worth," and a Beatles song. Which Beatles song did they play?

23. Name the only rock group to appear at both Woodstock and the One-To-One benefit concert.

24. Who was the last group to play the original Cavern?

25. Who was the first rock performer to play Los Angeles' Dodger Stadium after the Beatles' appearance there before 45,000 fans, 28 August 1966?

26. Who was the first major rock star to sing "Back In The U.S.S.R." in the U.S.S.R.?

27. In 1984, George and Ringo joined well-known bands onstage to liven things up a bit. Name the two respective bands George and Ringo jammed with.

28. On 21 October 1985, George Harrison came out of semi-retirement to join Carl Perkins, Ringo, Eric Clapton, and many others for the taping of the Cinemax special, "A Rockabilly Session - Carl Perkins and Friends." One highlight of many that evening was Carl's rendition of this Perkins classic, backed by the harmonies of Harrison and Dave Edmunds. What is the title of this song?

29. On 19 February 1987, George strolled onto the stage at the Palomino Club in North Hollywood with a couple of "good friends" to

jam with Jesse Ed Davis' Graffiti [sic] Band and Taj Mahal. Harrison ran through such Beatle cover classics as "Honey Don't," "Matchbox," and "Dizzie Miss Lizzie." Who, by the way, were Harrison's friends?

30. Where did Dhani Harrison first see his father perform live onstage before an audience? What songs did George perform?

WE HOPE YOU WILL ENJOY THE SHOW
(ANSWERS)

---

1. The McCartney Brothers performed at Butlin's Holiday Camp in Filey, Yorkshire. Paul and Mike sang the Everly Brothers' "Bye Bye Love," after which Paul launched into his best Little Richard rendition of "Long Tall Sally."

2. The Silver Beetles were hoping to back Ronald Wycherley, better known by his stage name, Billy Fury.

3. The Silver Beetles toured Scotland backing Johnny Gentle, the stage name for John Askew.

4. The Silver Beatles were asked to play the Indra Club (and later the Kaiserkeller) after Gerry Marsden, of Gerry and the Pacemakers, turned down the gig.

5. Also appearing with the Beatles at their first Star Club gig were Tex Roberg and the Graduates, and the Batchelors.
    (For two weeks of the Beatles' Star Club stint, they shared the bill with Little Richard, and later with Gene Vincent.)

6. The Stone mistaken for a Beatle was Brian Jones.

7. Ringo debuted his Ludwig "Beatles"-logo drums on an appearance of ABC's "Lucky Stars (Summer Spin)," filmed 23 June 1963 and transmitted 29 June 1963.

8. Bernstein was willing to pay the Beatles $25,000 to play Madison Square Garden.
    (Epstein turned down Sid's offer.)

9. "Hello Dolly"

10. John played the electric organ in public for the first time on "I'm Down."

11. The Beatles were featured performing "Hello Goodbye" in their Sgt. Pepper suits (courtesy of Berman's Theatrical Outfitters) in one of the three promotional films they shot for the song at London's Saville Theatre, 10 November 1967.

(During his solo career, George has twice donned Pepper suits for shots used in his promotional films/videos: first in 1974 for "Ding Dong, Ding Dong," then again in 1987 for "When We Was Fab.")

12. Allegedly because George would not let Yoko perform at the Bangla Desh concert, John would not appear.

13. Supposedly, Paul would have agreed to perform at the Bangla Desh concert if George had dropped his lawsuit against him.

(This suit was brought by Allen Klein on behalf of the other three Beatles and Apple, after Paul had sued them in order to dissolve the Beatles and pursue a solo career.)

14. The Bangla Desh concert raised nearly $11,000,000.

(On 9 February 1982, George presented UNICEF chairman Hugh Downs with a check for $8.8 million. In 1972, Apple sent out $2 million just before an IRS impoundment of its funds began a nine-year audit of the company.)

15. On 10 December 1971, John and Stevie Wonder appeared at the Ann Arbor, Michigan, rally for John Sinclair. On 30 August 1972, both were featured on the bill at the One-To-One Concert at Madison Square Garden.

16. Elton's Madison Square Garden material first appeared on the album **Here and There** (MCA).

17. A delay in Wings' 1976 North American tour occured when lead guitarist Jimmy McCulloch slipped in the bathroom, breaking his left pinky.

(Speculation has it that McCulloch's broken pinky was a story concocted for the media to cover McCartney's desire to delay the

58

Tour program.

Q & A #19

American tour following the death of his father, 18 March 1976.)

18. Ringo played drums with the Band at San Francisco's Winterland, 24 November 1976, on "I Shall Be Released."

19. Paul Newman's picture was part of a two-page advertisement for "Maxwell Blendy" instant coffee.

20. As the Beatles received their MBE's, the band of the Coldstream Guards played selections from "Bittersweet" and "Humoresque."

21. Brian wanted to set up a tour for the Velvet Underground.
(Before being fired and replaced by Moe Tucker, original VU drummer Angus MacLise was involved in the Fluxus artists group, of which Yoko was a member. MacLise collaborated with Ono on her "Music For Dance" piece.)

22. Led Zepp's "Communication Breakdown" medley included "I Saw Her Standing There."

23. Sha Na Na is the only group that appeared at both Woodstock and the One-To-One benefit.

24. The Hideaways were the last group to play the original Cavern.

25. Elton John was the next rock performer to play Dodger Stadium, 23 October 1975.

26. The first major rock star to sing "Back In The U.S.S.R." in the Soviet Union was Elton John, in May of 1979.
(Elton's Russian tour is chronicled in the film, "To Russia...With Elton." Elton's tour of the U.S. that September was called the "Back In The U.S.S.A." tour.)

27. On 4 July 1984, Ringo joined The Beach Boys onstage at shows in Washington, D.C., and Miami, Florida.
(Ringo played on several songs that day including "Back In The U.S.S.R," "Day Tripper," and "You Can't Do That." On The Beach Boys' 1985 Caribou album release, titled simply **The Beach Boys**, Ringo plays drums and timpani on Side two's opening cut, "California Calling.")
Playing Ritchie Blackmore's guitar on a rendition of "Lucille,"

George joined Deep Purple on stage in Sydney, Australia, 14 December 1984.

(Harrison was brought onstage by Ian Gillan, who introduced George as "Arnold From Liverpool," whom the audience had been led to believe was the winner of a contest to play with the band.)

28. Carl, George, and Dave played and sang together on "Your True Love."

(Other highlights of the special, titled "Blue Suede Shows: Carl Perkins and Friends" in Britain, were Ringo's renditions of "Honey Don't" and "Matchbox," with Perkins and Eric Clapton joining in on the latter song. George took a lead vocal on "Everybody's Trying To Be My Baby" and "Sure To Fall." Because of a time limitation, "Sure To Fall" had to be cut from the hour-long special.)

29. George jammed at the Palomino Club that night in the company of Bob Dylan and John Fogerty.

30. Dhani first saw his father perform live at the 1987 Prince's Trust Rock Gala, 5 June, at London's Wembley Arena. Backed by an all-star band which included Ringo, Eric Clapton, Elton John, and Phil Collins, Harrison sang "While My Guitar Gently Weeps" and "Here Comes The Sun."

(George also joined the all-stars singing backup for Ringo on his rendition of "With A Little Help From My Friends.")

The gate at Strawberry Field, Liverpool.
Previously unpublished photo by
Joyce Sanderson.

CHAPTER 9

FROM THE MAN IN THE CROWD
WITH THE MULTI-COLOURED MIRRORS

This is a quiz on the songs of the Walrus, Yer Bluesman, Old Flattop, a Peacenik, a Dreamer, and a Wheel Watcher. But you know I know this isn't a dream - all these people, and many more besides, were John Winston Ono Lennon. You, too, could be suffering from a severe case of Lennon Fever. You are not alone! While this quiz may not be as good as a drink from Dr. Robert's special cup, the songs of Dr. O'Boogie are guaranteed to keep you from having to go cold turkey.

1.   Which of John's Beatles songs did he once say he wanted to re-make, as he felt it was recorded too fast the first time?

2.   From which song did John borrow a line for "Run For Your Life"?

3.   How long did it take John to write "Strawberry Fields Forever"?

4.   "We just stuck two songs together...same as 'A Day In The Life'," said John, when asked who wrote this song, included on the **Magical Mystery Tour** LP. Which song is it?

5.   Name the two songs on "The White Album" on which Yoko Ono sings backing vocals.

6.   When the Beatles anthologies **1962-1966** and **1967-1970** were re-leased, John was not pleased. One song in particular, in its remixed form, he was particularly vocal about, calling it "a piece of ice cream." Which song was he referring to?

7.   List all the tracks comprising John and Yoko's **Wedding Album**.

8.   John plays a snippet of which Beatles song on the **Wedding Album**?

9.   Who did Yoko prefer as the piano player on the song "Imagine"?

10. What do John and Yoko whisper at the beginning of "Happy Xmas (War Is Over)"?

11. Name two songs, included on Adam VIII Records' unauthorized Lennon TV album, **Roots**, that did not appear on John's Capitol LP, **Rock 'N' Roll**.

12. Though John denied copying Chuck Berry's song "You Can't Catch Me" when he wrote "Come Together," on 8 October 1974, he met with music publisher Morris Levy to reach an out of court settlement on a suit filed by Levy which contended just that. Levy, who runs Big Seven Music, the publisher of "You Can't Catch Me," required as part of the settlement that John record three Big Seven songs. Which songs did John select?

13. Yoko described these two songs as "the backbone of **Double Fantasy**." What are the songs?

14. John's guitar lick for "Walking On Thin Ice" was based on what song?

15. What is the B-side of "Walking On Thin Ice"?

16. Name the song John gave Ringo to record for his **Can't Fight Lightning** album.

17. Though they are included on the U.K. version of the LP, in the U.S., which songs are only available on Geffen's cassette version of **John Lennon: The Collection**?

18. Which of his father's songs did Julian Lennon record in 1982, intending to release it?

19. This song, featured on his **Rock 'N' Roll** album, is one of John's all-time favorites. John has even gone on record as wishing he'd written it. What is the title of this song?

20. What is the title of the song John composed for Harry Nilsson?

21. What is the title of the song John produced in 1974, featuring Mick Jagger on vocals?

22. Name the only song (so far) that both John and Yoko have sung and released versions of.

23. Which of John's songs is subtitled "Freda People"?

24. Which of John's songs did he envision being played at weddings?

25. List all of the songs John has released that feature a reprise later in their respective albums.

**FROM THE MAN IN THE CROWD
WITH THE MULTI-COLOURED MIRRORS
(ANSWERS)**

1. "Help!"

2. John borrowed a line from the Arthur "Hardrock" Gunter song, "Baby, Let's Play House" for "Run For Your Life."
   ("I'd rather see you dead little girl than to be with another man.")

3. John has said it took him six weeks to write "Strawberry Fields Forever," according to an interview conducted by David Sheff for "Playboy" in September 1980.

4. "Baby You're A Rich Man"

5. Yoko's backing vocals can be heard on "The Continuing Story Of Bungalow Bill" and "Birthday."

6. John called the fast version of "Revolution" on the **1967-1970** anthology, "a piece of ice cream."

7. Side A: "John and Yoko"
   Side B: "Amsterdam"

8. "Goodnight"

9. While John insisted on playing piano, Yoko's first choice for pianist on "Imagine" was Nicky Hopkins.
   (Hopkins worked with John on 11 July 1968 when he played

John's framed gold record for the LP Imagine.

electric piano for an overdub on "Revolution" in Abbey Road's Studio Three.)

10. Yoko: "Happy Christmas, Kyoko."
John: "Happy Christmas, Julian."

11. "Angel Baby" and "Be My Baby"
("Angel Baby" was finally released by Capitol in October of 1986, along with two other songs from the **Rock 'N' Roll** sessions, "My Baby Left Me" and "To Know Her Is To Love Her," on the album **Menlove Avenue**, a collection of previously unreleased Lennon outtakes.)

12. John recorded "Angel Baby" and "You Can't Catch Me" from the Big Seven Music catalogue, and "Ya Ya," co-written by Levy and published by the Frost Music Corp.

13. "Grow Old With Me" and "Let Me Count The Ways"
(A Christmas deadline for the album's release, plus a delay in arranging "Grow Old With Me," kept both songs off **Double Fantasy**.)

14. John's guitar lick on "Walking On Thin Ice" is based on Sanford Clark's "The Fool" (1956).

15. Featuring a spoken intro by John, "It Happened" is the B-side of "Walking On Thin Ice."

16. John composed "Life Begins At Forty" for Ringo to include on **Can't Fight Lightning**. Ringo opted not to include the song on the album, later retitled **Stop And Smell The Roses**.

17. "Happy Xmas (War Is Over)" and "Stand By Me"

18. "I Don't Wanna Face It"
(Yoko asked Julian not to release it, as his father's version of the song had not (at the time) been issued.)

19. John wishes he had written "Bring It On Home To Me," the Sam Cooke song he sings in medley with "Send Me Some Lovin'."
(John made an obvious allusion to the song in "Remember," one of the songs on the LP **John Lennon/Plastic Ono Band**: compare the lines "If you ever change your mind/About leaving it all behind..." with Sam Cooke's "If you ever change your mind/About leaving

me behind....")

20. "Mucho Mungo"
(This song was recorded in medley with Nilsson's "Mt. Elga," and released on Nilsson's **Pussycats** album, which John also produced.)

21. "Too Many Cooks"
(As of this writing, this song has yet to be commercially released.)

22. "Every Man Has A Woman Who Loves Him"
(Yoko's version appears on **Double Fantasy**, while John's version was released posthumously on the **Every Man Has A Woman** album. Also recorded, but as yet unreleased, is John's version of "Hard Times.")

23. "Bring On The Lucie"
(From the **Mind Games** album.)

24. "Grow Old With Me"

25. "Give Peace A Chance"
(Featured on the **Shaved Fish** album, the reprise is a snippet of the song from John and Yoko's appearance at the One-To-One Concert at Madison Square Garden, 30 August 1972. The predominant voice on the reprise is that of Stevie Wonder.)

CHAPTER 10

GIVE THE LETTERS WHICH THOU FIND'ST ABOUT ME TO EDMUND EARL OF GLOUCESTER

(Liverpudlian recitation accent optional.)

I sat belonely 'neath a tree,
To write of Beatle poetry.
Of poems and plays and shorts of story,
All recall past Beatle glory.
So please forgive me grotty rhyme,
Indulge yourself a quiz this time.

1.   Where can you hear John recite his poems "Jock and Yono" and "Once Upon A Pool Table"?

2.   A is for Parrot which we can plainly see.
B is for glasses which we can plainly see.
Y is a crooked letter and you can't straighten it.
Z is for Apple which we can plainly see.

These letters of the alphabet, and all the ones in between, were part of a poem written by John as the introduction for what project?

3.   Which poem from *A Spaniard In The Works* did David Peel set to music and record?

4.   Which song, recorded by Wings, was based on a poem written by Edwin Arlington Robinson?

5.   What are the titles of the poems excerpted on "The Broadcast," a track on **Back To The Egg**?

6.   How is the poetry of Rabindranath Tagore related to Paul and one of his songs?

7.   Where did John's story "A Carrot In A Potatoe Mine" first ap-

pear in print?

8.   What is notable about the authorship of John's short story "On Safairy With Whide Hunter," first published in "Mersey Beat" newspaper and later in John's first book?

9.   What is the title of Gregory Benford's science fiction short story about a man who, after an extended period of hibernation, awakens claiming to be John Lennon?

10.   What is the title of John Weeks' short story about a Beatles reunion concert before 80,000 fans at the New Orleans Superdome, a gathering brought about by the abduction of the four men and the threat of harm to their families?

11.   Originally published in "The Best Of Omni," what is the title of Spider Robinson's short story detailing the first day of John's life - twenty-four years after his assassination?

12.   From what Shakespearean play, act, and scene is the fadeout of "I Am The Walrus" taken?

13.   Who were the authors of the sketch the Beatles performed as part of their 1963 Christmas show? What was the title of this sketch?

14.   "In His Own Write," the one-act play adapted from John's two books, was originally titled what?

15.   What is "Four In Hand"?

**GIVE THE LETTERS
WHICH THOU FIND'ST ABOUT ME
TO EDMUND EARL OF GLOUCESTER
(ANSWERS)**

---

1.   The Beatles' 1968 Christmas message features the poems "Jock and Yono" and "Once Upon A Pool Table."
      (Both of these poems first appeared in print in the 28 December 1968 issue of "New Musical Express." It was later included in first issue copies of the **Live Peace In Toronto** album as part of the text for

the "John And Yoko Calendar For 1970." In October of 1986, Harper & Row published the poems in a new collection of John's writings, ala *In His Own Write*, titled *Skywriting By Word Of Mouth*. The poems were featured in a chapter titled "Two Virgins.")

2.   This poem accompanied John's "Bag One" lithographs.
(The poem was also reprinted as the chapter "An Alphabet" in *Skywriting By Word Of Mouth*.)

3.   Peel included "My Fat Budgie" on his 1977 album, **Bring Back The Beatles**, released on Peel's own Orange Records label.

4.   Paul Simon's song, "Richard Cory."
(Sung by Denny Laine on the **Wings Over America** album.)

5.   "The Sport Of Kings" by Ian Hay, and "The Little Man" by John Galsworthy.

6.   Tagore wrote the line "In love all of life's contradictions dissolve and disappear," the basis for Paul's song "Pipes Of Peace."

7.   "A Carrot In A Potatoe Mine" appears in John's Quarry Bank school exercise book, "The Daily Howl."

8.   John coauthored "On Safairy with Whide Hunter" with Paul.
(Or, as John states in the book's index, "Written in conjugal with Paul.")

9.   Published in the April 1975 issue of "Analog" magazine, Benford's short story is titled "Doing Lennon."

10.   Published in the March 1978 issue of "Oui" magazine, Weeks' short story is titled, "The Beatles' Not-So-Magical Mystery Tour."

11.   An absolute treasure of Beatles-related puns and inside jokes, Spider Robinson's short story is titled "Rubber Soul."
("Rubber Soul" is currently available as a chapter in a paperback collection of Robinson's short stories titled, *Melancholy Elephants* (Tor, 1985).)

12.   The fade of "I Am The Walrus" is from BBC Third Programme's production of "King Lear," Act IV, scene vi, a radio broadcast from

29 September 1967.

("Walrus" contains two lengthy, audible passages from Shakespeare's tragedy, the first occuring after John sings the line, "If the sun don't come you get a tan from standing in the English rain." As Lennon begins to recite the chorus:

("I am the Eggman...")

Gloucester [Mark Dignam]: *"Now, good sir,* what are you?"

("They are the Eggmen...")

Edgar [Philip Guard]: "A *most poor man, made tame to fortune's* blows..."

The second, more familiar passage, the death of Oswald by Edgar's blade, is heard at the song's fade:

Oswald [John Bryning]: "Slave, thou hast slain me: - *villain, take my purse;*
If ever thou wilt thrive, *bury my body,*
And give *the letters which thou find'st about me,*
To Edmond earl of Gloster; seek him out
Upon the British party: - O, untimely death!"
　　　[Oswald dies]

Edgar: *"I know thee well: a serviceable villain;*
As duteous to the vices of thy mistress,
As badness would desire."

Gloucester: *"What, is he dead?"*

Edgar: *"Sit you down father; rest you - "*

(Note: I have indicated in italics the most audible spoken lines in the song.)

13.　The Beatles' 1963 Christmas show sketch, "What A Night," was written by Ireland Cutter and David Cumming.

14.　"Scene Three, Act One"

15. "Four In Hand" is the title (from the paperback adaptation of the play) of the group masturbation scene John wrote for "Oh! Calcutta!"

(It was Pete Shotton who suggested John contribute the story, drawn from a childhood memory. The scene features a group of men masturbating together while calling out the names of movie actresses.)

A SPANIARD IN THE WORKS

JOHN LENNON

Q & A #13

CHAPTER 11

TO BE OR NOT TO BEATLE

Over the years, there have been a lot of other loonies out there besides the Rutles taking playful swipes at the Beatles. Spike Milligan, writer Mark Shipper, and the "National Lampoon" have all had a go. For the most part, our heroes have been very good sports about it all; sometimes they've even been accessories to this peculiar madness. As the following quiz proves, these parodies run the gamut from complimentary to downright crude:

1.   Presented as a kind of fractured retelling of Mark Twain's "The Prince and the Pauper," who narrated Ringo's one-hour television special, first aired in the U.S. on NBC, 26 April 1978?

2.   Tony Hendra played John, and Melissa Manchester played Yoko on what recorded spoof, issued by the National Lampoon on two different albums?

3.   On which of Cheech and Chong's albums did George play guitar?

4.   In 1984, ATV Music sued Sesame Street Records for copyright infringement. Charges stemmed from Sesame Street's parodies of two Beatles songs, "Hey Jude" and "Let It Be," included on one of their children's albums. Name the album and the two song parodies.

5.   This comedy LP features pictures of Groucho Marx and John Lennon on its front sleeve. Name the title of this album and the comedy team who released it.

6.   Which Beatles song is briefly sung on the album mentioned in question #5 above? (Note: It is not sung by the Beatles.)

7.   What is the title of the song that John says he wrote as a Roy Orbison parody?

8.   What was Goon Spike Milligan's parody of "Yellow Submarine" titled?

9.   Which "Harrisong" did George parody on Eric Idle's "Rutland Weekend Television Christmas Show," aired in the British Isles on

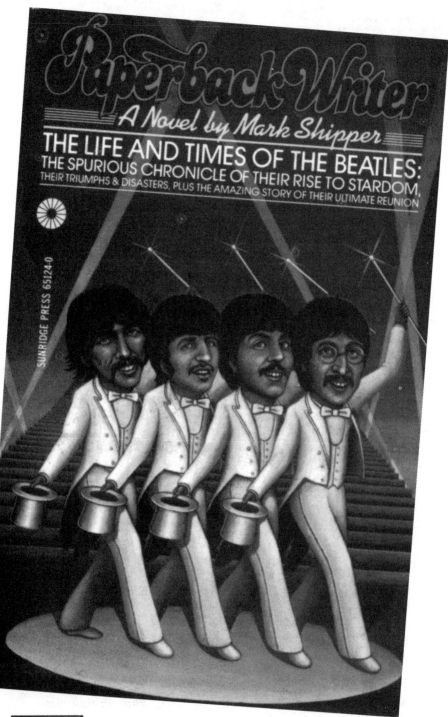

Paperback Writer

A Novel by Mark Shipper

THE LIFE AND TIMES OF THE BEATLES:
THE SPURIOUS CHRONICLE OF THEIR RISE TO STARDOM,
THEIR TRIUMPHS & DISASTERS, PLUS THE AMAZING STORY OF THEIR ULTIMATE REUNION

SUNRIDGE PRESS 65124-0

Q & A #21

26 December 1975?

10. What is the title of George and Eric's parody version of the song described above?

11. A snippet from which of Paul's songs is included on Dickie Goodman's "break-in" single, "Hey, E.T.!"?

12. In 1964, the "New Musical Express" reported that a record parodying the Beatles had been recorded by a group calling themselves "The Bumblers." Who were the members of "The Bumblers," according to the NME?

13. The title of John's second book, *A Spaniard In The Works* is a pun on what phrase?

14. On one of his comedy albums, this well-known stand-up comic thanked Ed Sullivan for bringing us the Beatles. Name him.

15. What is the title of Jane Oliver's underground comic parody of the Beatles?

The next five questions were drawn from articles that appeared in "National Lampoon" magazine's Beatles parody issue dated October 1977:

16. What is unique about Roger Huyssen's rendering of the front sleeve of **Abbey Road**, featured as the cover of the October 1977 issue of "National Lampoon"?

17. What is the title of George's unreleased solo album from 1969?

18. What is the title of Ringo's unreleased solo album from 1967?

19. What did the Lampoon say was to be the Beatles' follow-up to the movie "Help!"?

20. "Love Mao Do," "(Won't You) Please Police Me," and "Paperback Tiger" were all songs to be included on what unreleased Beatles album?

In the next five questions, recall the slightly twisted history of the Beatles as recounted in Mark Shipper's 1978 novel *Paperback Writer*.

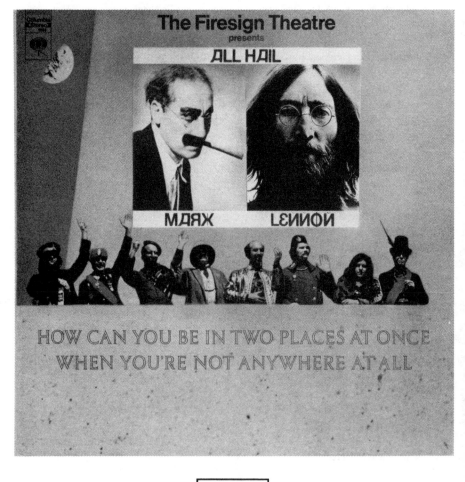

21. Why did Mark Shipper write his Beatle spoof, *Paperback Writer*?

22. According to *Paperback Writer*, what is the title of the Beatles' first album?

23. What was Paul trying to say in the title cut from Shipper's version of **Sgt. Pepper**?

24. What were the titles of George's two songs on **Get Back**, the Beatles' 1979 reunion album released on Columbia Records?

25. Who did the Beatles open for (!) at their final concert?

TO BE OR NOT TO BEATLE
(ANSWERS)

---

1. Ringo's "Ringo" special was narrated by George Harrison.

2. "Magical Misery Tour"
(From **Radio Dinner** and **Greatest Hits Of The National Lampoon**. **Radio Dinner** facetiously lists the cut as being from the album, **Yoko Is A Concept By Which We Measure Our Pain**.)

3. **Los Cochinos**
(George and his guitar guested on the song "Basketball Jones featuring Tyrone Shoelaces.")

4. **Born To Add** features "Letter B" and "Hey Food," as performed by the Sesame Street Beetles.

5. **How Can You Be In Two Places At Once When You're Not Anywhere At All** was released on Columbia Records in 1969 by the Firesign Theater.

6. A couple of lines from "I'm So Tired" are sung by Prof. Catherwood (David Ossman) on side two's "The Further Adventures Of Nick Danger."

7. "Please Please Me," the Beatles' first number 1 single in Britain,

#1 THE BAEGLES LOONEY HEARTS CLUB

$1⁰⁰

A KARMA KOMIX PRODUCTION.

S⁹ PEPPERS LOONEY HEARTS CLUB BAND

was written by John as a Roy Orbison parody.

8. Produced by George Martin and released as a single by Parlophone, Spike's take-off on "Yellow Submarine" is titled "Purple Aeroplane."

9. "My Sweet Lord"

10. "The Pirate Song"

11. "Take It Away"

12. "The Bumblers," as reported by the "New Musical Express," were Bing Crosby, Sammy Davis Jr., Dean Martin, and Frank Sinatra.

13. A "spanner" in the works, the British equivalent to the American expression which describes the disruption of smoothly running circumstances by "throwing a monkey wrench into" the process.

14. George Carlin thanked Mr. Sullivan on his comedy album **FM & AM** (Little David/Atlantic).

15. "The Baegles Looney Hearts Club"

16. The cover of the October 1977 issue of "National Lampoon" magazine, a variation on the cover of the **Abbey Road** LP, depicts the Beatles, apparently following their attempt to negotiate the famous zebra crossing, showing all the effects of having been flattened by a passing steamroller.

17. Featuring such cuts as "My Sweet He's So Fine" and "My Sweet Beethoven's Ninth Symphony," George's "unreleased" solo album is titled, **Lifting From The Material World.**

18. Suppressed by Beatles publicist Derek Taylor, Ringo's "unreleased" solo album is titled **Goodnight Vicar.**

19. Described as "a soft-core film with a jelly center," the Beatles' follow-up to "Help!" was to have been called "FUCK!"

20. Said to be inspired mainly by John, these songs were to be included on the Beatles' "unreleased" **Red Album**, also known as "The

Little Red Album."

21.   Shipper lost all the notes from his exclusive "tell-all" interview with Ringo, forcing him to make up his own version of the Beatles' story.

22.   **We're Gonna Change The Face Of Pop Music Forever.**

23.   "Sgt. Pepper" criticized the practice in the British Army of affording enlisted men higher quality condiments (such as a pepper for sergeants only) than that made available to privates.

24.   George's songs on **Get Back** were "Disco Jesus" and "Bring The Captain In To Kneel (Before The Altar)."

25.   At their final concert appearance, 2 August 1979, at L.A.'s Dodger Stadium, the Beatles opened for Peter Frampton.
      (Also supporting Frampton that night were The Sex Pistols.)

CHAPTER 12

EIGHT ARMS TO HOLD YOU (OR) GET BACK!

When you were younger, so much younger than today, were you and your mates looking forward to the release of the new Beatles motion picture?

"This time it'sa gonna be in colour," said George.

"Green," a quick-witted John added.

Will John live to sleep in his pit once more? Will Paul ever get back to his electric organ? Will George be reunited with his ticker-tape machine? And Ringo, will he ever play the drums again? And what about you? Are you still wearing your "HELP!" band-aid? Well take it off, your skin is turning green!

And while you're looking for a sympathetic nurse to give it a quick rip, why not have a go at this quiz on the Beatles' last two (theatrically premiered) films, "Help!" and "Let It Be."

1.   "In the weeks that followed, five more attempts were made to steal the ring," noted this caption, a prelude to the myriad plots carried out by Clang (played by Leo McKern) and his devotees in their efforts to recover the sacrificial ring of the dreaded Kaili. Prior to attempt number five, the Beatles are shown in the studio doing take five of "Your Gonna Lose That Girl." What instruments are the boys seen playing?

2.   Seeking enlightenment as to the ring's origins, our heroes pop into an Eastern restaurant, unaware that the staff of this public house are being systematically replaced by Clang's thugs. After the "Indian" house band is spirited off, what do Clang's replacements begin playing?

3.   Following the events at the restaurant, Clang appears outside the Beatles' Ailsa Avenue flats in Twickenham disguised as a manhole cover. What song are the Beatles playing during this scene?

4.   During "the exciting adventures of Paul on the floor," what brand of gum wrapper did Paul wrap himself in when, following an accidental injection of Priestess Ahme's "minor medical secret," he suddenly finds himself shrunk to the size of a beetle?

5.   During the curling scene in the Austrian alps, Professor Tiberius Foot (a mad scientist played by Victor Spinetti), arranges for a curling stone laden with explosives to be put into play. What does George call this booby trap when warning the others?

6.   Following the explosion of the curling stone, a lost Channel swimmer (played by Mal Evans) emerges from the broken ice to inquire of the Beatles if he has reached his destination. Where was he headed?

7.   Back in London following their Austrian escapades, our heroes seek out Scotland Yard for protection. What is the name of the superintendent who takes on their case?

8.   While the Beatles are singing "The Night Before" on the Salisbury Plain, what other Beatles song is Ahme playing on a portable tape recorder?

9.   What scene from "Help!" was filmed in the Madame Pompadour room at the Cliveden home of Lord Astor?

10.   At Buckingham Palace, Professor Foot tries to slow the Beatles' escape down a palace hallway with what device?

11.   How does Clang transport himself to the Bahamas for his final confrontation with the Beatles in Nassau?

12.   Paul plays (as his bass) a bikini-clad girl during what song?

13.   Who is Sam Ahab and what is his connection to "Help!"?

14.   Why did the Beatles choose Michael Lindsay-Hogg to direct "Let It Be"?

15.   As early as 1966, plans had been made for the Beatles to work with Michael Lindsay-Hogg on a promotional film for what song?

16.   Filming on "Let It Be" began 2 February 1969 at Twickenham Film Studios, London. In his book, "The Love You Make," Peter Brown writes that the Beatles "were brought there early every morning...and put under the scrutiny of two 16mm-cameras filming

their every move." What brand of cameras were used to film the Fabs?

17. What was the first scene shot for "Let It Be"?

18. Who plays anvil during the film's rehearsal scene for "Maxwell's Silver Hammer"?

19. Which song did John and Yoko waltz to in "Let It Be"?

20. "They said our love was just fun,
The day that our friendship begun.
There's no blue moon that I can see,
There's never been in history."

During a discussion of the merits of early Lennon and McCartney songwriting, Paul sings this verse from what unreleased Beatles song?

21. What is the title of the first song featuring an onscreen appearance by Billy Preston?

22. Which song was not originally intended for the "Let It Be" soundtrack album, but was quickly recorded when it was decided to leave in the corresponding film segment?

23. Lindsay-Hogg and the Beatles once discussed fictionalizing a sequence in "Let It Be." What were they planning to do?

24. What is the connection between Stephen King, chief accountant at the Royal Bank of Scotland in January of 1969, and the filming of "Let It Be"?

25. What is "Bluthner"?

```
EIGHT ARMS TO HOLD YOU
(OR) GET BACK!
(ANSWERS)
```

1. On "You're Gonna Lose That Girl," John plays acoustic guitar, Paul alternates between his Hofner bass and piano, George plays lead

on his electric guitar, and Ringo switches off between his drum kit and a pair of bongos.

2. Clang's replacement band launches into an instrumental version of "A Hard Day's Night," identified on Capitol's **Help!** soundtrack LP as "Another Hard Day's Night."

3. While Clang bided his time, John serenaded Priestess Ahme (Eleanor Bron) with "You've Got To Hide Your Love Away."

4. Paul covered himself with the Wrigley's spearmint gum wrapper previously discarded by George.

5. George called the smoking curling stone "a fiendish thingy."

6. Mal's character is trying to reach the White Cliffs of Dover.

7. Superintendent Gluck of Scotland Yard (played by Patrick Cargill) directed the efforts to protect the Beatles, alternately, from Clang and Professor Foot.

8. "She's A Woman"

9. Lord Astor's home in Cliveden doubled as Buckingham Palace in the film. The scene where George and Ringo are shown playing poker, while Paul and John discuss the merits of Mr. Starkey cutting off his ring-laden digit, was filmed in the Madame Pompadour room of the Astor home.

10. Foot tries to slow the Beatles' escape with a Relativity Cadenza he acquired from Harvard.

11. Clang arrives in Nassau via the Goodyear blimp, "Mayflower."

12. "Another Girl"
(While Paul is "playing" left-handed girl in this scene, the other Beatles have taken the opportunity to switch instruments as well. John is playing Ringo's drum kit, George is playing Paul's bass, and Ringo is playing John's acoustic guitar.)

13. In *The Beatles in HELP!*, Al Hine's novelisation of the movie based on Marc Behm's screenplay, Sam Ahab was a dramatic arts

teacher from whom the Beatles were taking acting lessons.

14. The Beatles chose Michael Lindsay-Hogg to direct "Let It Be" after the two Beatles promotional films he directed, "Hey Jude" and "Revolution" (shot at Twickenham Film Studios on 4 September 1968), significantly boosted sales of that single.
     (In England, the films were televised on David Frost's "Frost On Sunday" show, 8 September. In the U.S., "Hey Jude" was broadcast on the "Smothers Brothers Comedy Hour," 6 October, with the "Revolution" clip airing the following Sunday, 13 October.)

15. Plans were made (which later fell through) for Lindsay-Hogg to direct a promotional film for "Paperback Writer."

16. The Beatles were filmed at Twickenham on two Beaulieu 16-mm outfits.

17. The first scene shot for "Let It Be" was the one which opens the film, a shot of Mal Evans picking up the "Beatles"-logo bass drumskin.

18. The man at the anvil during "Maxwell" was Mal Evans.

19. John and Yoko waltzed to "I Me Mine."

20. Paul offhandedly sings a verse from "Just Fun."

21. Billy Preston is seen for the first time in "Let It Be" while playing the organ on a version of "You Really Got A Hold On Me."

22. "I Me Mine"
     (Recorded without John on 3 January 1970.)

23. Lindsay-Hogg and the Beatles discussed plans to fictionalize part of the rooftop sequence by featuring an actor in a London bobby's uniform who would "...shake his fist and say something about 'getting those bastards'."
     (Such a sequence was, of course, unnecessary, as the real thing showed up during filming. Lindsay-Hogg's quotation was taken from an interview with the director included in "Rolling Stone," No. 62, 9 July 1970.)

24.   Mr. King called in the "black marias" to halt the Beatles' first live performance together on the roof of the Apple building, 3 Saville Row, 30 January 1969.

25.   Bluthner is the brand of grand piano McCartney is seen playing in the film, most notably in the formal performance sequences and for "Let It Be" and "The Long And Winding Road."

CHAPTER 13

SO KEEP ON PLAYIN'
THOSE MIND GAMES

Bloody hell, it's just like those bleedin' story questions I had to solve in school! Don't know 'bout you lads, but it's goodnight Vienna! Hold on now, stop, oh yes, wait a minute! These look like Beatles story questions. Should make 'em a mite simpler, shouldn't it?

1. When the Beatles, in a letter written on their behalf by Stuart Sutcliffe, informed Allan Williams he was no longer their manager, Williams wrote them back, in a letter dated 20 April 1961, admonishing them for refusing to pay him his weekly commission on their current Hamburg gig at Peter Eckhorn's Top Ten Club. Among his threats, Williams wrote that if they failed to pay him his fee, he would forget about considering them as the backing group for what singer, arriving soon (in England) from America?

2. When Ringo checked into University College Hospital in London to have his tonsils removed (1 December 1964), The Official Beatles Fan Club was able to get updated information on Ringo's condition. This was made possible because of a prearranged code word the hospital agreed to acknowledge. What was that code word?

3. During their final world tour in 1966, the Beatles unknowingly slept through Imelda Marcos' luncheon party, 4 July, while playing in Manila, the Philippines. On an earlier world tour, the Beatles slept through a similar reception, though the consequences weren't nearly as traumatic. Name the year and the country the Beatles were appearing in when the earlier incident occurred.

4. Dominique Chevalier, in her book, *Viva Zappa!*, described Frank Zappa's December 1967 release of the album, **We're Only In It For The Money**, as "...an allusion to the fortune that the Beatles were making from their hippyish new look." Indeed, "Money's" artwork is a direct parody of the **Sgt. Pepper** sleeve. Designed by Calvin Schenkel, Zappa's cover features likenesses of Harry Truman, Lyndon Johnson, Lee Harvey Oswald, Jimi Hendrix, Elvis Presley, and Rod Serling, among others. There is, however, one person who appears on both the covers of "Pepper" and "Money." Who is he?

When British fans bought those first Beatle LPs and EPs, from 1963 to 1965, they could look forward to copious liner notes penned by Tony Barrow or Derek Taylor. They were usually pretentious affairs, often structured as favourable reviews, gushing over with the praises of each Beatles' musical merits. While the practice didn't catch on with quite as much fervor on early Beatles albums here in the states, we Yanks do have our share of pompous liner notes.

Excerpts from some of these texts comprise the next eight questions. Please identify from which album or EP these quotations were taken. (Hint: Four excerpts are from British discs, three from American LPs, and one was featured text from a disc released in both countries.)

5.   "Their own built-in tunesmith team of John Lennon and Paul McCartney has tucked away enough self-penned numbers to maintain a steady output of all original singles from now until 1975!"

6.   "...preserve this sleeve for ten years, exhume it from your collection somewhere around the middle of 1973 and write me a very nasty letter if the pop people of the 70's aren't talking with respect about at least two of these titles as 'early examples of modern beat standards taken from The Lennon & McCartney Songbook'."

7.   "People old enough to know worse - and who often do - can be overheard saying: 'It's about time they did another one.' And so it is and here it is and aren't we all very proud of it?"

8.   "At the same time it is interesting to remember that the LP housed within this sleeve is the first-ever album release to be made up entirely of self-composed and self-performed Beatle compositions."

9.   "And here in this album are five hit vocals from that movie, United Artists' 'A Hard Day's Night' which is, of course, the Beatles' first! Now their fans can see John, George, Paul and Ringo giant-size on the screen *and* play the big hits from the picture on their HiFi and Stereo sets between trips to the movies!"

10. "But you, the Beatles' fans, knew all along. You knew that the Beatles really do have a style and a sound like there's never been before. And it's simply because you like them (and they like you) that this fantastic success story has happened, and continues to happen

more and more all the time."

11. "The four boys find time to pop into the club headquarters despite their hectic schedule of tours, television appearances, recording sessions, film work and broadcasts. The girls in the office still retain vivid memories of the morning Paul dropped in for a chat, joined in with the gang to stamp up a batch of membership cards and then treated the entire staff to an excellent lunch in a nearby steakhouse!"

12. "In the multiplatinum, sophisticated world we live in today, it is difficult to appreciate the excitement of the Beatles' breakthrough. My youngest daughter, Lucy, now nine years old, once asked me about them, 'You used to record them, didn't you daddy?' She asked, 'Were they as great as the Bay City Rollers?'. 'Probably not,' I replied. Some day she will find out."

13. Following Paul's departure from the Beatles in 1970, John, George, and Ringo briefly toyed with the idea of asking bassist and longtime mate, Klaus Voormann, to join them. This new line-up was to be called "The Ladders." Did this considered line-up ever record anything?

14. On 26 April 1974, following the departure of Wings drummer Denny Seiwell (9 August 1973), Paul auditioned fifty drummers at the Albery Theatre, London, to find Seiwell's replacement. As the initial eliminations began, these fifty drummers were asked to play what old jazz standard?

15. "We the People of the United States, in order to further advance the causes of international artistry and human relations, do ordain one John Lennon with a most prized and coveted 'Green Card' which shall enable said Lennon to remain within the territorial boundaries of these here United States of America."
    Where is this statement, a reference to John's permanent resident alien status, granted on 27 July 1976, located?

FROM ME TO YOU · THANK YOU GIRL
PLEASE PLEASE ME · LOVE ME DO

mono

PARLOPHONE

THE BEATLES'HITS

THE BEATLES

Photo: Angus McBean

Q & A #6

1.   Ray Charles was the carrot that Allan Williams tried unsucessfully to dangle in front of the Beatles.

2.   The Ringo update code word was "keystar."

3.   On 5 June 1964, during their world tour stop in Holland, the Beatles unknowingly slept through a civic reception held at a local restaurant, as well as the planned tour of a traditional Dutch village which was to follow.

4.   Albert Einstein is the only person to appear on both the covers of **Sgt. Pepper** and **We're Only In It For The Money**.
     (Hidden behind John on the Sgt. Pepper cover, Einstein's white hair and the top of his forehead can be seen in left profile, just over the right epaulet on John's suit. Two other figures hidden or so obscured as to be unidentifiable include Bette Davis, dressed as Queen Elizabeth I, and Sigmund Freud. The top of Davis' head can be seen just over George's left epaulet, while Freud's forehead and graying hair can be seen just below Bob Dylan.)

5.   This quotation is from Tony Barrow's liner notes for the **Please Please Me** album.

6.   This Barrow excerpt is from the 1963 EP **The Beatles' Hits**.

7.   This memorable verbiage was written by Derek Taylor for the 1964 EP **Long Tall Sally**.

8.   Tony Barrow wrote these liner notes to accompany the release of the U.K. LP **A Hard Day's Night**.

9.   From author (or authors) unknown comes this excerpt from the U.S. compilation LP, **Something New**.

10.   Taken from the back cover of the LP, **Beatles '65**.

11. This account of Paul's morning with the girls of the Official Beatles Fan Club was penned by Tony Barrow for the back sleeve of **Another Beatles Christmas Record,** released to fan club members in mid-December 1964.

12. This paragraph was taken from the liner notes written by George Martin for **The Beatles at the Hollywood Bowl** album.

13. The line-up for "The Ladders," together with Billy Preston, recorded, "I'm The Greatest" for the **Ringo** album.

14. "Caravan"
(The drummer selected by Paul from that audition was Geoff Britton.)

15. This statement appears on the front of John's **Shaved Fish** album, illustrating the song, "Power To The People."

CHAPTER 14

BE AT LESO

Scholars of the "Paul is dead" rumor will recognize BE AT LESO as the phrase supposedly written in the hyacinth floral arrangement on the front cover of **Sgt. Pepper**. According to theorists, Leso is an underwater island (part of Atlantis, perhaps?) purportedly owned by the Beatles. Is this where Paul was buried after his fatal car accident of 9 November 1966? Perhaps the real Paul is living there still, so disfigured that he can't bear to show his face to the world (along with James Dean, Jim Morrison, and Elvis Presley).

Instead of sinking a Greek island, why couldn't the Beatles really want us to be at Lesotho, a South African kingdom and a former British protectorate? Maybe it would explain why Peter Blake and Jann Haworth didn't have enough hyacinths to spell out the country's full name (you gotta admit, that "o" in Leso is awful scrawny).

Is Paul dead? While you're deciding which of his solo albums to play, have a go at this quiz. A word of advice, though. While solving these questions, it might be a good idea if you didn't discover the answers barefoot while holding a cigarette in your right hand and wearing an outdated suit with a black rose in the lapel.

1. The night of Paul's "death," he was said to have picked up a hitchhiker who, upon recognizing her famous driver, caused the fatal accident in her enthusiasm. What was her name?

2. Staged as a mock trial in December 1969, who moderated this TV special to determine if Paul was dead, featuring testimony from such "witnesses" as Peter Asher and Allen Klein?

3. The centerfold photograph of the Beatles in their **Magical Mystery Tour** booklet features Ringo playing his infamous "Love 3 Beatles" drum kit. (A death clue signifying that there were only three Beatles left alive to love.) Prior to this, where else had Ringo been seen playing this kit?

4. When "Revolution 9" is played backwards, what are the two most discernable messages it is claimed one can hear?

5. By early November 1969, several "Paul is dead" novelty singles had been released, including "So Long, Paul," recorded by Jose Fe-

Q & A #6

liciano (under the pseudonym Werbley Finster), "Saint Paul," by Terry Knight (released on Capitol Records, no less!), and "Brother Paul," by Billy Shears and the All-Americans. "Brother Paul" was originally commissioned by a southern U.S. radio station as the theme song for their coverage of the rumor. What are the call letters of this station, and from what city did it broadcast?

6.   Okay, we all know now that the patch on the left sleeve of Paul's Sgt. Pepper jacket doesn't stand for Ontario Police Department. What does it stand for? (Hint: It's not "Officially Pronounced Dead.")

7.   What message is allegedly to be heard when John's mumbling at the end of "I'm So Tired" is played backwards?

8.   One of the most eclectic death clues, included on U.K. copies of **Sgt. Pepper,** was a two-second snippet of gibberish at the end of Side two. Titled the "Sgt. Pepper Inner Groove," when released in 1980 on Capitol's **Rarities** LP, some have interpreted the voices on the track as saying, "Lucy Abbey all the way," or "He's Found Heaven." When WKBW, a radio station in Buffalo, New York, played the cut backwards, they claimed it said, "We'll all be back here soon." When Paul talked to rock journalist Paul Gambaccini in December 1973, he claimed to have heard something completely different. What did Paul say he heard?

9.   The cover of **Abbey Road** is cited by theorists as an absolute hotbed of clues. When Iain Macmillan was preparing to photograph the Beatles for that cover the morning of 8 August 1969, he tried to have this "future clue" removed because, as he later told WMCA D.J. Alex Bennett, he found it "aesthetically unpleasant." What clue was that?

10.   One of the first printed accounts of the "Paul is dead" rumor was an article headlining this Des Moines, Iowa, college newspaper, 17 September 1969. Its author, a sports editor named Tim Harper, would later garner national attention, including credit in a "Is Paul dead?" article on page one of the 21 October edition of the "Chicago Sun-Times." What was the title of Harper's story, and the name of the paper it was printed in?

11.   "Paul McCartney was killed in an automobile accident in early November 1966, after leaving EMI recording studios tired, sad and

dejected." This was the opening line from a record review for **Abbey Road** printed 14 October 1969 in the "Michigan Daily," the newspaper of the University of Michigan at Ann Arbor. This student's article is more frequently cited as one of the earliest printed accounts of the rumor, notably one of the first to include death clues from the **Abbey Road** cover. Who was the writer of this review?

12.   Paul McCartney's replacement, so the story goes, was the winner of a Paul McCartney look-alike contest held in 1965, one William "Billy" Campbell of Scotland, also known as Billy Shears. What was the name of Billy Shears' dad?

13.   Some claim that the Beatle costumed as a walrus on the cover of **Magical Mystery Tour** is actually Paul instead of John. Cite two clues which support this theory.

14.   What are the three interpretations of the phrase attributed to the fade of "Strawberry Fields Forever"?

15.   On the afternoon of 12 October 1969, this man was disc-jockeying his show on WKNR-FM, an underground radio station in Detroit, Michigan, when he received a call from a young man who claimed that Paul's "death" could be proven by examining "clues" on the Beatles' albums. What is the name of this Detroit DJ, a person pivotal to spreading the death rumor to a national level? Also, what was the name of the young man who called him?

**BE AT LESO
(ANSWERS)**

1.   Paul's passenger was named Rita.
     (This clue allows the song "Lovely Rita" to be tied in as a death clue because of the line, "I took her home/I nearly made it.")

2.   Presiding over the mock trial was noted lawyer, F. (Francis) Lee Bailey.

3.   Ringo was behind this drum kit when the Beatles recorded "All You Need Is Love," the British contribution to the "Our World" TV special.

4. "Turn me on dead man" and "Let me out, let me out."

(Two other backward messages, mentioned in William Pound-stone's book, *Big Secrets*, are "She used to be assistant" and "There were two men.")

5. "Brother Paul" had originally been commissioned by New Orleans radio station WTIX. Listener demand for the song was so great during the rumor that a single was rush-released. Distributed by Silver Fox Records, "Brother Paul" had an advance order in the New Orleans area alone of 40,000 copies.

6. Long interpreted as reading "O.P.D.", the initials on Paul's "Pepper" patch actually read "O.P.P.", an abbreviation for the Ontario Provincial Police.

7. "Paul is dead man, miss him, miss him."

8. "I went inside...and played it studiously, turned it backwards with my thumb against the motor, turned the motor off and did it backwards. And there it was, plain as anything. *"We'll fuck you like Supermen."* I thought, Jesus, what can you do?" (Quotation by Paul from "Rolling Stone" No. 153, 31 January 1974. The "Sgt. Pepper Inner Groove" is also available on CD pressings of the **Sgt. Pepper** album.)

9. Macmillan, thwarted in his efforts to locate a tow truck owner in time for the 10:00 a.m. photo session, was unable to remove the white Volkswagen Beetle, license plate "LMW 281F."

(According to the clue associated with this license plate, Paul would have been 28 years of age in 1969 IF he had lived, and if you counted the time he'd spent before his birth inside mother Mary. On 28 August 1986, the Sotheby's auction house in London sold this V.W. bug for $3,795.)

10. Tim Harper's article, "Is Beatle Paul McCartney Dead?," appeared in the 17 September 1969 issue of the "Drake Times-Delphic."

(Following his brief fling with the national press, Harper was later quoted in the 24 October 1969 issue of the "DTD" as saying, "I think I stunned people by saying I didn't believe he was really dead. Actually, I think the whole thing was a hoax deliberately perpetrated by the Beatles.")

11.   The "Michigan Daily's" **Abbey Road** review was penned by Fred LaBour.

(LaBour was also one of the "witnesses" at F. Lee Bailey's TV trial. In an article run in the "The (Portland) Oregonian," 16 January 1987, LaBour, when asked about his part in the rumor, admitted that while he had never met McCartney: "I'm sure that if I told him I was the one who started the hoax, he'd probably punch me in the nose." Since 1978, Fred "Too Slim" LaBour has played bass in a Western/ Comedy band known as "Riders In The Sky.")

12.   Though there exist several variations on the Campbell legend, including one version that says that William was an orphan from Edinburgh, according to a "story" by Lee Merrick on the front page of the 29 October 1969 issue of "RAT" (an underground paper touted as featuring "Subterranean News"), Billy Campbell's father, living at the time of the article "in the quiet Chelsea section of London," was named Philip Shears.

13.   The first of two clues pointing to Paul as the Walrus instead of John, can be found in the song title/composer credit listings opposite page one of the **Magical Mystery Tour** booklet. In parentheses below the listing for "I Am The Walrus" it reads, "'No you're not!' said Little Nicola." Little Nicola's denial is repeated on page 9 of the booklet: "'I AM THE WALRUS' says John. 'NO, YOU'RE NOT' cries Nicola, laughing at his funny feathery hat." The second clue can be found in the song "Glass Onion," the third track on Side one of "The White Album." In it, John sings, "Well here's another clue for you all/The Walrus was Paul."

(Theorists' obsession with the symbolism of the walrus stems from the supposed belief that, among other things, the word "walrus" is Greek for "corpse.")

14.   "Cranberry sauce."

(This is the interpretation most widely accepted and the phrase Lennon himself states he said.)

"I buried Paul."

(This is the interpretation most Paul is dead theorists embrace.)

"I'm very bored."

15.   On 12 October 1969, WKNR-FM DJ, Russ Gibb, received a phone call from a listener named Tom.

100

CHAPTER 15

Do Me a Favour, Open the Door

Someone's knockin' at the door; are they lovers and friends you still can recall? Major leads and minor characters, the Beatles have known enough people to fill twenty different **Sgt. Pepper** covers. This quiz covers but a fraction of their number.

Too many people, you say? Though you feel as if you're in a play - relax - you are anyway.

1.   Besides the Beatles with Pete Best, who else has been a member of Tony Sheridan's Beat Brothers backup band?

2.   Name ten people who have been tagged the "Fifth Beatle."

3.   Who comprised the "famous five"?

4.   Name ten people considered for record release on Apple's experimental label, Zapple.

5.   On Saturday, 6 July 1957, the Quarry Men played the summer fete at St. Peter's Parish Church in Woolton. It was early in the evening, between the Quarry Men's sets, that John Lennon was first introduced to Paul McCartney. Who made this historic introduction? Also, who secured the Quarry Men their booking at this venue?

6.   What are the names of Julia Lennon's three daughters (John's half sisters)?

7.   What are the names of Cynthia Lennon's two brothers?

8.   What are the names of Yoko Ono's younger brother and sister?

9.   What was the maiden name of Paul and Mike's mother, Mary?

10.   What is Mike McCartney's first name?

11.   What are the names of Mike McCartney's children?

Country • Western • Rock 'n' Roll • Skiffle

The Quarry Men

LEOSDENE,
VALE ROAD, WOOLTON.
LIVERPOOL.

OPEN FOR ENGAGEMENTS

12. What is the most commonly retold fallacy about Linda McCartney?

13. What are the names of Pattie Harrison Clapton's two younger sisters?

14. Who is known as "the Teacher"?

15. Who did Derek Taylor call "the American Beatle"?

16. A new and better man? Who once described himself to the Beatles as an "Eminent physicist, polyglot classicist, prize-winning botanist, hard-biting satirist, talented pianist..." (and a good dentist, too!)?

17. Who bought John his first musical instrument?

18. Who thought up the name Quarry Men?

19. What group did former Quarry Man Nigel Whalley briefly manage in 1957?

20. Who thought up the name "Beatals," the first version of the Beatles' name?

21. Recorded at Akustik Studio, Hamburg, on 15 October 1960, the Beatles cut a version of the George Gershwin song, "Summertime," backing what singer?

22. Which Beatle did Cavern D.J. Bob Wooler once describe as "a sort of teenage Jeff Chandler"?

23. What three names did Ringo's old group, Rory Storm and the Hurricanes, first go by?

24. While Freda Kelly ran the northern region of the Official Beatles Fan Club (from Liverpool), who ran the southern region (from London)?

25. Which Beatle(s) attended the funeral service for Brian Epstein, 29 August 1967, at Liverpool's Longlane Jewish Cemetary?

26. Who played at the party launching the Beatles' new film, "Magi-

cal Mystery Tour," 21 December 1967?

27.   What was the original name of the "Black Dyke Mills Band"?

28.   When George and Pattie got busted for possession of hashish at their home in Esher, 12 March 1969 (the same day as Paul and Linda's wedding), who did they ask (unsuccessfully) to exert their influence in hopes of getting the charges dismissed?

29.   Who were listed as the witnesses to the marriage certificate for John Lennon and Cynthia Powell, married 23 August 1962.

30.   Whose picture was in John's FBI file, updated July 1972? (Hint: It was not John Lennon.)

31.   Of the ten artists featured on Yoko's **Every Man Has A Woman** album, which one did Ms. Ono initially refuse to consider using?

32.   For his thirty-fourth birthday, Paul was willing to pay $600 for this man to perform at his party. Who is this famous comedian, and what did Paul want him to perform?

33.   While Paul is credited with creating the term "C-Moon," who first sang of its antonymous term, L7?

34.   Name all the "fugitives" pictured on the cover of **Band On The Run**.

35.   According to the inner sleeve notes for this McCartney album, this group was "returned virtually intact to John Foster and Sons Ltd." What group was that?

36.   This group auditioned the same day as the Beatles (1 January 1962) for a spot on the Decca Records roster. Name the group, which Decca A&R man Mike Smith signed over the Beatles.

37.   When the Beatles held down the top five spots on "Billboard's Hot 100," 4 April 1964, who was at number 6? Artist and song title, please.

38.   When this woman decided she didn't want to be included in a "lonely hearts club," the Beatles wrote her personally for permission

to include her image on the **Sgt. Pepper** cover. Who is she?

39. Name the four people comprising "The Fool."

40. Why would the names John and Roy Boulting be of interest to Paul?

41. Paul once read in "Melody Maker" that this group had just recorded "...the loudest, most raucous rock 'n' roll, the dirtiest thing they've ever done." This news item inspired Paul to write "Helter Skelter" in an effort to top this claim. What is the name of the rock group that got Paul so worked up?

42. In 1968, it was reported that Vic Lewis, a British concert promoter, was hoping to organize a show in Moscow featuring the Beatles and what two other performers?

43. Which country/rock group of the sixties thanked (among other people) the Nurk [sic] Twins & George and Ringo on the back of one of their albums, "for their influence and inspiration."

44. Whose fan club could you join by sending "...a stamped, undressed elephant"?

45. In 1968, this popular comedian helped form Tetragrammaton Records, the label that distributed John and Yoko's **Two Virgins** album in the U.S. Who is he?

46. What did sewing machine magnate Edward Clark open in New York City in 1884 that would be of importance to John and Yoko in 1973?

47. A lavatory attendant at The Indra Club (and later at Peter Eckhorn's Top Ten Club), Rosa was always there for the Beatles with clean towels when they came off stage. Rosa also kept the boys (except Pete Best) supplied with Preludins, the German-made diet pills nicknamed "Prellys," which they took to get them through hours of "making show." What was the Beatles' affectionate nickname for Rosa?

48. What was the "Liverpool One Fat Lady All-Electric Show"?

49. Who designed the Beatles' collarless jackets?

Q & A #2

50. Who set up Brydor Cars, where many a Beatles auto was acquired?

DO ME A FAVOUR,
OPEN THE DOOR
(ANSWERS)

1. The "other" Beat Brothers included: Rikki Barnes (sax), Colin Milander (bass), Johnny Watson (drums), and Roy Young (organ and piano).

(According to Iain Hines, leader of the "Jets," noted for being the first British group to play in Hamburg, Peter Wharton and Ringo Starr were also Beat Brothers.)

2. "Fifth" Beatles abound in Beatle lore. Inductees include: Neil Aspinall, Pete Best, Leslie Bryce, Norman Chapman, Brian Epstein, Mal Evans, George Martin, Tommy Moore, Murray the K, Chas Newby, Jimmy Nicol, Billy Preston, Ed Rudy, and Stuart Sutcliffe.

(In the Beatles' actual pecking order, Stu Sutcliffe was the fourth Beatle and Pete Best the actual fifth Beatle. Leslie Bryce was a photographer for "The Beatles Book" magazine. Norman Chapman played drums with the Silver Beatles for a short time in the summer of 1960. Chas Newby played bass for the Beatles on four occasions in December 1960. In their Beatles parody issue, the "National Lampoon" named Charles Manson the fifth Beatle.)

3. "The Famous Five Through Woenow Avenue," a short story from *In His Own Write*, are: Tom, Stan, Dave, Nigel, Berniss, Arthur, Harry, Wee Jockey, Matoombo, and Craig? [sic].

4. The Zapple Records Hall of (Almost) Fame includes: Daniel Cohn Bendit, Richard Brautigan, Lenny Bruce, Lord Buckley, Charles Bukowski, Eldridge Cleaver, Lawrence Ferlinghetti, Hermione Gingold, Allen Ginsberg, Ken Kesey, Norman Mailer, Michael McClure, Charles Olson, Kenneth Patchen, Pablo Picasso and Ken Weaver.

(Only George Harrison and John & Yoko had albums released on Zapple, the label once envisioned as the phonographic equivalent of paperback books. Richard Brautigan did actually spend six days in early 1969 recording an album for Zapple, the initial costs of the LP's studio time reportedly paid out of the author's own pocket. Scheduled for release in the U.K. on 23 May 1969 as Zapple 03, **Listening To Richard Brautigan** was subsequently withdrawn due to the shakeup within Apple following the appointment of Allen Klein's ABKCO Industries Inc. as the company's manager, 8 May. Brautigan's LP was released in the U.S. on Capitol's Harvest label, 21 September 1970. Hermione Gingold's Zapple release was to have been a spoken children's LP with a Moog music background. Ken Kesey's spoken-word LP was to have been called **Paperback Records**, while Michael McClure had planned to contribute an album of his own songs.)

5.   John was introduced to Paul by the Quarry Men's tea chest bassist, Ivan Vaughan. The Quarry Men's booking at the Woolton fete was secured by Pete Shotton's mother, Bessie.

6.   John's three half sisters are Julia, Jaqueline "Jacqui" Gertrude, and Victoria Elizabeth.
     (John's third sister, Victoria, whose existence was only recently discovered, is believed to be living in Norway. John's half brothers, by Alfred Lennon's second wife, Pauline (nee Jones), are named David Henry and Robin Francis.)

7.   Cynthia Lennon's brothers are named Tony and Charles.

8.   Yoko's younger sister is named Setsuko; her younger brother's name is Keisuke.

9.   Mary Patricia McCartney's maiden name was Mohin.

10.   Mike McCartney's first name is Peter.

11.   Mike's children are named Benna, Theran, Abbi, Joshua, and Max.
     (Mike's three daughters are by his first wife, Angela, while Joshua and Max were borne by his second wife, Rowena.)

12.   The most commonly retold fallacy about Linda McCartney is that she is an heiress to the Eastman Kodak fortune.
     (Linda's father, Lee Eastman, changed his last name to Eastman from Epstein.)

13.   Pattie's younger sisters are named Paula and Jenny.

(Donovan's Epic album, **The Hurdy Gurdy Man**, contains the song "Jennifer Juniper," which he wrote for Jenny Boyd.)

14. "The Teacher" is Anthony Esmond Sheridan McGinnity, better known as Tony Sheridan.

("The Teacher" was a monicker bestowed upon Sheridan by Liverpool bands because of the influence his musicianship and style had on them, including the Beatles.)

15. Harry Nilsson was dubbed "the American Beatle" by Derek Taylor.

16. The preceeding resume was for Jeremy Hillary Boob, Phd. (Phud), the nowhere man in the animated feature "Yellow Submarine."

17. John's Uncle George Smith bought John his first instrument - a harmonica.

(Ray Coleman, in his book, *Lennon*, claims Julia was the first to buy him an instrument, a guitar given him when he was four.)

18. Associating the group's name with Woolton's sandstone quarries, and the fact that most of its members attended Quarry Bank High School, Pete Shotton named the group in which he played washboard bass, "Quarry Men."

(For about a week's time prior to being rechristened the Quarry Men, John called his first group the "Black Jacks.")

19. After a stint on tea chest bass for the Quarry Men, Nigel Whalley decided his musical expertise would never measure up and, for a brief time, he opted to manage the group.

(At various times, members of the Quarry Men included: Rod Davis, Eric Griffiths, Colin Hanton, John Lennon, Pete Shotton, Ivan Vaughan, Nigel Whalley (the original lineup), Ken Brown, Len Garry, George Harrison, John "Duff" Lowe, Paul McCartney, and Bill Smith.)

20. Stu Sutcliffe thought up the name "Beatals" as a parallel to Buddy Holly's Crickets.

(In one of his many asides in Derek Taylor's limited edition autobiography, *Fifty Years Adrift*, George stated his belief that Stu could have gotten the name "Beatles" from the Marlon Brando film "The Wild One," after having seen a gang in the film (led by Lee Marvin) named the "Beetles."

In John Goldrosen's book *The Buddy Holly Story*, former Crickets rhythm guitarist, Nikki Sullivan, recalls that when Holly's group was deciding on a name, the monicker "Beetles" was considered, but quickly dropped because, as Crickets' drummer, Jerry Allison, remarked at the time, "That's just a bug you'd want to step on.")

21. The Beatles were backing Walter Eymond (stage name: Lou "Wally" Walters), bassist for Rory Storm and the Hurricanes.

(This recording marked the first time all four Beatles played together, with Ringo - at the time drumming for the Hurricanes - sitting in for Pete Best. According to Allan Williams, in his book, *The Man Who Gave The Beatles Away*," the B-side of the Beatles' first record, cut at 78 rpm, "...was a sales spiel by some guy selling leather goods like handbags and shoes.")

22. Bob Wooler was describing Pete Best.

(A book of Pete's Beatle reminiscences, *Beatle! The Pete Best Story*," was published in 1985.)

23. Alan Caldwell (Rory Storm) started his first group under the name "Al Caldwell's Texans." When Ringo began drumming for the band, they were known as the "Raving Texans," then "Al Storm and the Hurricanes," followed by "Jett Storm and the Hurricanes," and finally "Rory Storm and the Hurricanes."

24. Bettina Rose ran the southern region.

(The Beatles' Fan Club had first been established in Liverpool in May 1962 by Bobbie Brown.)

25. Asked to stay away so as not to turn the service, in the words of Peter Brown, "...into a media circus," none of the Beatles attended Brian's funeral.

(All of the Beatles, however, did attend a memorial service for Brian, held 17 October 1967 at the New London Synagogue, London.)

26. The McPeake Family and the Bonzo Dog Doo Dah Band performed at the "Magical Mystery Tour" party, held at the Royal Lancaster Hotel.

27. "The Alan Wharton Reed and Brass Band," as they were known in 1836, changed their name to the "Black Dyke Mills Band" in 1851.

28. George and Pattie appealed unsuccessfully to Princess Margaret.

29. John and Cynthia's wedding certificate, as executed by the hand of Eric Williams, Registrar for the District of Liverpool, was witnessed by James Paul McCartney and Margery Joyce Powell, the wife of Cynthia's brother, Tony.

30. David Peel's picture, from an ad for his Apple album, **The Pope Smokes Dope**, was the FBI's file photo of John Lennon!

31. Initially, Yoko declined Harry Nilsson's offer to sing on the **Every Man Has A Woman** album. Yoko, associating Harry with John's Beatle past, did not want to impose on him by asking.

32. On 18 June 1976, John Belushi did his Joe Cocker impersonation at Paul's thirty-fourth birthday party, held at the old Harold Lloyd estate in Beverly Hills.

33. Sam the Sham and the Pharaohs' song "Wooly Bully" referred to L7 (someone who is unhip or square).

34. The "Band On The Run" were: James Coburn (actor), John Conteh (boxing champion), Clement Freud (member of Parliament), Denny Laine, Christoper Lee (actor), Linda McCartney, Paul McCartney (noted bass player) and Michael Parkinson (English talk show host).

35. The "Black Dyke Mills Band" was returned virtually intact.
    (On the **Back To The Egg** album, this band is featured on "Love Awake.")

36. Dick Rowe, head of A&R at Decca, instructed his assistant, Mike Smith, that he could only sign one of the two groups he auditioned on 1 January 1962. Smith signed Brian Poole and the Tremeloes to Decca over that Northern group, the Beatles.

37. Terry Stafford was at number 6 the week of 4 April 1964 with "Suspicion."

38. The Beatles' letters were addressed to Mae West.
    (In 1977, Mae starred with Ringo in the movie "Sextette." Paul

A girl,
a boy,
a tender, funny, terrible wedding night...

The BOULTING BROTHERS' Production

the ♀♂
family
way

Starring
HAYLEY MILLS · JOHN MILLS · HYWEL BENNETT · MARJORIE RHODES

AVRIL ANGERS · LIZ FRASER · WILFRED PICKLE
JOHN COMER · BARRY FOSTER · MURRAY HE

Music by
PAUL ("Beatle") McCARTNEY

From
BILL ("Alfie") NAUGHTON'S
"All In Good Time"

Adaptation by ROY BOULTING and JEFFREY DELL . Screenplay by
Produced and Directed by JOHN and ROY BOULTING · BILL NAUGHTON
TECHNICOLOR® · Distributed by WARNER BROS.

ORIGINAL SOUND TRACK ALBUI
AVAILABLE ON LONDON RECORD

Q & A #40

included a lyrical encounter with Ms. West in "Move Over Busker," a song from his 1986 Capitol LP **Press To Play**.)

39. "The Fool" were Simon Posthuma, his wife at the time, Marijke, Joskje Leeger, and their British manager and publicist (and Joskje's husband), Barry Finch.

40. The Boulting Brothers' 1967 film "The Family Way" features a soundtrack composed by Paul.

41. The Who
(Pete Townshend comments on John's death in a chapter titled "Winston," from his book *Horse's Neck*, published in 1985.)

42. Lewis' Moscow dream ticket included the Beatles, Donovan, and Nina Simone.

43. The Buffalo Springfield thanked the Beatles on the back of their **Buffalo Springfield Again** album.

44. The Jim Keltner Fan Club
(From the back of George's **Living In The Material World** album. Harrison's announcement of the Keltner Fan Club was intended (at least in part) as a parody of the announcement on the back of **Red Rose Speedway** for the Wings Fun Club (note the wings to either side of Keltner's name). Another way of joining Jim's fan club, according to the booklet in the **Ringo** album, was to "send a stamped, undressed envelope.")

45. Bill Cosby helped form Tetragrammaton Records.

46. Edward Clark opened the Dakota apartment building, located at One West 72nd Street.

47. The Beatles' nickname for Rosa was "Mutti."

48. The "Liverpool One Fat Lady All-Electric Show" was the forerunner of the "Scaffold" musical/comedy troupe.
("One Fat Lady" included among its members: Mike McCartney, Celia (his girlfriend at the time), Celia's friend, Jenny Beattie, Adrian Henri, and the two other members of the "Scaffold," Roger McGough and John Gorman.)

49. Pierre Cardin designed the Beatles' trademark collarless suits.

50. Brydor Cars was set up by Brian (Br) Epstein and Terry (ydor) Doran.

Q & A #1 ▶

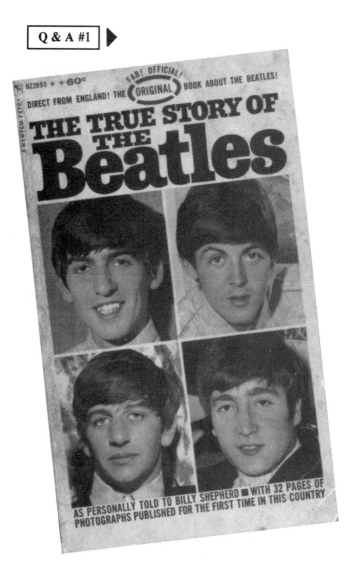

CHAPTER 16

EVERYONE KNEW HER AS NANCY

Scorecards! Scorecards! Get your official Beatle scorecards here! You can't tell one Beatle alias from another without a scorecard!

Tis true, tis true, Beatle peedles! What with Paul running around writing songs as Bernard Webb, and George galavanting around on Cream and Jack Bruce albums as rhythm guitarist L'Angelo Misterioso, and many of their friends and acquaintances donning aliases and nicknames left and right, why, it's enough to write a quiz category about!

1.   Author of *The True Story Of The Beatles*, one of the first Beatles biographies, what is Billy Shepherd's real name?

2.   Who did Paul nickname "Two D-B's Smith"?

3.   Eric Clapton's guitar work on "While My Guitar Gently Weeps" was kept secret for a time. What pseudonym did Eric use on the session?

4.   Who did John nickname "Superchicken"?

5.   Who was Stuart de Stael?

6.   Who did John once dub "Mother Superior"?

7.   Who did Yoko nickname "Milkman"?

8.   Who was nicknamed "Twitchy"?

9.   Who are Winnie and Snowball?

10.   Who are Spiggy Topes and Okay Yoni?

11.   What was Ringo's grandfather's nickname for him as a child?

12.   While Billy Shears was a Ringo alias from **Sgt. Pepper** and the singer of "With A Little Help From My Friends," where else did Mr. Starkey don this monicker?

13.   On what album is Ringo credited under the alias "R.S."?

14. On what song is Ringo credited as simply "Richie"?

15. For what auspicious occasion did the Quarry Men briefly change their name to "Johnny and the Moondogs"?

16. On which Beatles or post-Beatle recording did John refer to himself as Johnny Rhythm?

17. On which song is John credited as the Hon. John St. John Johnson?

18. What is John's alias on the **Walls And Bridges** version of "Ya-Ya"?

19. When the Beatles and their wives/girlfriends split into two groups to embark on their 1964 holidays, elaborate security precautions were observed to insure the Beatles' privacy. Code names were assigned each Beatle and his respective companion. What were these code names?

20. During the seventies, what names did John and Yoko frequently travel under?

```
EVERYONE KNEW HER
AS NANCY
(ANSWERS)
```

1. Billy Shepherd was the pen name of former "Record Mirror" editor, Peter Jones.

2. "Two D-B's Smith" was Paul's nickname for Beatles recording engineer Norman "Hurricane" Smith.
(John's nickname for Norman was "Normal" Smith.)

3. Clapton's alias on "While My Guitar Gently Weeps" was Eddie Clayton.

4. "Superchicken" was John's nickname for his former assistant, Anthony Fawcett.

5. Stuart de Stael was the stage name taken by Stuart Sutcliffe

when the Silver Beetles toured Scotland backing Johnny Gentle, 20-28 May 1960.

(Stuart took the surname "de Stael" after the Russian artist, Nicholas de Stael. While John decided not to adopt a stage name, Paul became Paul Ramon, and George became Carl Harrison, in honour of his idol, Carl Perkins.)

6.   May Pang is credited as "Production Coordinator and Mother Superior" on the **Rock 'N' Roll** album.

(Yoko is also the "Mother Superior" who "jumped the gun" in the lyrics to "Happiness Is A Warm Gun.")

7.   Yoko's nickname for Harry Nilsson was "Milkman."

8.   "Twitchy" was John's nickname for Bobby Dykins, Julia Lennon's lover and the father of two of John's half sisters, Jacqui and Julia.

(As Julia notes in her book, *John Lennon, My Brother* (Henry Holt, 1988), John never called Dykins "Twitchy" to his face.)

9.   Winnie and Snowball are the first nicknames John and Pete Shotton gave each other.

("Winnie" was derived from "Winston," John's middle name, while "Snowball" was John's description of Pete's head of white hair.)

10.   "Private Eye," a British left-wing magazine, used the names "Spiggy Topes" and "Okay Yoni" to refer to John and Yoko in their articles.

(The Beatles were often referred to in "Eye" as "The Turds.")

11.   Grandfather Starkey's nickname for Ringo as a child was "Lazarus," a biblical reference to Ringo's constant sickliness.

12.   Ringo plays drums under the alias "Billy Shears" on the 1974 Dark Horse album, **Shankar Family & Friends**.

13.   Ringo's finger clicks on "Step Lightly" are credited to "R.S." on David Hentschel's 1975 Ring O' Records album, **Sta*rtling Music**, an instrumental synthesizer version of the **Ringo** album.

14.   Ringo is credited as "Richie" on "I Ain't Superstitious," a cut from **The London Howlin' Wolf Sessions** LP.

15.   The Quarry Men became "Johnny and the Moondogs" when they went through four rounds (in Liverpool and Manchester) of the Carol Levis' Star Search in October and November of 1959; the Moondogs were hoping to win a two-minute spot on Levis' ATV show, "Discoveries."

16.   At the conclusion of the 1965 Christmas message, John refers to himself as Johnny Rhythm.

17.   John plays guitar as the Hon. John St. John Johnson on "Whatever Gets You Through The Night," from his **Walls And Bridges** album.

18.   "Dad"
(Julian Lennon made his first recorded appearance on "Ya Ya" playing the drums.)

19.   For their May '64 holidays, Mr. Manning (Paul) and Mr. Stone (Ringo) and their companions, Miss Ashcroft (Jane Asher) and Miss Cockroft (Maureen), flew to St. Thomas, the Virgin Islands. With their ultimate destination Papeete, Tahiti, John and Cynthia traveled as Mr. and Mrs. Leslie. They were accompanied by Mr. Hargreaves (George) and his future wife, Miss Bond (Pattie Boyd).

20.   During the seventies, John and Yoko frequently traveled as the Rev. Fred and Ada Gerkin.

CHAPTER 17

M~AKE~ Y~OUR~ M~OTHER~ S~IGH~

By all indications, the children of the Beatles (and their wives) have shown themselves to be a talented and intelligent lot (must be in the genes). Two of them, in fact, have inherited their respective fathers' hunger for rock 'n' roll. So hello, Julian, Sean, Mary, Stella, James Louis, Dhani, Zak, Jason, and Lee: this quiz is dedicated to you! As you grow older, I hope you will be appreciated for your individual talents and abilities, and not merely for being born the son or daughter of a famous musician.

1.   While Heather McCartney is not Paul's natural daughter (he adopted her in 1969), this quiz on Beatle siblings wouldn't be complete without her. With that in mind, what is the title of the photograph shot and printed by Heather that won her Ilford's "Young Printer Of The Year" award for 1981?

2.   George and Olivia named their first son, born 1 August 1978, Dhani. What is the origin of his name?

3.   Name four bands Zak Starkey has played drums in.

4.   What is the name of Zak's wife, whom he married in a civil ceremony, 22 January 1985?

5.   What is the name of Ringo's first grandchild, born to Zak and his wife, 7 September 1985?

6.   Zak was one of seven drummers who performed on Roger Daltrey's musical tribute to the late Keith Moon. What is this song's title?

7.   In 1977, Kyoko Cox, Yoko's daughter by her second marriage to Tony Cox, was enrolled by her father in Walter Reed Junior High School in North Hollywood, California. What assumed name was she taught under?

8.   When Sean Lennon was asked in 1984 what he wanted to be when he grew up, what was his answer?

9.   How did Sean first learn of his father's fame as a Beatle?

JULIAN LENNON
VALOTTE

JULIAN LENNON
VALOTTE

The first single
"VALOTTE"

Produced by Phil Ramone
Management: Dean Gordon/D.A.G. Promotions LTD., London

On Atlantic Records and Cassettes

Q & A #17

10. At age nine, where did Sean attend school?

11. List Sean's performances on record.

12. What noted artist did Yoko Ono once refer to as Sean's "mentor"?

13. What is the name of the short-lived band Julian helped form in 1983?

14. How did John tell his eldest son he would make contact with him after his death?

15. Who has Julian cited as a critical influence on his piano playing?

16. Which song of his father's has Julian said was an inspiration for many of the songs on his debut LP, **Valotte**?

17. Which album, produced by Phil Ramone, convinced Julian he wanted Ramone to produce **Valotte?**

18. Pins distributed during the promotion of **Valotte** featured a photo of Julian's head uttering something contained within a cartoon balloon. What was Julian saying?

19. Who directed Julian's first two videos?

20. In the opening scenes of his "Stick Around" video, Julian's girlfriend (played by Jami Gertz) has just packed her bags and is out the door. Before her return, Jules will have entertained three other young women. What are their names?

MAKE YOUR MOTHER SIGH
(ANSWERS)

---

1. Heather McCartney's winning photo, "Waterfall," shows drummer Steve Gadd and his wife, Carol, standing under a waterfall in Montserrat.

2.   While the press has reported for some time that the name Dhani meant "wealthy" in Hindi, the name is actually derived from two ascending tones of the Indian musical scale, "dha" and "ni."

3.   Zak has banged the skins for "The Next," "Monopacific," "Nightfly," "The Rock" (the post-Who band of bassist John Entwistle), and "Ice."

4.   Zak's wife is named Sarah, nee Menikides.

5.   Born to Zak and Sarah Starkey, 7 September 1985, in Windsor, England, a girl, Tatia Jayne, making Ringo the first (gasp!) Beatle grandfather. Tatia weighed in at 7 lbs, 2 oz.

6.   Playing alongside such noted drummers as Martin Chambers (late of The Pretenders), Queen's Roger Taylor, and former Police drummer Stewart Copeland, Zak was featured on "Under A Raging Moon," the title track from Roger Daltrey's 1985 Atlantic album.

7.   Tony Cox enrolled Kyoko as Ruth Holman.
     (Kyoko is the associate producer of "Vain Glory," a 32-minute documentary film produced by her father about his involvement with the Church of the Living Word, also known as the Walk. Tony and Kyoko sought refuge with the Walk from 1972 to 1977.)

8.   In an answer displaying the classic Lennon wit, Sean said that he wanted to be "a toothpick maker" when he grew up.

9.   Sean learned his father was once a Beatle when, after having just seen "Yellow Submarine" on TV, he asked Warner LeRoy, a Dakota neighbor and restaurateur whom Sean was visiting, why his Daddy was famous.

10.   At the age of nine, Sean attended the Ethical Cultural School.

11.   Sean's vocal performances include "It's Alright," with Yoko on her album of the same name, and as a soloist on the **Every Man Has A Woman** album; "Little Story," a recitation included on **Season Of Glass**; two spoken-word passages on "Never Say Goodbye," also from **It's Alright,** and the role of the alien voice heard at the opening of the title track of Yoko's 1985 LP, **Starpeace.**

Concerts Coors et FM93 Présentent:

Julian Lennon

12 JUIN, 20h
COLISÉE DE QUÉBEC
Sièges réservés: 17⁵⁰

Venez vivre
la musique

Coors
CONCERTS

DONALD K DONALD

En vente au Colisée, magasins la Baie, Place Laurier et Galeries de la
Capitale, Bibliothèque Gabrielle-Roy, Palais Montcalm et com-
mandes téléphoniques, de 9h à 16h: 691-7211.

Q & A #13

12.   Ono referred to Andy Warhol as Sean's mentor at a memorial mass for the artist held in New York's St. Patrick's Cathedral, 1 April 1987. Warhol died 22 February 1987.

13.   Julian drummed briefly in a band dubbed "Quasar."

(Despite reports in the English press, Julian never played in bands named "the Lennon Drops," or "the (Julian) Lennon Kittens." Julian's band for his first North American tour, in February and March of 1985, included "Quasar" alumnus Justin Clayton (guitar), whom Julian first met when both were schoolboys at Kingsmeade in Hoylake; Carlton (Carlos) Morales (guitar); Carmine Rojas (bass); Chuck Kentis (keyboards and backing vocals); Frank Elmo (sax); and Alan Childs (drums).)

14.   John told Julian he would float a white feather across the room.

15.   Jazz pianist Keith Jarrett is cited by Julian as a major influence on his piano playing.

16.   Many of the songs on **Valotte** were inspired by "Isolation," a track from John's **Plastic Ono Band** album.

17.   Phil Ramone's production of Billy Joel's album **The Nylon Curtain** convinced Julian that Ramone should produce **Valotte**.

(Ramone also produced Julian's second album, **The Secret Value Of Daydreaming**, which features a cameo appearance by Billy Joel on "You Get What You Want.")

18.   "Thanx Valotte"

("Valotte" is the name of a chateau in France where most of the album's songs were written.)

19.   The late Sam Peckinpah directed Julian's first two videos.

(Phil Ramone can be seen in the "Valotte" video, while former Wings-man Steve Holley plays drums behind Julian in the video promoting "Too Late For Goodbyes.")

20.   In the video for "Stick Around," Julian entertains (and is entertained by) Daphne, Venus, and Barbi.

CHAPTER 18

YOU'RE MUCH TOO
COMMON FOR ME

A well-rounded Beatles fanatic may soon realize that one cannot live by Beatles music alone. The well-versed "fab-natic" will find it's to his or her advantage to delve into the group's musical roots. You might start by spinning the records of Buddy Holly, Carl Perkins, the Everly Brothers, Chuck Berry, Little Richard, and of course, Elvis Presley. Perhaps a taste of the Mersey Beat is in order, including the Swinging Blue Jeans, Gerry and the Pacemakers, Billy J. Kramer and the Dakotas, and the Fourmost. To round it off, try a bit of Harry Nilsson, Badfinger, the Raspberries, Emitt Rhodes, Cheap Trick, Squeeze, and XTC to name but a few.

Keeping in touch with the Beatles means pretty much keeping abreast of the entire pop music scene. The Beatles have touched base with a lot of people over the years, either through direct contact or indirectly, as a source of inspiration to their music. Likewise, the musical heritage the Beatles as a group contributed to continues to influence countless musicians to this day. This quiz tests your knowledge of these special musical relationships.

1.   The Beatles, Jeff Beck, the Mahavishnu Orchestra, Neil Sedaka, and Jimmy Webb all have this talented gentleman's services in common. Who is he?

2.   What well-watched event do the following people have in common: Georgia Brown, Tessie O'Shea, Whitehall-Pillsbury, and the Beatles?

3.   What do Prince and former soft-porn star Koo Stark have in common with the Beatles?

4.   What do The Beatles, Marc Chagall, Van Cliburn, and Franco Zeffirelli all have in common with Expo '67?

5.   Who is the woman that the Beatles and Woody Allen have in common?

6.   Arthur Kelly, Elizabeth Kelly, Luke Kelly, Sylvia Nightingale, and Bill Wall all did something with the Beatles in September of 1967. What was it they all did?

125

7.   Besides their general association with one or more members of the group, what do Neil Aspinall, Ewa Aulin, Brian Epstein, George Martin, Yoko Ono, Elizabeth Taylor, Harold Wilson, and the Maharishi Mahesh Yogi have in common with the Beatles?

8.   What do the album covers for **The Beatles' Second Album** and the double-disc album **Rock 'N' Roll Music** have in common?

9.   What does the cover of **"Yesterday"...And Today** have in common with the cover of the Rolling Stones' album, **Beggar's Banquet**?

10.   What two people share something in common with both the **Sgt. Pepper** album and Band Aid's 1984 single "Do They Know It's Christmas?"?

11.   To a record collector, the Rolling Stones, Frank Sinatra, and the Beatles are the only musicians (as of 1989) to be honored in this fashion. What exclusive "revolver" honor do they share?

12.   The Beatles, ELO, Led Zeppelin, Pink Floyd, and Prince have all used (or been accused of employing) this recording technique on one or more of their songs. What have all these people done?

13.   Had Brian Epstein gotten his wish, what would the album sleeve for **Sgt. Pepper** have had in common with the cover of **Two Virgins**?

14.   **Double Fantasy** has what in common with Aerosmith's album **Rock In A Hard Place**?

15.   What does John Lennon's **Rock 'N' Roll** album have in common with John Cougar Mellencamp's album **American Fool**?

16.   Billy Joel, Michael Sembello, Paul Simon, Phoebe Snow, Barbra Streisand, Julian Lennon, and Paul McCartney all have this talented gentleman in common. Who is he?

17.   Besides knowing Ringo and starring together in "Give My Regards To Broad Street," what theatrical film series do Barbara Bach Starkey and Paul have in common?

18.   The sleeve for The Reddings' album **Back To Basics** shares some-

thing in common with the cover of Wings' album **Venus and Mars**.
What is that?

19. From a creative standpoint, what do these songs - "It's All Too
Much," "See Yourself," and "Here Comes The Moon" have in common?

20. George, Dolly Parton, Richard Pryor, and Tom Selleck all own
property here. Where?

21. What do "A Dose Of Rock and Roll," from **Ringo's Rotogravure**, and "Ram On," from side two of Paul's **Ram** LP, have in common?

22. Cinematically speaking, Tom Cruise, Ryan O'Neal, Ringo, and
Henry Winkler have this actress in common. Who is she?

23. Besides being rock and roll songs common to the Quarry Men's
repertoire, Bill Justis' instrumental, "Raunchy," and Eddie Cochran's
"Twenty Flight Rock" share a special distinction in the history of the
Beatles. What is it?

24. Before the Beatles, what group did Dick Lester and George Martin have in common?

25. "A Hard Day's Night," "Eight Days A Week," and "Tomorrow
Never Knows" - what do these Beatles song titles have in common?

26. What does the movie "Help!" have in common with the cover of
Pink Floyd's 1977 album **Animals**?

27. Mohandas "Mahatma" Ghandi, Adolf Hitler, and Bowery Boy
Leo Gorcey all share a Beatle-related distinction. What is it?

28. What do the phrases "Pushing and Pulling," "Come Together,"
and "One World, One People" have in common?

29. The Residents, Roolgalator, the Rutles, the Stone City Band,
and Utopia have all done something Beatle-related. What?

30. Two of Genesis' singles, "Paperlate" b/w "You Might Recall,"
from their 1982 Atlantic album **Three Sides Live**, and "Land Of Con-

127

fusion" b/w "Feeding The Fire," from their 1986 Atlantic LP **Invisible Touch,** share a Beatles connection. What is it?

```
YOU'RE MUCH TOO COMMON
        FOR ME
      (ANSWERS)
```

1.   All these artists have had one or more of their albums produced by George Martin:
(The Beatles - **Please Please Me, With The Beatles,** et al.; Jeff Beck - **Blow By Blow** and **Wired** (both on Epic); Mahavishnu Orchestra - **Apocalypse** (Columbia); Neil Sedaka - **A Song** (Elektra); Jimmy Webb - **El Mirage** (Atlantic).)

2.   These people were the featured acts on the 9 February 1964 CBS Television Studio 50 marquee.
(This was, of course, the date of the Beatles' first live TV appearance in the U.S. on "The Ed Sullivan Show.")

3.   Prince, Koo, and the Beatles have all made movies with Victor Spinetti.
(The Beatles - "A Hard Day's Night" and "Help!"; Koo Stark - "Emily"; Prince - "Under The Cherry Moon." In "Cherry Moon," Spinetti plays Johnny, listed in the film's credits as one of "The Jaded Three.")

4.   Produced in Canada as a part of Expo '67, the two-hour "Our World" TV special, aired 25 June 1967, featured appearances by all the aforementioned people.

5.   Mia Farrow.
(Farrow, Woody's current companion, has starred in several Allen-directed films, including "Hannah and Her Sisters" and "Radio Days." On 23 January 1968, Mia, then 22, and her sister, Prudence (later the subject of "Dear Prudence"), accompanied the Maharishi on a flight from New York to his ashram at Shankaracharya Nagar (near Rishikesh), India, to begin a course in transcendental meditation; the Beatles arrived shortly thereafter in two groups, on 16 and 20 February. Farrow also starred in the film "Rosemary's Baby," which features exterior shots of the Dakota apartment building.)

6. These people were all passengers on the "Magical Mystery Tour" bus.

(On page 14 of the "MMT" album booklet, Bill Wall is the elderly gent wearing glasses and standing next to Victor Spinetti. In the cast photo on page 24, Sylvia Nightingale, in 1967 the Beatles' Sussex-area fan club secretary, is the second woman to Derek Royle's right. Just below Sylvia is the Beatles' national fan club secretary, Freda Kelly.)

7. All these people are pictured on the White Album's poster photo collage, assembled by Richard Hamilton.

8. The sleeve for **Rock 'N' Roll Music** is based on a photograph that first appeared on the sleeve of **The Beatles' Second Album**.

9. Both of these albums were to be released in then-controversial covers.

(While the Beatles' "dead babies" cover, as John once called it, was released (15 June 1966) and then quickly withdrawn, the original sleeve for **Beggar's Banquet**, a photograph of a graffitied bathroom wall above a toilet, never got past Decca/London record execs in 1968. Decca finally issued the album in this sleeve when the LP was digitally re-mastered in 1984.)

10. **Sgt. Pepper** and the single "Do They Know It's Christmas?" both feature Paul (who says hello on single's flip side, "Feed The World"), as well as the artistic talents of Peter Blake. (Blake designed the picture sleeve for "Do They Know," and co-designed the **Sgt. Pepper** cover with Jann Haworth.)

11. The Beatles, the Stones, and Frank Sinatra have all had collections of their music presented in Mobile Fidelity Sound Lab box sets.

12. All these artists have included messages on their respective albums that are only discernable when played backwards.

13. Both albums were considered for packaging under a brown paper wrapper.

(While **Two Virgins** did receive such treatment, the Beatles nixed Epstein's suggestion for **Sgt. Pepper's** cover. Epstein believed that the row of green above the hyacinth floral arrangement of the name "Beatles" were marijuana plants, a oft-retold rumor refuted by Peter Blake, who claims they were just "plants from a regular nursery.")

14. **Double Fantasy** and **Rock In A Hard Place** were both produced by Jack Douglas.

15. **American Fool** and **Rock 'N' Roll** both feature cover photographs by Jurgen Vollmer.

16. These artists have all had one or more of their records produced by Phil Ramone:
     (Billy Joel - **An Innocent Man** (Columbia); Julian Lennon - **Valotte** and **The Secret Value of Daydreaming** (Atlantic); Michael Sembello - **Bossa Nova Hotel** (Warner Bros.); Paul Simon - **Still Crazy After All These Years** (Columbia); Phoebe Snow - **Never Letting Go** (Columbia); Barbra Streisand - **A Star Is Born** and Yentl (Columbia); Paul McCartney - "Once Upon A Long Ago" b/w "Back On My Feet" (single, Parlophone).)

17. Paul and Barbara have both participated in movies in the James Bond series.
     (In 1973, Paul wrote and sang the title track for Roger Moore's debut as Bond, "Live and Let Die." In 1977, Barbara co-starred with Moore as Major Anya Amasova (Agent Triple X) in "The Spy Who Loved Me." The Beatles were first connected to a Bond film when Sean Connery, in 1964's "Goldfinger," noted to Jill Masterson (Shirley Eaton) that drinking 1953 Dom Perrigon champagne above 38 degrees is "...as bad as listening to the Beatles without earmuffs.")

18. The titles: "The Reddings" and "Back To Basics" employ the same style lettering as is featured on the **Venus and Mars** album.
     (The graphics for **Venus and Mars** are credited to George Hardie.)

19. These songs were supposedly written by George following LSD experiences.

20. George, Tom, Richard, and Dolly all own homes on the Hawaiian island of Maui.

21. Both "A Dose Of Rock and Roll" and "Ram On" end with short renditions of other songs either featured in whole elsewhere on the

130

LP or on a subsequent album.

("A Dose Of Rock and Roll," which opens side one of **Rotogravure**, includes a snip of Bruce Channel's "Hey Baby," which Ringo then covers in full as the LP's second track. Just before the fade of "Ram On," Paul sings a bit of "Big Barn Bed," which he later released a complete version of as the opening cut of Wings' 1973 LP **Red Rose Speedway**.)

22. Each of these actors have starred in movies opposite Shelley Long: Tom Cruise - "Losin' It"; Ryan O'Neal - "Irreconcilable Differences"; Ringo - "Caveman"; Henry Winkler - "Night Shift."

23. When Paul first met John, it was his skill on guitar while performing Eddie Cochran's "Twenty Flight Rock" that was a major factor in John's decision to allow Paul to join the Quarry Men. (Other deciding factors included McCartney's rendition of Gene Vincent's "Be-Bop-A-Lula," and his ability to tune a guitar.) George's flawless rendering of "Raunchy" convinced John and Paul that they should allow George to join the Quarry Men.

24. Before the Beatles, George Martin and Richard Lester both worked with Spike Milligan, Peter Sellers, and Harry Secombe, known collectively as the Goons.

(Martin was the producer of their records, including **Bridge on the River Wye**, while Dick Lester directed the Goons' television show, "Idiot's Weekly," and their movie, "The Running, Jumping And Standing Still Film.")

25. These song titles were all malapropisms first uttered by Ringo.

26. Pink Floyd's album cover and the Beatles' second film both make use of the Battersea Power Station in London.

(In "Help!", the Queen's Royal Fuse blows at Battersea. While driving across the Waterloo Bridge in his custom hot rod during the "Band On The Run" sequence from "Give My Regards To Broad Street," Paul passes by Battersea.)

27. Gorcey, Ghandi, and Hitler were all considered for inclusion on the cover of **Sgt. Pepper**, but were dropped from the final photograph.

(Leo Gorcey, whose image was photographed next to fellow Bowery Boy, Huntz Hall, requested a fee for his appearance on the cover, which EMI refused to grant. Gorcey's face was summarily airbrushed

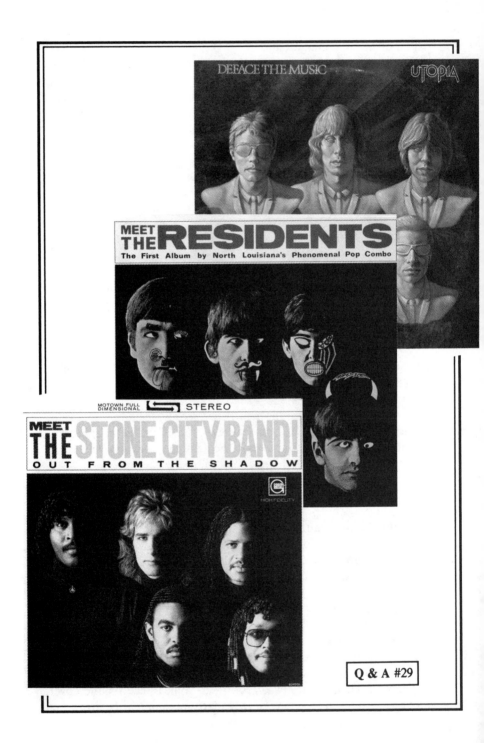

Q & A #30

from the cover. Ghandi, who was photographed next to Lewis Carroll, was also airbrushed out so as not to offend EMI India's record buyers. A left profile shot of Hitler was at one point positioned next to Larry Bell, but the decision was made to remove his likeness. He was replaced by Johnny Weissmuller in the final photo. Also under consideration for cover inclusion were Jesus Christ, Jean Cocteau, and Elvis Presley.)

28. These phrases were etched in the runoff wax of solo singles or albums issued by John and Paul.
("Pushing And Pulling" can be read on both sides of the **Tug Of War** LP. "Come Together" is etched into the "Woman" single, while "One World, One People" is on the single for "(Just Like) Starting Over." John and Yoko had originally planned to end the **Double Fantasy** album with the Benny Cummings Singers and the Kings Temple Choir - who can be heard on "Hard Times Are Over" - chanting "One World, One People" over and over again.)

29. All these artists have released records in album sleeves that parody Robert Freeman's **Meet The Beatles/With The Beatles** album cover photo:
(Utopia - **Deface The Music** (Bearsville); the Rutles - **The Rutles** (Warner Bros.); the Residents' jacket for **Meet The Residents** (Ralph) actually defaces the **Meet The Beatles** sleeve. The Roogalator's album, **With The Roogalator** (Dynamite), was only issued in Holland. The album concept for the Stone City Band's album, **Out From The Shadow** (Gordy), is credited to the record's producer, Rick James.)

30. The picture sleeves for "Paperlate" and "Land Of Confusion" are parodies, respectively, of the U.K. Beatles EP's **Twist and Shout** and **All My Loving**.
(The attention to detail is so exacting on the sleeve for "Paperlate" that it even includes liner notes written by Tony Barrow, who penned the notes for the **Twist and Shout** EP in 1963. The half-shadowed faces of Genesis on the sleeve for "Land Of Confusion" come from the Spitting Image puppets featured in the song's promotional video. This video also includes a cameo by a Spitting Image puppet of Paul.)

Chapter 19

Walrus Gumboots,
Looking Glass Ties,
and Polythene Bags

So there you are Beatle fans, you're writing what you hope will be a gear trivia quiz book on the world's greatest rock group. At this point, you're trying to sequence your questions into logical categories. Perhaps you end up with some questions that just don't fit anywhere. Perhaps you end up with 35 such questions - a veritable potpourri of Beatles topics and trivia. Like this chapter for instance:

1. What were the occupations of each of the Beatles' fathers at the time their respective sons were born?

2. Paul and Mike McCartney, George Harrison, and Neil Aspinall should all rightly be considered Liobian boys. What is a Liobian boy?

3. Why would the names Everett, Pecan, Bones, and Slim be of interest to students of early Beatleology?

4. Mike McCartney owns a home tape recording of the Beatles doing something? What is it?

5. Whatever became of John and Paul's earliest compositions ("One After 909" is one of the few from that period ever recorded)?

6. When the Beatles arrived at San Francisco International Airport, 18 August 1964, to begin their first tour of the U.S., Ed Sullivan passed on the chance to present them on his show because Brian Epstein wanted too much money for an appearance. Sullivan did, however, do something for the group during their stay in New York City. What did Ed do?

7. Who were the primary sponsors for "The Beatles" Saturday morning cartoon?

8. For the cover of his instrumental album, **The Beatle Girls**, George

Martin is seen surrounded by four beautiful women, and the sleeves of which three Beatles albums?

9.   Ringo once told Max Weinberg, "...it's the best (drumming) out of all the records I've ever made. (This song) blows me away." What song was Ringo referring to?

10.   When George and Pattie spent six weeks in Bombay, India, with sitar master Ravi Shankar (beginning 14 September 1966), Shankar suggested to George that he adopt a disguise, so as not to be immediately recognized. What did George do?

11.   In November of 1966, Berkeley students held a demonstration against the presence of a Navy recruiting table on campus. During this demonstration, what Beatle song was sung on the picket line?

12.   During the legendary Monterey Pop Festival, 16-18 June 1967, a souvenir program was made available featuring messages from various bands. What was the Beatles' message?

13.   When Victor Spinetti's one-act production of "In His Own Write" opened at London's Old Vic, 18 June 1968, two other one-act plays, staged by the National Theatre, played with it. What were their titles?

14.   The scenario: John is playing slide trombone, Paul is playing flute, George is on tuba, and Ringo is blowing a mean trumpet. Where did all this take place?

15.   Who displaced the Beatles as Top Group in the 1970 "Melody Maker" poll, a category they had dominated during the previous eight years?

16.   This group used to call themselves "Pogo" before John suggested they change their name. What new name did they adopt?

17.   What is the significance of this phrase: "Well Leo! what say we promenade through the park?"

18.   Which Beatles records are credited to "Lyntone Recordings"?

19.   Sounds Greek to me: What are the appropriate English translations of these Beatle-related foreign phrases: "En Flagrant delire"

and "4 Garcons Dans Le Vant" (French); "Tutti Per Uno" and "Il Sottomarino Giallo" (Italian); "Na Pomoc!" (Polish).

20. According to John, when did Elvis die?

21. When Denny Laine sang "Richard Cory" on the **Wings Over America** album, whom did he wish that he could be?

22. Who are Thunder and Lightning?

23. Before writing a rejected McCartney film script, Willy Russell wrote something else Beatle-related. What was it?

24. Pink Floyd's Dave Gilmour plays guitar on "No More Lonely Nights," but that wasn't the first time he's played for Paul. What was the previous occasion?

25. Featuring topless Andy Warhols on motorcycles, which song did John illustrate for Bernie Taupin's book of lyrics, *The One Who Writes The Lyrics For Elton John*?

26. Which song by the B-52's provoked John to comment, upon hearing it for the first time, that it sounded like Yoko?

27. During the **Tug Of War** sessions in Montserrat, Carl Perkins wrote a song for Paul that they recorded, but has yet to be released. What is the title of this song?

28. When Mick Jagger recorded his first solo album, **She's The Boss**, in 1984, which track did Paul want to play on?

29. What albums do the following catalogue numbers represent?
    a.) Apple PCS 7067/68
    b.) Apple 3356
    c.) Apple PCSP 718
    d.) Capitol ST 12373

30. What is the significance of this phrase to Paul: "What did you do when you were made deputy sheriff?"

31. According to Yoko, what is "bagism" inspired by?

32. What color is John's green card? Who took the picture of John that appeared on his card?

33. What unusual instrument is George Martin credited with playing on "Through Our Love," from the **Pipes Of Peace** album?

34. What did John get Yoko for Christmas in 1980?

35. To McCartneyites, what is the significance of the following titles:
     "Burning Bush"
     "Lucky Spot And Fence"
     "On The Pier"
     "Wasteland"

**WALRUS GUMBOOTS,
LOOKING GLASS TIES,
AND POLYTHENE BAGS
(ANSWERS)**

---

1. Freddie Lennon was a ship's steward when John was born, 9 October 1940. At the time of Paul's birth, 18 June 1942, Jim McCartney was a cotton salesman for A. Hannay and Co. Harold Harrison was a city bus driver when George came along, 25 February 1943, and Richard Starkey, Sr. worked in a bakery when Jr. arrived, 7 July 1940.

(John Best was an Army physical training instructor when his first son, Randolph Peter, was born, 24 November 1941. Charles Sutcliffe was a senior civil servant in Edinburgh, Scotland, when his only son, Stuart, was born, 23 June 1940.)

2. A Liobian boy is a member of the Liverpool Institute Old Boys Association.

(Since Paul, Mike, George, and Neil were all graduates of The Liverpool Institute High School for Boys (or "The Inny," as it was affectionately known), and all have certainly gone on to distinguish themselves in the field of entertainment, all four rightly deserve a place within its ranks.) (See *The Macs*, page 44.)

3. Everett, Pecan, Bones, and Slim made up the Royal Caribbean Steel Band. Their enticement away from Allan Williams' Jacaranda Club to Bruno Koschmider's Hamburg night club, the Kaiserkeller, in

late June of 1960, paved the way for the Beatles and other Liverpool groups.

4. The younger McCartney owns a tape recording of the Beatles playing at the Cavern.

5. Jane Asher accidentally threw out many of Lennon and McCartney's earliest compositions during a spring cleaning.

6. Unable to find a hotel willing to put them up (the prospective innkeepers no doubt recalling the frenzied scenes at the Plaza), the Beatles stayed at the Sullivan-owned Delmonico because of Ed's personal intercession with the hotel's management.

7. Toy manufacturer A.C. Gilbert, Quaker Oats, and Mars Candy were the primary sponsors of "The Beatles" cartoon, which premiered on ABC-TV, 25 September 1964. The last program aired 7 September 1969.

8. The "Beatle Girls" display copies of **Beatles For Sale, Rubber Soul,** and **Revolver.**

9. Ringo believes "Rain" to be the best example of his drumming.
(See *The Big Beat - Conversations With Rock's Greatest Drummers*, by Max Weinberg with Robert Santelli.)

10. At Ravi's suggestion, George grew a moustache and cut his hair.

11. Berkeley's Navy table picketers sang "Yellow Submarine."

12. The Beatles' message in the Monterey Pop Festival program reads: "Peace to Monterey from Sgt. Pepper's Lonely Hearts Club Band."

13. "A Covent Garden Tragedy" and "An Unwarranted Intrusion" played with "In His Own Write," 18 June 1968.

14. This musical performance can be seen in the animated feature, "Yellow Submarine."
(The animated Beatles were playing the instruments and roles of the members of "Sgt. Pepper's Lonely Hearts Club Band.")

15. Led Zeppelin was voted Top Group in the 1970 "Melody Maker"

readership poll.

(In addition, Robert Plant was voted Best British Male Vocalist, while **Led Zeppelin II** was voted Best British Album.)

16. At John's suggestion, "Pogo" became "Poco."

17. This phrase is contained in a cartoon balloon issuing from Peter Sellers' mouth (Sellers is talking to George) in the Terry Doran gatefold photograph for the **Dark Horse** album.

(This line was first spoken in Mel Brooks' 1968 comedy, "The Producers," a film which Harrison cites as one of his favorites. In the film, after dining "alfresco" on a park vendor's hot dogs, Max Bialystock (Zero Mostel) says this line to his partner Bloom (Gene Wilder).)

18. The Beatles' fan club Christmas messages are credited to "Lyntone Recordings."

(Lyntone Records was the company that pressed the original 7-inch Christmas-message flexi-discs issued between 1963 and 1969.)

19. "En Flagrant delire" is the title of the French translation of *In His Own Write*. "4 Garcons Dans Le Vent" and "Tutti Per Uno" are the French and Italian translations, respectively, for "A Hard Day's Night." "Il Sottomarino Giallo" is the Italian title for the film "Yellow Submarine." "Na Pomoc!" is the title "Help!" was released under in Poland.

20. John has said that Elvis died in 1958, the year Presley went into the Army.

21. Denny wished that he could be Richard Cory and John Denver.

22. Thunder and Lightning are the drumming duo of Ringo and Jim Keltner.

(Ringo refers to their duo in "Drumming Is My Madness.")

23. Russell's other Beatle-related script is for the 1974 play, "John, Paul, George, Ringo... and Bert."

(Russell also wrote the screenplay for the film "Educating Rita.")

24. Gilmour played guitar for Paul previously as a member of "Rockestra."

25. John's photo collage illustrates Taupin's lyrics to "Bennie and the Jets."

(Ringo also contributed a quick line drawing to this book. As he had written "Snookeroo Snookeroo" on the sketch, it was probably intended to illustrate the lyrics to "Snookeroo," a Taupin/John song Starr included on his **Goodnight Vienna** LP. The sketch is added as a "P.S." to Taupin's author biography page.)

26. "Rock Lobster"
(Single release from the group's first album, **B-52's**.)

27. Perkins' unreleased duet with Paul is "My Old Friend."
(Paul did not release this song on **Tug Of War** as he felt it was too country to fit the album.)

28. Paul wanted to play on "Hard Woman."
(The track, which features Pete Townshend, was already finished by the time Paul asked.)

29. a.) Apple PCS 7067/68 is the U.K. record number for **The Beatles** album.

b.) Apple 3356 was a U.S. record number never assigned to a release.

c.) Apple PCSP 718 is the U.K. record number for **The Beatles 1967-1970**.

d.) Capitol ST 12373 was the record number assigned by the label to the aborted **Sessions** album.

30. This question begins side one of the last Wings album, **Back To The Egg**.

31. "Bagism" was inspired by Antoine De Saint-Exupery's book *The Little Prince*.
("The essential is invisible to the eye.")

32. John's green card is really blue. The picture of John on his card was taken by Bob Gruen.

33. George Martin's instrument on "Through Our Love" was a bicycle.
(Martin struck a revolving cycle wheel with a rachet.)

34. For Christmas 1980, John got Yoko a portrait and some original handwriting of poetess Elizabeth Barrett Browning framed side by side.

(John gave Sean an Akita puppy. Sean named it Merry, after "Merry Christmas.")

35. These are the titles of photographs taken by Linda McCartney.

(They were among the thirty-one prints displayed in galleries across the United States in 1982-83. "On The Pier" is a picture of Paul and Heather. "Wasteland" is a photograph of Paul's son, James Louis. Lucky Spot is the name of an Appaloosa residing at the McCartney's Scottish farm. "Burning Bush" is a photograph of a bush engulfed in flames.)

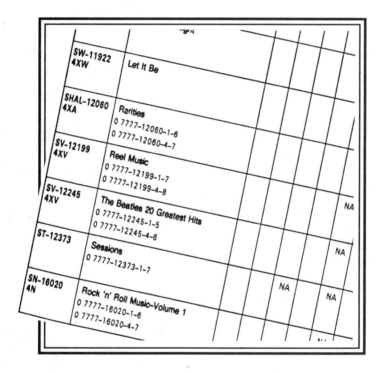

◀ **Q & A #29** Sessions LP listing in Capitol Records August 1987 alphabetical catalog.

CHAPTER 20

FROM THE MAN
OF A THOUSAND VOICES

And there followed a series of flaming pies, screaming jelly babies, and comments like:

"God is more popular than the Rolling Stones."

Crossing Abbey Road together for the last time, people soon realized that the Beatles (which they cleverly called themselves) were more than just four boys joined at the hair. Tucked into all this madness was John (who was called O'Leannain), George (a man of no visible middle name), Richard (late of "Ringo Starrtime"), and a lad named Paul. When people heard his name was also a McCartney, they exclaimed in high glorias:

"Ah, Mr. Paul (who is really James), you will soon take Wings, win rhodium records, and write many clever and engearing pop tunes." (And he did.)

In this quiz are questions based on songs he composed.

Can you dig it?

1. Written by Paul when he was just sixteen, who was "Love Me Do" written for?

2. While Paul, Jane, Ringo, and Maureen holidayed in St. Thomas, the Virgin Islands, in May of 1964, Paul wrote two songs, one of which the Beatles later recorded. Name the songs.

3. What is the name of the imaginary character Paul composed "Paperback Writer" for?

4. Which three songs from the **McCartney** album has Paul said he made up as he went along?

5. Which song from the **McCartney** album did Paul say he wrote the bulk of while on holiday in Benitses, Greece, in 1969?

6. "If when she tries to run away,
   And he calls her back, she comes.
   If there's a next time, he's okay,
   Cause she's under both his thumbs."

Paul McCartney playing guitar with Hamish Stuart
and Robbie McIntosh, taken at the L.A. Forum, 28 November 1989.
Previously unpublished photograph by Janet D. Ragsdale.

Paul's lyrics for the above song have never been commercially released, but a line from this song's chorus has. What is the song's title?

7.   Name two Macca songs chronicling Wings' adventures in the Caribbean. (This was at the time Wings was recording the songs for their **London Town** LP.)

8.   This song from **Back To The Egg** was originally recorded by Wings merely as a demo for the Mills Brothers. What is this song's title?

9.   List all of the songs released in the short career of the supergroup "Rockestra."

10.   When **McCartney II** was released in Japan, which song did Paul have retitled?

11.   When Paul released this song, he referred to himself as "a drycleaner." What is the song's title?

12.   Which of Paul's songs did he sing with the King's Singers and the St. Paul's Boys Choir?

13.   After many years apart, producer George Martin was reunited with Paul in the studio in the fall of 1980. What is the title of the song that brought them together?

14.   What are the respective B-sides of the twelve-inch singles featuring "Ebony and Ivory" and "Take It Away"?

15.   Which song is available on the cassette version of **Give My Regards To Broad Street**, but not on the album?

16.   What is the title of the bonus cut available only on compact disc versions of the **Give My Regards To Broad Street** soundtrack?

17.   Which of his songs did Paul say he wrote after hearing the Rolling Stones sing it in his dream?

18.   Paul has said that a line from the chorus of "Press" was "a subtle update" from this song by Gary Glitter. What's the title of the song he

was referring to?

19. The compact disc version of Paul's 1986 album, **Press To Play,** contains three bonus cuts not available on the LP. What are the titles of these songs?

20. Name all the songs Paul has released that feature reprises later in their respective albums.

21. What is the title of the song by Steve Miller for which Paul plays bass, drums, and contributes backing vocals?

22. What are the names of the songs written by James Taylor on which Paul and Linda sing backing vocals?

23. What is the title of the song Paul wrote for Rod Stewart?

24. What is the title of the song Paul wrote with Michael Jackson in mind?

25. Were Paul to become stranded on a desert island, which of John's songs has he said he would want with him?

**FROM THE MAN
OF A THOUSAND VOICES
(ANSWERS)**

---

1. Paul wrote "Love Me Do" for Iris Caldwell.
(Iris is the sister of the late Rory Storm.)

2. During his Virgin Island holiday, Paul wrote "Things We Said Today" and "Always and Only."
(The latter song has yet to be released.)

3. Paul wrote "Paperback Writer" to Ian Iachimoe.

4. Paul made up the instrumentals "Valentine Day" and "Momma Miss America," and the song "Oo-You" as he went along.

5. Paul wrote most his song "Every Night" while on holiday in

Benitses, Greece.

6.   A line from the chorus of "Suicide" is included at the tail end of the "Hot As Sun/Glasses" instrumental medley, a cut from Side one of the **McCartney** album.
(Paul sings "Suicide" on the unreleased McCartney and Wings documentary from 1974, "One Hand Clapping.")

7.   Paul's Caribbean chronicles in song are "Morse Moose and the Grey Goose," from the **London Town** album, and "Wanderlust," included on the **Tug Of War** LP.

8.   "Baby's Request" was originally intended to be recorded by Wings merely as a demo for the Mills Brothers.

9.   "Rockestra's" recorded output includes the "Rockestra Theme," "So Glad To See You Here," "Let It Be," and "Lucille."
("Rockestra" recorded these songs for the albums **Back To The Egg** and **The Concerts for the People of Kampuchea**.)

10.   In Japan, "Frozen Jap" was retitled "Frozen Japanese" so as not to offend Paul's fans there.

11.   Paul's drycleaner song is "Bogey Music," from the **McCartney II** album.
(In Raymond Briggs' book, *Fungus The Bogeyman*, Bogeys refer to people living above ground as "drycleaners.")

12.   Paul sang "We All Stand Together" (from the Rupert Bear featurette) with the King's Singers and the St. Paul's Boys Choir.

13.   The song reuniting Paul and George Martin in the studio was also "We All Stand Together," recorded 31 October and 3 November 1980.

14.   The B-side of the "Ebony and Ivory" twelve-inch single includes "Rainclouds" and Paul's solo version of "Ebony and Ivory." The B-side of the "Take It Away" twelve-inch includes "I'll Give You A Ring" and "Dress Me Up As A Robber."

15.   A new version of "So Bad" kicks off side two of the **Give My Regards To Broad Street** cassette.

148

16.   The instrumental track "Goodnight Lonely Princess" is only available on the **Broad Street** CD.

17.   Paul wrote "No Values," included on the **Broad Street** LP, after hearing the Stones sing it in a dream.

18.   The line "Right there, that's it. Yes." from "Press," is described by Paul as a "subtle update" from the Gary Glitter song "Do You Wanna Touch Me."

19.   The **Press To Play** CD bonus songs are "Write Away," "It's Not True," and "Tough On A Tightrope."

20.   Paul's reprise songs include:
      "Bip Bop"/(reprise) (From the **Wild Life** album.)
      "Band On The Run"/(reprise) (From the **Band On The Run** album. Though not listed, this reprise follows the song "Nineteen Hundred And Eighty-Five.")
      "Venus and Mars" (From the **Venus And Mars** album.)
      "No More Lonely Nights" (ballad)/(ballad reprise - instrumental)
      "Silly Love Songs"/(reprise - instrumental) (From the **Give My Regards To Broad Street** album.)

21.   Donning his Silver Beetle stage name, Paul Ramon, as a pseudonym, Paul demonstrated his musical diversity on "My Dark Hour," a cut from Steve Miller's 1969 Capitol LP, **Brave New World**.

22.   Paul and Linda's backing vocals can be heard on "Night Owl," written by Taylor and sung by his wife at the time, Carly Simon; the song is included on her 1972 Elektra album **No Secrets**. The McCartneys also lend backing vocals to "Rock 'n' Roll Is Music Now" and "Let It All Fall Down," from Taylor's 1974 Warner Bros. album **Walking Man**.
      (Paul's earliest appearance on a Taylor recording was as bassist on "Carolina In My Mind," first released in the U.S. by Apple on the album **James Taylor**, 17 February 1970. In an interview printed in "Rolling Stone," 11 June 1981, Taylor told Timothy White that the line in the song referring to the "...holy host of others standing 'round me," is a reference to the Beatles.)

23. Paul wrote the song "Mine For Me" for Rod Stewart.
(Paul also supplies backing vocals for this cut, released in 1974 on Stewart's Mercury LP **Smiler.**)

24. Paul wrote "Girlfriend" with Michael Jackson in mind.
(Paul's version of this song appears on his **London Town** LP. Michael Jackson covered the song on his 1979 Epic album **Off The Wall.**)

25. Paul's desert island Lennon song would be "Beautiful Boy."
(Paul gave this answer to Roy Plomley on BBC Radio's "Desert Island Discs" show.)

CHAPTER 21

BEHIND A WALL OF ILLUSION

For better or worse, the music video has changed how we see and hear music. For recording artists, it is very nearly a prerequisite to release your new single with a companion video. In some instances, entire albums have been translated into video images.

While this quiz will question you in the finer points of noted post-Beatle videos, it should be pointed out that before Paul and Michael Jackson ever teamed up as Mac and Jack in "Say Say Say," and "Coming Up" introduced us to a multitude of McCartneys all playing together, the sixties saw the Beatles pioneering the field of music video with their promotional films, notably the clips directed by Peter Goldman for "Penny Lane" and "Strawberry Fields Forever."

While many critics roasted "Magical Mystery Tour" as amateurish, when viewed as a series of promotional film clips (particularly "I Am The Walrus" and "Your Mother Should Know"), "Magical Mystery Tour" holds up quite well.

1. In George's video for "Ding Dong, Ding Dong," what flag is lowered from the flagpole? What flag is raised in its place?

2. As the "Crackerbox Palace" video opens, George is seen emerging from a pram his nanny has been pushing. Who played George's nanny?

3. What is the name of the boat in which George and his lady companion were riding in the "True Love" video?

4. What is the name of the newspaper that the angel is reading in "True Love"?

5. In which of George's videos can he be seen playing his guitar while sitting atop a bobbing-head bulldog toy?

6. At one point in the video for "Stop and Take The Time To Smell The Roses," Ringo is seen dressed as a traffic cop marching in a parade complete with marching band. As he marches past a line of cars, who is driving the Rolls Royce he looks into?

7. In a scene from the video for "Nobody Told Me," John and

Yoko are shown playing chess. Who is using the black pieces?

8. Which of John's videos includes footage from "Let It Be"?

9. Which Lennon video utilizes footage from John and Yoko's appearance at the 1971 Oz/IRA demonstration in London?

10. Which Lennon video features cameos by Dick Cavett and Jack Palance?

11. Which of Paul's videos was taped in and around The Fountain pub in Brickwoods?

12. In his video for "Coming Up," Paul is made up to resemble musicians from such noted bands as the Shadows, Roxy Music, and Sparks. Which members from these respective units does Paul ape?

13. What is the name of the polar bear Paul borrowed from Chipperfield's Circus for his "Waterfalls" video?

14. What is the name of the reggae band that appears with Paul and Stevie Wonder in their video for "Ebony and Ivory"?

15. What was George Butler's role in the making of the video for "Take It Away"?

16. Name two McCartney videos where Paul can be seen playing his Hofner Beatle bass.

17. In "Say Say Say," Paul and Michael Jackson play con men selling an elixir of questionable value. What is the name of their product?

18. What event is the "Pipes of Peace" video based upon?

19. Which of Paul's videos features a clip of artist Salvador Dali?

20. What is the brand and model number of the keyboard Chevy Chase plays in the "Spies Like Us" video?

21. What did Paul, Dan Aykroyd, and Chevy Chase do as a finale to their "Spies Like Us" video?

22. Which of Paul's videos was taped in and around the Half Way Station in Amado, Arizona?

23. Which of Paul's videos includes a snippet of the Beatles' "She's Leaving Home"?

24. Which video by Tracey Ullman did Paul appear in?

25. Which video based on a song by the late Bob Marley did Paul make an appearance in?

BEHIND A WALL OF ILLUSION
(ANSWERS)

---

1. In the "Ding Dong, Ding Dong" video, a Jolly Roger pirate flag is lowered and replaced by the symbol for Om, in red on a yellow field.

2. "Baby" (the name of George's nanny) was played by Neil Innes.

3. George's boat was called the "True Love."

4. The angel in "True Love" was reading "The Guardian," making him, in essence, a "Guardian angel."

5. Through the magic of video, George can be seen sitting atop a toy bulldog in a sequence from "Blow Away."

6. The driver of the Rolls that Ringo looks into is - Ringo!

7. John and Yoko are both using white chess pieces.
    ("Nobody Told Me" takes its chess sequence from the scene for Yoko's song "Don't Count The Waves" in the Lennons' 1972 film, "Imagine.")

8. Footage from "Let It Be," showing John and Yoko leaving the Twickenham film studios (with George also visible in the background) is included in the video for "I'm Stepping Out."
    (Black-and-white outtake footage from "Let It Be" is also included in the video for "Grow Old With Me.")

Q & A #14

Q & A #16

9. "Living On Borrowed Time" includes footage of John and Yoko marching up London's Oxford Street in the Oz/IRA demonstration, 11 August 1971.

10. "Nobody Told Me"
("Nobody Told Me" took this footage from the "Imagine" film, a scene originally used to accompany Yoko's song "Mind Train." The shot of John whispering to someone lying on a park bench was from a scene accompanying Yoko's song "Midsummer New York.")

11. The video for "Wonderful Christmas Time" was filmed at The Fountain in Brickwoods.

12. Paul parodies Shadow Hank Marvin, Roxy Music saxophonist Andy Mackay, and Sparks keyboardist Ron Mael in his "Coming Up" video.

13. Olaf was the name of the polar bear appearing in "Waterfalls."

14. The Cimarons appeared with Paul and Stevie Wonder in the "Ebony and Ivory" video.
(In 1982, The Cimarons released **Reggaebility** (Pickwick), an LP of largely MPL-controlled tunes, including "Love Me Do," "With a Little Luck," "C Moon," and "Mull of Kintyre.")

15. George Butler, who bears a striking resemblance to drummer Steve Gadd, stood in for Gadd when it wasn't possible for him to attend one day during the "Take It Away" shooting schedule.

16. Paul played his Hofner violin bass in videos released for "Coming Up" and "Take It Away."

17. Guaranteed to give you "the strength of a raging bull" is the "Mac and Jack Wonder Potion & Cure All."
(Besides appearances by Paul and Linda, the scene at Mrs. Ensign's Orphanage features an appearance by Heather McCartney. Heather also makes a brief appearance as a saloon girl.)

18. The "Pipes of Peace" video is based on the Christmas Day truce of 1914 between British and German troops in the lines around Ypres, France.

19. A clip of Spanish surrealist painter Salvador Dali is included amongst the footage in the video for the disco version of "No More Lonely Nights."

20. Chevy Chase played an Emulator II digital sampling keyboard. (As a joke, an extra "I" was added to the front of the keyboard, creating the non-existent Emulator III.)

21. A barefoot Aykroyd, Macca, and Chase conclude the "Spies Like Us" video (shot at Abbey Road Studios) by walking across the same "zebra" crossing, at the intersection of Abbey Road and Grove End Road, that a certain bare-footed Beatle once negotiated with his mates, 8 August 1969.

22. Redubbed the "Cactus Club" for the video, "Stranglehold" was filmed at the Half Way Station in Amado, Arizona (near Nogales).

23. The video for "Pretty Little Head" opens with the final bars from "She's Leaving Home."

24. Paul's cameo for Tracey Ullman was in her video for "They Don't Know," the first single from her MCA album **You Broke My Heart In 17 Places.**

25. Paul makes a cameo appearance in the video for "One Love," from Marley's posthumously released Island album **Legend.**

WRACK MY BRAIN

You say you've got no time for trivialities? After this quiz, many of you may wish you were up a tree in Strawberry Field. No words of love whispered soft and true for the lot of you college puddings that have made it this far. These questions are designed to test your Beatle lyric recall.

Ready? All the same, you'll play the game.

1. In several songs the Beatles released, the names of the individual members are mentioned. List at least three songs that, in total, mention each of our fabulous foursome by name.

2. Name two songs that have the Beatles on "bended knee(s)."

3. List three songs the Beatles composed with a reference to diamond(s) in their lyrics.

4. List three songs the Beatles composed with a reference to "wine" in their lyrics.

5. Name four yellow objects the Beatles have sung about.

6. List the titles of eight songs the Beatles composed with a reference to "rain" in their lyrics.

7. List the titles of fifteen songs the Beatles composed that contain a reference to "sun" or "sunshine."

8. With the entire globe fair game, name ten cities the Beatles have sung about; please limit your list to songs written by members of the group.

9. Name five countries the Beatles have mentioned in their songs.

10. What two bodies of water have the Beatles made reference to in their songs?

11. Name two songs the Beatles recorded that make a reference to "grandchildren."

12.   List the titles of three Beatles or post-Beatle songs that mention the man that taught the band to play - Sgt. Pepper.

13.   Which solo Beatle song contains the line "All you need is love"?

14.   Which Beatles songs mention, respectively, a sweater and a t-shirt?

15.   According to John and Paul, what are two things that money can't buy?

WRACK MY BRAIN
(ANSWERS)

---

1.   JOHN:

"I'm Down"
(Paul sings, "Hurry up John.")

"For You Blue"
(George sings, "Go, Johnny, go!")

PAUL:

"Glass Onion"
(John sings, "The Walrus was Paul.")

GEORGE:

"Boys"
(Before this song's instrumental break, Ringo says, "All right, George ...")

"Honey Don't"
(Ringo says, "Rock on, George, one time for me.")

RINGO:

"Honey Don't"
(Ringo says, "Rock on George for Ringo one time")

"You Know My Name (Look Up The Number)"
(John announces, "Featuring Dennis O'Fell...and Ringo!")

2. Bended Knee(s):

    "Tell Me Why"
    ("Well I beg you on my bended knees.")

    "One After 909"
    (Well I begged her not to go and I begged her on my bended knee.")

3. Diamond(s):

    "Can't Buy Me Love"
    ("Say you don't need no diamond rings...")

    "I Feel Fine"
    ("...he buys her diamond rings...")

    "Lucy In The Sky With Diamonds"

4. Wine:

    "Her Majesty"
    ("But I gotta get a belly full of wine.")

    "I Me Mine"
    ("Flowing more freely than wine.")

    "Norwegian Wood (This Bird Has Flown)"
    ("I sat on a rug, biding my time, drinking her wine.")

    "When I'm Sixty-Four"
    ("...birthday greetings, bottle of wine.")

5. Yellow:

    "Yellow Submarine"

"Lucy In The Sky With Diamonds"
("Cellophane flowers of yellow and green...")

"I Am The Walrus"
("Yellow matter custard...")

"You Never Give Me Your Money"
("Yellow lorry slow, nowhere to go.")

(The color yellow is also mentioned in "All Together Now.")

6. Rain:

"Across The Universe"
("...endless rain into a paper cup.")

"Fixing A Hole"
("I'm fixing a hole where the rain gets in...")

"Hey Bulldog"
("Sheepdog standing in the rain.")

"I'm A Loser"
("My tears are falling like rain from the sky.")

"The Long And Winding Road"
("The wild and windy night that the rain washed away.")

"Love Of The Loved"
("So let it rain, what do I care...")

"Penny Lane"
("And the fireman rushes in from the pouring rain.")

"Please Please Me"
("...you know there's always rain in my heart.")

"Rain"

("Two Of Us" also makes a reference to "wearing rain coats....")

7. Sun/Sunshine:

"Across The Universe"
("...shines around me like a million suns.")

"Anytime At All"
("If the sun has faded away ...")

"Dear Prudence"
("The sun is up...")

"The Fool On The Hill"
("...sees the sun going down.")

"Good Day Sunshine"

"Goodnight"
("Now the sun turns out its light...")

"Here Comes The Sun"

"I Am The Walrus"
("Sitting in an English garden waiting for the sun.")

"I'll Be On My Way"
("The sun is fading away...")

"I'll Follow The Sun"

"It's All Too Much"
("Sail me on a silver sun...")

"I've Got A Feeling"
("Everybody saw the sun shine.")

"Julia"
("...shimmering, glimmering in the sun.")

"Lucy In The Sky With Diamonds"
("Look for the girl with the sun in her eyes...")

"Mother Nature's Son"
("...a lazy song beneath the sun.")

"Nobody I Know"
("Everywhere I go, the sun comes shining through.")

"Sun King"

"Two Of Us"
("...standing solo in the sun.")

"The Word"
("It's so fine, it's sunshine...")

"Yellow Submarine"
("So we sailed up to the sun.")

8. Cities:

Amsterdam
("The Ballad Of John And Yoko")

Blackburn (in the county of Lancashire)
("A Day In The Life")

Hollywood
("Honey Pie")

Kirkcaldy
("Cry Baby Cry")

London
("The Ballad Of John And Yoko")

Los Angeles (L.A.)
("Blue Jay Way")

Miami Beach
("Back In The U.S.S.R.")

Moscow
("Back In The U.S.S.R.")

Paris
("The Ballad Of John And Yoko")

Southampton
("The Ballad Of John And Yoko")

Tucson (Arizona)
("Get Back")

(Although Liverpool is mentioned in "Maggie Mae," this song was not written by the Beatles. Kirkcaldy is located in Eastern Scotland on the Firth of Forth. Southampton is located in South Central England on an inlet of the English Channel opposite the Isle of Wight. Georgia and the Ukraine, mentioned in "Back In The U.S.S.R.," are not cities, but the names of Soviet Republics.)

9. Countries:

England
("Honey Pie")

France
("The Ballad Of John And Yoko")

Holland
("The Ballad Of John And Yoko")

Spain
("The Ballad Of John And Yoko")

U.S.A.
("Honey Pie")

U.S.S.R.
("Back In The U.S.S.R.")

(Gibraltar, mentioned in "The Ballad Of John And Yoko," is classified as a British colony, not a country.)

10. Bodies of Water: Paul mentions the Atlantic Ocean in "Honey Pie," while John sings of honeymooning down by the river Seine (in

the North of France) in "The Ballad Of John And Yoko."

(Other geographic locations mentioned in Beatles songs include two states (Arizona and California in "Get Back"); one U.S. territory (Dakota, which in 1889 was divided into the states of North and South Dakota, from "Rocky Raccoon"); one island (the Isle of Wight, located in the English Channel off south central England, from "When I'm Sixty-Four"); one mountain range (the Black Hills, located in Southwest South Dakota and Northeast Wyoming, from "Rocky Raccoon"); one noted Liverpool landmark (Strawberry Field orphanage, from "Strawberry Fields Forever" and "Glass Onion"), and two streets (Liverpool's "Penny Lane," and Los Angeles' "Blue Jay Way" - three, if you count Lime Street mentioned in "Maggie Mae.")

11.   Grandchildren: "When I'm Sixty-Four" ("Grandchildren on your knee..."), and "Hey Bulldog" (after John howls like a dog, Paul enthusiastically replies, "You got it! That's it, you have it! That's it man, that's it - ya got it! What do you mean, man, I already have grandchildren?")

12.   Sgt. Pepper: "Sgt. Pepper's Lonely Hearts Club Band," "Sgt. Pepper's Lonely Hearts Club Band (Reprise)," "How Do You Sleep?"
("How Do You Sleep?" is from John's **Imagine** album.)

13.   George's tribute to John, "All Those Years Ago," from the album **Somewhere In England,** includes the line "But you point the way to the truth when you say/*All you need is love.*"

14.   "When I'm Sixty-Four" ("You can knit a sweater by the fireside."), and "I Am The Walrus" ("Corporation t-shirt...").

15.   The two things that money can't buy are "love" ("Can't Buy Me Love") and "fun" ("She's Leaving Home").

CHAPTER 23

CRIMBLE MAYBE?

And so this is Christmas...and what have we here? Amid all the pretty wrapping paper, ribbons, empty boxes, and playing cards made out of knickers - a Beatles Fan Club Christmas message quiz! Really now, you shouldn't have! Here, open mine. It's full of some interesting facts pertaining to those hilarious recorded holiday greetings, facts like these:

* When Paul announces to his fans during the 1963 message that people are telling him to "stop," amid a chorus of "stops!" John declares, "Stop shouting those animoles!"

This is a line from John's short story "On Safairy With Whide Hunter." "Safairy" would appear a few months later in John's first book.

* A full-length bootleg recording exists of "Christmas Time Is Here Again," the song used as the unifying theme to the Beatles' 1967 message. Recorded 28 November 1967 at Abbey Road's No. 2 studio, this version clocks in at just over 6 1/2 minutes.

* Ringo's reference to "Ken" in the 1969 message, following a plug for his latest film, "The Magic Christian," alludes to D.J. Kenny Everett. Everett (whose real name is Maurice Cole) edited together that year's message, as well as the one released in 1968.

Yes, everywhere it's Christmas.

1. In what geographic locale does the 1966 Christmas message open?

2. Who is Count Balder?

3. Where does the Count live?

4. What did Podgy the Bear and Jasper have to remember to get?

5. What is the name of the woman "gradually injured" in heavy fighting near Blackpool?

6. What is the title of the song this woman wanted "for all the people in hospital," and the name of the fictitious group who sings it?

7. Snippets from which Beatles songs can be heard on "The Beatles' 1968 Christmas Record"?

8. What does John like to eat, according to the message he re-

corded for "The Beatles' Seventh Christmas Record" (December 1969)?

9.   What type of wall does John tell Yoko he favors?

10.   What title does **The Beatles Christmas Record** compilation LP go by in England?

CRIMBLE MAYBE?
(ANSWERS)

---

1.   "The Beatles' Fourth Christmas Record Pantomime: Everywhere It's Christmas" opens in Corsica.

2.   Count Balder is the son of Baron Lansberg, inventor of the rack.

3.   The Count lives in Felpin Mansions.

4.   Podgy and Jasper had to remember to get matches, candles, and buns.

5.   Mrs. G. Evans was gradually injured.

6.   Mrs. G. Evans requested "Plenty of Jam Jars," by the Ravellers.
     (From "The Beatles Fifth Christmas Record - Christmas Time Is Here Again.")

7.   The Beatles' 1968 Christmas message features snippets of "Ob-La-Di, Ob-La-Da," "Helter Skelter," and "Yer Blues."

8.   John likes to eat "corn flakes prepared by Persian hands" and "blessed by a Hare Krishna mantra."

9.   John favors the "...Elizabethan high wall."

10.   In England, the compilation album of the Beatles' seven fan club Christmas flexidisc messages was titled **From Then To You.**

CHAPTER 24

On the Wings of an Angel

When the Beatles officially called it quits in April 1970, Paul made his first solo albums by himself with help from Linda. It seemed only natural that by 1971 Paul had formed his own band - "Wings." Alas, Wings is no more, perhaps because Paul has outgrown the need to be surrounded by a set group of musicians. Some could argue that Wings was nothing more than Paul's constantly rotating lineup of session men. Despite the example set by the **Wings At The Speed Of Sound** album, the music of Wings was really that of Paul McCartney. Even elder Wing Denny Laine couldn't be thought of as Paul's new partner.

Whatever your opinion of the group's purpose to Paul and the musicians who played with him, the Wings banner did very well for McCartney, garnering him a string of hit records and new fans beyond the Beatles.

1.   Without examining the record or the record label it was released on, what is the easiest way to tell if your copy of **Band On The Run** is American or British?

2.   Paul, Linda, and Denny worked on **Band On The Run** in Africa for three weeks in September of 1973. In what suburb of Lagos, Nigeria, did they record it?

3.   Following their three weeks in Lagos, Paul, Linda, and Denny arrived back in London on 26 September 1973. What airport did they arrive at, and what was their flight number?

4.   What was the title of the first song Wings recorded for **Back To The Egg**?

5.   What are sides one and two, respectively, of **Back To The Egg** referred to as?

6.   On the morning of 11 June 1979, Wings held a party to promote **Back To The Egg**. Where did this party take place?

7.   What was the name of Denny Laine's first group, which he formed back in 1963?

8.   What was the original line-up of Wings, assembled in 1971?

9.   What was the line-up for Wings in 1972?

10.   List the personnel of Wings '73, prior to the recording of **Band On The Run**.

11.   Following the release of **Band On The Run** in 1973, who filled the Wings roster?

12.   Including the members of their four-piece horn section, please run through the line-up for Wings 1975-76.

13.   Who was in Wings Mach V (1978-79)?

14.   Name the 1982 line-up of Wings.

15.   Who are the musicians who comprised the Wings hybrid dubbed "The Country Hams"?

16.   When Paul and Wings toured the U.S., 3 May - 23 June 1976, they "commuted" between four base cities to each night's concert. Name the four cities Wings used as home bases during this tour.

17.   Who is "Po," and what is his connection to Wings' 1976 U.S. Tour?

18.   List eight songs Denny Laine has recorded and released under the Wings banner.

19.   This instrumental, written by former Wings guitarist Laurence Juber and recorded during the sessions for the **Back To The Egg** album, was released in 1982 on **Standard Time**, Juber's first solo album. What is the title of this instrumental?

20.   Why would Jules Shear's band "Reckless Sleepers" and their 1988 album **Big Boss Sounds** (IRS) be of interest to Wings fans?

168

Wings 1975-76 world tour program.

1.   Only American copies of the **Band On The Run** LP include the song "Helen Wheels."

2.   A large part of **Band On The Run** was recorded at ARC Studio in the Lagos suburb of Apapa.

3.   Flight No. BR364 arrived at London's Gatwick Airport, 26 September 1973.
    (The Macs were flying economy class, by the way. All information for this question is located on the back of the **Band On The Run** album sleeve.)

4.   "To You" was the first song recorded for **Back To The Egg** at Paul's "Spirit of Ranachan" studio in Scotland.

5.   Side One - "Sunny Side Up"; Side Two - "Over Easy"

6.   Paul's "Back To The Egg" promo party was held at Abbey Road's No. 2 studio.

7.   Denny Laine's first group was "Denny and the Diplomats."
    (Denny [whose given name was Brian Arthur Hines] and his Diplomats once supported the Beatles on a bill at the Plaza Ballroom in Old Hill, Staffordshire, 5 July 1963.)

8.   Wings 1971 was Paul and Linda McCartney, Denny Laine, and Denny Seiwell (drums).
    (Seiwell can count among his pre-Wings drumming experiences four years in the U.S. Army as a bandsman.)

9.   Wings 1972 was Paul and Linda McCartney, Denny Laine, Denny Seiwell, and Henry McCullough (lead guitar).
    (Prior to joining Wings, McCullough was a member of Joe Cocker's Grease Band.)

10.   Wings 1973, pre-**Band On The Run**, were Paul and Linda McCartney, and Denny Laine.

170

11. Wings 1973, post-**Band On The Run,** were Paul and Linda Mc-Cartney, Denny Laine, Jimmy McCulloch (lead guitar), and Geoff Britton (drums).

(Prior to joining Wings, Jimmy played guitar for Stone The Crows, while Britton was the percussionist for East of Eden.)

12. Wings 1975-76 was Paul and Linda McCartney, Denny Laine, Jimmy McCulloch, Joe English (drums), Steve "Tex" Howard (trumpet, flugelhorn), Thaddeus Richard (soprano and alto saxophones, clarinet, and flute), Howie Casey (tenor saxophone), and Tony Dorsey (trombone).

(Prior to joining Wings, English played drums for Jam Factory.)

13. Wings 1978-79 was Paul and Linda McCartney, Denny Laine, Laurence Juber (lead guitar), and Steve Holley (drums).

(Wings' horn section - Howard, Richard, Casey, and Dorsey - appeared with Wings Mark VI on their 1979 tour of Britain.)

14. There was no line-up for Wings 1982; Wings' last recording sessions took place in October of 1980.

15. "The Country Hams" were Chet Atkins, Geoff Britton, Vassar Clements, Floyd Cramer, Denny Laine, Linda McCartney, Paul McCartney, and Bobby Thompson.

(The Hams recorded Jim McCartney's "Walking In The Park With Eloise" b/w "Bridge Over The River Suite.")

16. Wings' 1976 U.S. tour base cities were Chicago, Dallas, Los Angeles, and New York.

17. "Po," alias photographer Aubrey Powell, accompanied Wings on their 1976 American tour. His photographic account of this tour was published in the 1978 book *Hands Across The Water - Wings Tour USA.*

18. Denny Laine's songs for Wings:

"I Lie Around"
(Written by Paul and sung by Denny, "Around" is the B-side of the "Live and Let Die" single);

"No Words"
(Released on the **Band On The Run** album, this duet between Paul and Denny is a McCartney/Laine composition);

"Spirits Of Ancient Egypt"
(Released on the **Venus and Mars** album, "Spirits" is another trade-off of lead vocals between Denny and Paul. The song was written by Paul);

"The Note You Never Wrote"
(Written by Paul and sung by Denny, "Note" is from the **Wings At The Speed Of Sound** album);

"Time To Hide"
(Written and sung by Denny, "Time" is also from **Wings At The Speed Of Sound**);

"Richard Cory"
(Sung by Denny as a medley with "Picasso's Last Words," "Richard Cory" was written by Paul Simon, and was released on the **Wings Over America** triple album);

"Go Now"
(Denny sings lead on this blast from his Moody Blues past, written by Milton Bennet and Larry Banks. It is also included on the **Wings Over America** album);

"Children Children," "Deliver Your Children"
(Both songs, credited as McCartney/Laine compositions, are featured on the **London Town** LP. Denny handles lead vocals on both);

"Again And Again And Again"
(Denny's last song on a Wings album, this Laine composition and lead vocal is featured on **Back To The Egg**).

19. Featuring Paul on bass, Juber's instrumental from **Standard Time** (Breaking Records) is titled "Maisie."

20. Former Wings drummer Steve Holley handles drums, percussion and backing vocals for the Reckless Sleepers on **Big Boss Sounds**.

CHAPTER 25

SHE'S THE KIND OF
A GIRL THAT MAKES
THE NEWS OF THE WORLD

There is probably no other rock group in the history of music journalism so frequently written about as the Beatles. Acting on a suggestion from Dezo Hoffman, Peter Jones became the first to interview the group for a national music paper, London's "Record Mirror," in August of 1962.

A well-educated Beatles fan will have plowed through millions of words spoken by and written about the group over the years, from books to the contents of a myriad of newspapers and magazines. This quiz highlights just a few of the most notable and quotable in news, reviews, and startling interviews!

1.   Whose picture is on the front page of the first issue of "Mersey Beat" newspaper (6-20 July, 1961)?

2.   What article of Beatle note was featured in that first issue of "Mersey Beat"?

3.   Who were the writers responsible for these regularly featured "Mersey Beat" columns: "The Roving 'I,'" "Mersey Roundabout," and "Beatcomber"?

4.   Commenting in "Rolling Stone" on the demise of this magazine, John was quoted as saying, "For the last few years I've been with Yoko, they've been kicking the hell out of us." What magazine was John referring to?

5.   For a short time, what other Merseyside group had its own monthly magazine, similar in format to "The Beatles Book"?

6.   London's "Daily Herald" once offered this breakdown of the composition of Beatlemania: "75% publicity, 20% haircut and five percent...." What?

7.   What Beatle-related event did "Time" magazine call "a serious

lapse in taste"?

8.   Why was Pete Best unhappy with the interview Jean Shepherd conducted with the Beatles in the February 1965 issue of "Playboy"?

9.   Besides David Sheff's memorable interview with John and Yoko in the January 1981 issue of "Playboy," what other feature made this issue of interest to Beatle fans?

10.   Which of the Beatles was interviewed in Vol. 1, No. 1 of "Hustler" magazine?

11.   Who was the first Beatle to be interviewed in "Rolling Stone"?

12.   In late 1982, MGM/United Artists sponsored a contest to promote its home release of "The Compleat Beatles" video. Printed in newspapers, what form did the contest take?

13.   In what "publication" did John's poetry and sketches first appear?

14.   In which periodical could one have read John's short story of the adventures of Ralph the Elephant, Sydney Shoe, and Carol Cow?

15.   Which newspaper is pictured on the cover of Two Virgins?

16.   According to an interview in the 26 September 1980 issue of "Newsweek," what year did John first consider leaving the Beatles?

17.   Which Lennon single did "Billboard" say possessed a "breezy island atmosphere..."?

18.   When Julian Lennon was asked by "Rolling Stone" in 1984 for his list of the ten best albums and/or singles, which Beatles album did he include?

19.   For what magazine (issue dated August 1980) did Paul grant an interview, the tapes from said interview later being released on a record?

20.   Besides the "News of the World" (noted in "Polythene Pam"), what other newspaper have the Beatles mentioned in their lyrics?

21. Which song, written by Paul, did "Rolling Stone" call "...a two-and-a-half-minute definition of great rock songwriting"?

22. In 1963, the "New Musical Express'" year-end poll made the Beatles the world's top group. Who was the first runner-up?

23. In 1964, "Billboard" magazine ran an article that Brian Epstein was about to make his "disc debut." What was going to be on Brian's record?

24. In the 90th anniversary special edition of "Billboard," the Beatles shared a heading with two other people in a listing of "The 90 Who Made It Happen" in the music and home entertainment industry. Who were the two other people who shared a listing with the Beatles?

25. Whose fiberglass and papier-mache rendering of the Beatles graces the cover of the 22 September 1967 issue of "Time" magazine?

26. What is the title of Timothy Leary's 1968 essay on the Beatles?

27. Why is the cover of "Rolling Stone" No. 22 of note to Beatle fans?

28. What is unique about "Rolling Stone" No. 415, featuring a cover story on the 20th anniversary of the Beatles' arrival in the U.S.?

29. Who said, in a January 1985 "Rolling Stone" interview, "I think we're the Eighties Beatles."

30. "Frankly, we feel we're a publicity pawn in a longstanding legal battle between two record companies." This quote, taken from a full-page ad run in the "Oregonian," 6 August 1987, accused Apple Records of using this Beaverton, Oregon, company as a "pawn" in their "longstanding legal battle" with EMI/Capitol. What is the name of this company and why were they being sued by Apple Records?

1.   Gene Vincent appeared on the cover of the first "Mersey Beat."

2.   The premiere issue of "Mersey Beat" features John's article, "Being A Short Diversion On The Dubious Origins Of Beatles."
    (In this version, the Beatles receive their name from a man on a flaming pie.)

3.   "The Roving 'I'" was written by Bob Wooler. Bill Harry's wife, Virginia, wrote "Mersey Roundabout," while "Beatcomber" was the handiwork of John Lennon.

4.   In a "Rolling Stone" article from 21 January 1970, Lennon was referring to "The Beatles Book" on the occasion of their last issue (No. 77), published the previous December.

5.   Gerry and the Pacemakers.

6.   The other 5% was "lilting lament."

7.   "Only once did they show a serious lapse of taste: the cover of their 1966 album **Yesterday And Today** was a photograph of the four wearing butcher's smocks and laden with chunks of raw meat and the bodies of decapitated dolls."
    (Quoted from "Time" magazine's 22 September 1967 cover story on the group.)

8.   Ringo's flippant comment that Best "took little pills to make him ill," was interpreted by Pete as an implication that he was a drug addict. Best filed a $45 million lawsuit against the Beatles, Brian Epstein, and NEMS Enterprises, which was later settled out of court.

9.   The January 1981 "Playboy" issue included a steamy pictorial on Barbara Bach, who also graced the magazine's cover.

10.   The premiere issue of Larry Flynt's "Hustler" magazine featured

an interview with Paul.

11.   Ringo and George were the first Beatles interviewed in "Rolling Stone" in issue No. 5, 10 February 1968.

(Ringo's interview was conducted in a seafood restaurant in Soho by "Melody Maker" editor Jack Hutton, while George's interview (which ran in two parts, concluding in issue No. 6, 24 February 1968) was conducted by Nick Jones.)

12.   MGM/United Artists' promotion for "The Compleat Beatles" home video release took the form of a Beatles crossword puzzle.

13.   John's poetry and sketches first appeared in "The Daily Howl," his Dovedale Primary School workbook.

14.   The adventures of Ralph, Sydney, and Carol are in John's short story "The Toy Boy," first printed in the December 1965 issue of "McCall's."

15.   The newspaper pictured on the cover of **Two Virgins** is "The Times Business News."

16.   John first considered leaving the Beatles in 1966.

("I was always waiting for a reason to get out of The Beatles from the day I filmed "How I Won The War" [intermittently through September-November 1966]. I just didn't have the guts to do it.")

17.   Lennon's single with the "breezy island atmosphere" is "Borrowed Time."

(Quotation from the 26 May 1984 issue of "Billboard.")

18.   Julian's favorite Beatles album in 1984 was **Sgt. Pepper.**

(Among Julian's other favorites were ZZ Top's **Eliminator, Van Halen II, Synchronicity** by The Police, and **Pretzel Logic** by Steely Dan. Regarding the latter group, which Jules has frequently cited as a major influence on his music, Lennon has stated that he was first exposed to Steely Dan's music by his mother Cynthia.)

19.   Columbia Records' release of **The McCartney Interview** is based on tapes from an interview first conducted (by Vic Garbarini) for "Musician" magazine.

(Garbarini also conducted the interview with Ringo that appeared in the February 1982 issue of "Musician.")

20. The "Daily Mail" is mentioned in "Paperback Writer."

21. Paul's "two-and-a-half-minute definition of great rock songwriting" is "On The Wings Of A Nightingale," sung by the Everly Brothers on their reunion album, **EB '84**.
(Statement made by Kurt Loder.)

22. The 1963 NME year-end poll first runner-up as world's top group was the Everly Brothers.

23. The 3 October 1964 issue of "Billboard" reported that Brian's disc debut would have been readings from his autobiography *A Cellarful Of Noise*.

24. The Beatles share their listing with George Martin and Brian Epstein.
(Their listing reads: "Revolutionized pop music in '60's." Sid Bernstein and Ed Sullivan also made the "Billboard" list, in part because of their involvement with the Beatles. Bernstein is credited as a "Pioneer concert promoter, brought Beatles to U.S.," while Sullivan's listing reads: "CBS-TV m.c. for introducing key recording acts including Beatles to U.S. audience.")

25. The fiberglass and papier-mache rendering of the Beatles was done by Gerald Scarfe.
(Scarfe's rendering of the group was the only time the Beatles ever appeared together on the cover of "Time." Scarfe dressed his papier-mache Beatles in clothing from London's "In Savita" shop, owned by Mrs. Meher Vakeel.)

26. Leary's Beatles essay is titled "Thank God For the Beatles."

27. The cover and centerspread of "Rolling Stone" No. 22 (23 November 1968) features the cover art for **Two Virgins**.
(John himself sent in the photographs to "Rolling Stone" editor/publisher Jann Wenner via Ethan Russell.)

28. Two different photographs of the group were used for the covers of the "Rolling Stone" "Special Beatles Anniversary Issue," one for the East Coast, and the other for the West Coast.

CAN WE TALK?

You may have heard reports that NIKE is being sued by the Beatles.

That's not exactly true.

NIKE, along with our ad agency and EMI-Capitol Records, is being sued by Apple Records. Apple says we used the Beatles' recording of "Revolution" without permission.

The fact is, we negotiated and paid for all the legal rights to use "Revolution" in our ads. And we did so with the active support and encouragement of Yoko Ono Lennon. We also believe we've shown a good deal of sensitivity and respect in our use of "Revolution," and in how we've conducted the entire campaign.

So why are we being sued? We believe it's because we make good press. "Beatles Sue NIKE" is a much stronger headline than "Apple Sues EMI-Capitol for the Third Time." Frankly, we feel we're a publicity pawn in a long-standing legal battle between two record companies.

But the last thing we want to do is upset the Beatles over the use of their music. That's why we've asked them to discuss the issue with us face-to-face. No lawyers, critics, or self-appointed spokespersons.

Because the issue goes beyond legalisms. This ad campaign is about the fitness revolution in America, and the move toward a healthier way of life.

We think that's a message to be proud of.

NIKE®

Q & A #30

29.   Daryl Hall told "Rolling Stone" that he thinks Hall and Oates are "the Eighties Beatles."
     (Quoted from an interview published in the 17 January 1985 issue.)

30.   Apple sued Nike Inc., Nike's ad agency, Wieden and Kennedy, and EMI/Capitol for $15 million for allegedly using the Beatles' version of "Revolution" in their "Revolution In Motion" television commercials without permission.
     (Nike's ad marks the first time a Beatles recording has been used in a commercial. The "Revolution" spot (for their "Air" brand sport shoe) was first aired 26 March 1987, during "The Cosby Show.")

CHAPTER 26

I KNOW YOU, YOU KNOW ME

If, in the words of Shakespeare, "all the world's a stage," then a play called "The Beatles" has one of the largest supporting casts ever assembled. (Imagine all the extras the producers needed just for some of those concert sequences!)

"The Beatles" is still an ongoing play, however, enjoying a very successful run (even though the main characters have gone their separate ways). Their music and philosophies are still touching and influencing millions of actors, actresses, and playwrights - including me!

Over forty of the more prominent personae are presented here in this (sorry, Mick) "pleased to meet you, hope you guess my name" type of quizzical.

1.   Before I was John's Aunt Mimi, this was my maiden name.

2.   I was the part-time salesman who sold John his first Hessy's guitar back in 1957.

3.   The three of us were the first steady girlfriends that Paul, John, and George ever had.

4.   I was a waiter at Hamburg's Star Club. You can hear me singing "Be-Bop-A-Lula" and "Hallelujah, I Love Her So" on the 1977 Lingasong album **The Beatles Live! At The Star Club In Hamburg, Germany; 1962**.

5.   Together with Ringo Starr, we formed the Eddie Clayton Skiffle Group, Richard's first band.

6.   For a brief time in 1968, I was Led Zeppelin's press officer, though Beatle fans are more likely to remember me as the publisher of a certain Merseyside music paper. Who am I?

7.   I was the Liverpool concert promoter responsible for the Operation Big Beat shows at New Brighton's Tower Ballroom. In the course of an evening's entertainment, the bill might've included such acts as Gerry and the Pacemakers, Rory Storm and the Hurricanes, the Big Three, the Four Jays, and of course, the Beatles.

8. I wrote "How Do You Do It?"; the Beatles rejected my song as their follow-up single to "Love Me Do," but later it became a hit for Gerry and the Pacemakers. Who am I?

9. I was the Beatles' music publisher, Dick James. What was my given name?

10. At just four years of age in 1963, I was the youngest member of the Beatles Fan Club. My real last name is Jamieson; what was my famous nickname?

11. I'm the character John played in a skit featured in the Beatles' 1963 Christmas show. Who am I?

12. I was the heroine played by George in the Beatles' 1963 Christmas show skit. Who am I?

13. The three of us narrated **The Beatles' Story** documentary album.

14. In 1964, I was a sergeant on Miami's police force. I was assigned to be the Beatles' personal bodyguard during their stay in our city, which began 13 February 1964.

15. I was Brian Epstein's personal lawyer.

16. Along with my partner Gordon Waller, I enjoyed several hit records in the sixties, including four penned by Paul McCartney. I was named "Producer Of The Year" in 1977 by "Rolling Stone" magazine. Who am I?

17. When Ringo Starr married Maureen Cox, 11 February 1965, I was the photographer who took their wedding pictures. Who am I?

18. My film roles include the 1953 sci-fi classic "War of the Worlds" and 1954's "Suddenly," with Frank Sinatra. I am best known to Beatle people for doing the voices of two of the Fabs in the Saturday morning cartoon that ran on ABC-TV from 1965 to 1969. Who am I?

19. In George Martin's absence, I scored the harp and strings for "She's Leaving Home."

20. We are the four gurus selected by George for inclusion on the

cover of the **Sgt. Pepper** LP. Can you name us?

21.   My choices for the cover of **Sgt. Pepper** included Bobby Breen, Tony Curtis, Dion DiMucci, W.C. Fields, Shirley Temple, and Johnny Weissmuller. Who am I?

22.   I was the assistant director for the Beatles' "Magical Mystery Tour" TV special.

23.   We were the tailors hired to manufacture The Fool's clothing for the ill-fated Apple Boutique.

24.   I sang "Nowhere Man" on "The Beatles' 1968 Christmas Record." The world knows me as Tiny Tim. What is my given name?

25.   We're two members of the California chapter of the Hells Angels motorcycle club. When George visited the Haight-Ashbury district of San Francisco, 7 August 1967, he invited us to come visit Apple HQ in London, which we and our entourage did in December of 1968. Who are we?

26.   The first time I photographed John and Yoko was in 1968 while Jonathon Cott interviewed them for "Rolling Stone." In 1980, the scenes I directed of John and Yoko making love were used in Yoko's promotional video, "Walking On Thin Ice." Who am I?

27.   In the early sixties, I was a singer and band manager for a group called the Presidents. As a noted British recording engineer/producer, my credits include albums by the Stones, the Who, Led Zeppelin, and the Beatles. Who am I?

28.   In 1971, I released the soundtrack to the movie "El Topo" on the Apple label. Who am I?

29.   My trusty bulldozer and I demolished the original Cavern warehouse in June of 1973. Who am I?

30.   I am the father of Jane Asher's two children, Kate and Alexander. I am perhaps better known as the artist who illustrated Pink Floyd's album **The Wall**. What's my name?

31.   My name is May Pang. When John and I were seeing each other,

he'd sometimes call me by my Chinese name, especially when we were alone. What is my Chinese name?

32.   I'm the singer that John Lennon, Jim Keltner, Jesse Ed Davis and friends came to see at L.A.'s Troubadour the night of the infamous "Kotex" incident.

33.   I did the neon lettering for the cover of John's **Rock 'N' Roll** album.

34.   Along with John and David Bowie, I helped write David's first number one U.S. single.

35.   In 1979, I was the Secretary General of the United Nations. At that time I tried to organize a Beatles reunion concert to benefit the Boat People fleeing Vietnam. Who am I?

36.   I'm the New York immigration attorney who John and Yoko turned to when the Nixon administration tried to have John deported, beginning in 1972.

37.   In song, George called me "the devil's best friend."

38.   I am the Dutch musician whose Lennon vocal impersonation appears on the "Stars On 45" Beatles medley.

39.   My mother's name is Erika. She has told me that my father is Paul McCartney. Who am I?

40.   We helped Julian Lennon write "Valotte" for his debut album.

**I KNOW YOU, YOU KNOW ME
(ANSWERS)**

---

1.   Aunt Mimi's maiden name was Mary Elizabeth Stanley.

2.   John's first guitar from Frank Hessy's Music Store, a steel-stringed Spanish model, was sold to him by Jim Getty.

3.   Dot Rohne was Paul's first steady girlfriend; John and George's

FOLLOW THE MERSEYBEAT ROAD

Written and compiled by **SAM LEACH**

first steadies were, respectively, Barbara Baker and Ruth Morrison.

4. The Star Club's singing waiter was Horst Fascher.

5. The three other founding members of the Eddie Clayton Skiffle Group were Johnny Dougherty, Eddie Miles, and Roy Trafford.

6. Bill Harry was the publisher of "Mersey Beat" newspaper, an early chronicler of Beatle goings-on in Liverpool and Hamburg.

7. Sam Leach organized, among other events, the Operation Big Beat shows.
(Sam's early Beatle memories were published by Eden Publications in 1983 in the oversized booklet *Follow The Merseybeat Road*.)

8. The composer of "How Do You Do It?" was Mitch Murray.

9. Richard Leon (Dick) James' given name was Isaac Vapnick.

10. Young Jamieson's nickname was "Russell Beatle."
(Russell's picture appears in "The Beatles Book" #2.)

11. John's character in the Beatles' 1963 Christmas show skit was Sir John Jasper.

12. Erymntrude was the name of the heroine played by George in the Beatles' 1963 Christmas show skit.

13. **The Beatles' Story** documentary double LP was narrated by John Babcock, Al Wiman, and Roger Christian.

14. The Beatles' personal bodyguard during their 1964 stay in Miami was Sgt. Buddy Dresner.
(Now retired from the Miami police force, Dresner owns a construction business.)

15. David Jacobs was Brian Epstein's personal lawyer.

16. "Rolling Stone" named Peter Asher its "Producer Of The Year" in 1977, notably for his work with Linda Rondstadt, and with another artist he signed while the head of Apple's A&R department, James Taylor.

17. The photographer at Ringo and Maureen's wedding was Robert Freeman.

18. Character actor Paul Frees did the voices of John and George in "The Beatles" cartoon series.

19. Mike Leander scored the harp and strings on "She's Leaving Home," the only time a Beatles music score was done by anyone other than George Martin.

20. George's four gurus included Sri Yukteswar Giri, next to Aleister Crowley; Sri Mahavatara Babaji, between William S. Burroughs and Stan Laurel; Sri Paramahansa Yogananda, next to H.G. Wells; and Sri Lahiri Mahasaya, between Albert Stubbins and Lewis Carroll.

21. These people were included on the **Sgt. Pepper** album at the behest of the cover's co-designer, Peter Blake.
   (Shirley Temple is included three times on **Pepper**, more than anyone else; she is first seen hidden between the wax figures of John and Ringo, and then appears on both sides of Diana Dors, once as a cutout and next as the doll wearing the "WMPS Good Guys Welcome The Rolling Stones" pullover.)

22. Andrew Burkin was the assistant director on the "Magical Mystery Tour" TV special.

23. Gublick and Schlickstein were the two tailors hired to manufacture The Fools' clothing creations for Apple.

24. Tiny Tim's real name is Herbert Khuarty.

25. An event lovingly recalled in Richard DiLello's book *The Longest Cocktail Party*, it was Billy Tumbleweed, Frisco Pete, and their entourage who visited Apple in December of 1968.

26. Ethan Russell
   (In 1985, Houghton Mifflin published a collection of Ethan's photographs coupled with his reminiscences. Titled *Dear Mr. Fantasy: A Diary Of A Decade*. Russell dedicated his book to the memory of John Lennon.)

She was the woman who shared John's love.

LOVING JOHN

The Untold Story
by May Pang and Henry Edwards

"The hottest thing around. A weird love triangle for our times..."
—Liz Smith

Now in Quality Paperback WARNER BOOKS

Q & A #31

27.   Former Presidents member Glyn Johns engineered the **Get Back** recordings produced by George Martin.

(In early March of 1969, Johns was given all the tapes recorded during the "Get Back" sessions and asked to make them into an album. Johns compiled two different versions of **Get Back**; the first was completed on 28 May 1969, the revised lineup compiled on 5 January 1970. Neither version was ever officially released. Phil Spector was brought in beginning on 23 March 1970 to remix the tapes, completing on 2 April 1970 the lineup that was finally released in May of 1970 as **Let It Be**.)

28.   The **El Topo** soundtrack was released by Alexandro Jodorowsky.

29.   Terry Balmer demolished the warehouse that was the site of the original Cavern.

30.   Cartoonist Gerald Scarfe is the father of Jane Asher's children.

31.   May Pang's Chinese name, Fung Yee, means "phoenix bird" in translation.

32.   John was at the Troubadour to hear Ann ("I Can't Stand The Rain") Peebles.

33.   John Uomoto created the neon lettering on **Rock 'N' Roll**.

34.   Carlos Alomar, along with David Bowie and John Lennon, wrote what would become David's first U.S. number one single, "Fame."

(Originally titled "Shame," "Fame" was based on a guitar riff from the Shirley & Company song "Shame, Shame, Shame." It only took Bowie half an hour to write the song's lyrics after being inspired by John and Carlos' guitar riffs. Alomar also worked with Paul on his 1986 LP, **Press To Play**.)

35.   Currently the President of Austria (as of 1990), Kurt Waldheim tried unsuccessfully to reunite the Beatles in a concert to benefit the Vietnamese Boat People.

36.   The Lennons enlisted the legal counsel of attorney Leon Wildes.

(The U.S. Court of Appeals overturned the Immigration and Naturalization Services' deportation order on 7 October 1975.)

37. Mark David Chapman

38. Bas Muys is the Lennon impersonator on the "Stars On 45" Beatles medley.
(The vocal impersonations of Paul and George were supplied by Okkie Huysdens and Hans Vermeulen, respectively.)

39. Bettina Huebers believes her father is Paul McCartney.

40. **Valotte's** title cut was co-written by Julian, Justin Clayton, and Carlton Morales.

CHAPTER 27

WITHIN THE LIMITS
OF BRITISH DECENCY

One of Julian Lennon's earliest memories of his father's Beatle days was riding on the Magical Mystery Tour coach. "Paul is dead" theorists allege that the "24-page full color picture book," now deleted from current Capitol pressings of the **Magical Mystery Tour** album, was crammed full of death clues. One of the more popular clues appears on page 23. (Get your album out now, if you haven't already done so - I'll wait.)

While John, George, and Ringo wear red roses in their lapels, Paul's rose is colored a deathly black. A careful examination of the three red roses reveals that only John's rose is completely red, while George and Ringo's roses both have patches of black on them.

Page 11 of the "Tour" booklet makes reference to a "marvelous lunch" sequence during which Happy Nat eats too much, falls asleep, and subsequently "has a HAPPY DREAM...all about his adventures with a bunch of pretty girls beside the seaside!" (John had directed such a scene at a swimming pool at the Atlantic Hotel in Newquay. The Atlantic Hotel, incidently, is where the cast picture on page 24 of the "MMT" booklet was taken.) Don't know about you, but I'd have fancied seeing all that; it was cut from the final version of this TV special, first shown in Britain on Boxing Day 1967.

At this point, let's give the red balloon to George and take the "Magical Mystery Quiz."

Are you ready?

SPLENDID! The quiz begins with Question 1...or 2...

1.   What was the inspiration for Paul's idea to do a "Magical Mystery Tour"?

2.   What role did the Beatles originally want Victor Spinetti to play in the special?

3.   During filming of "MMT," a narrow bridge the bus encountered forced the cast to turn back and film elsewhere. Where was the coach headed at the time?

4.   What was Alf Mandera's role in the "Magical Mystery Tour"?

5. What role did Nat Jackley play?

6. Which song from the TV special had its accompanying film segment shot in France?

7. Which scene in "MMT" did John write?

8. On what day of the week does the Magical Mystery Tour take place?

9. According to John's voice-over narration, what is Richard Starkey's middle initial?

10. As the tour gets under way, Ringo and his Aunt Jessie begin to argue. At one point he laments that his Aunt hasn't been the same since a certain someone died. Who was Ringo referring to?

11. Following Aunt Jessie's dream, the audience sees two hunters firing their weapons at an offscreen target. As the magical mystery tourists, the Beatles among them, enter the shot, what song are they singing?

12. George can be seen "playing" a chalk-drawn keyboard during his "Blue Jay Way" sequence. What is written in chalk next to the keyboard?

13. Where was the strip club sequence filmed?

14. What name does John's magician character go by? What name does Mal Evans' magician character go by?

15. Fueled by a bit of ale, a sing-a-long commences on the bus. What song does Ringo start things off with?

16. What medley of songs comprises the sing-a-long?

17. What is the title of the last song heard on the "Magical Mystery Tour" film soundtrack?

18. Originally, plans had been announced for the inclusion in "MMT" of a film segment featuring a performance by Traffic. What song were they planning to do?

192

19. A costume party was held 21 December 1967 to launch the film. What did the Beatles and their wives/girlfriends come dressed as?

20. Who is Jerry Perencio and what was his connection to the "Magical Mystery Tour" film?

WITHIN THE LIMITS
OF BRITISH DECENCY
(ANSWERS)

1. Ken Kesey's Merry Pranksters inspired Paul's "Magical Mystery Tour."
(Tom Wolfe's 1968 book, *The Electric Kool-Aid Acid Test,* documents the Pranksters' own magical mystery tours.)

2. The Beatles originally wanted Victor Spinetti to play the courier.
(The role of Jolly Jimmy Johnson was played by Derek Royle.)

3. A narrow bridge across the River Dart forced the Beatles to cancel plans to film segments of "Magical Mystery Tour" at Dartmoor's Widdicombe Fair.

4. Alf played the driver of the tour bus.

5. Jackley played "Happy Nat The Rubber Man."
(Happy Nat also played an "Eggman" in the "I Am The Walrus" sequence.)

6. Paul's "Fool On The Hill" sequence, the last to be filmed for "MMT," was shot in Nice, France, 6-8 November 1968.

7. John's scene detailed Aunt Jessie's nightmare.
(A waiter - played by John - is seen shoveling spaghetti onto Aunt Jessie's plate as Buster Bloodvessel looks on. Originally, John had planned to co-write this scene with Monty Pythoner Michael Palin.)

8. The Magical Mystery Tour took place on a Sunday.

9. Richard's middle initial is "B."
(While narrator John never elaborated on what the letter B stood for, perhaps it stands for "Beatle.")

10. Aunt Jessie (played by Jessie Robins) hadn't been the same since her husband, Ringo's Uncle Jack, died.

11. Before the cast entered the pup tent to view the "Blue Jay Way" film, there was a rousing chorus of "There's No Business Like Show Business."

12. "Two Wives And Kid To Support"

13. The striptease sequence was filmed at Paul Raymond's Revue bar, Soho. As Janice disrobed, the Bonzos performed "Death Cab For Cutie."
(Featuring Viv Stanshall on vocals, "Death Cab For Cutie" was first released on the Bonzo's 1967 Liberty album, **Gorilla**.)

14. John's magician character, who took half an hour to find the sugar, is named Reggie. During the film's second segment with the magicians, John refers to Mal the magician as "Bonzo."

15. Ringo sings a slightly drunken rendition of "I've Got A Lovely Bunch Of Coconuts."

16. The sing-a-long medley, to Shirley Evans' accordion accompaniment, includes "Toot, Toot, Tootsie! (Goo' bye)," "Happy Wanderer," "When Irish Eyes Are Smiling," and "Never On Sunday."

17. A portion of "Hello Goodbye" is the last song on the film's soundtrack, played over the special's closing credits.

18. At one point it had been announced that Traffic were to film a segment performing their latest single, "Here We Go Round The Mulberry Bush."

19. At the "Magical Mystery Tour" costume party, John was dressed as a Teddy Boy, while Cynthia, dressed in Quality Street crinolines, came as an Edwardian lass. Paul and Jane arrived as the Cockney Pearly King and Queen. Pattie, dressed as an Eastern belly dancer, was escorted by George, who was dressed as a swordsman in the Errol

Flynn mold. Ringo came as a Regency Buck, while Maureen was decked out as an Indian princess.

(Other notable costumes that night included those worn by Freddie Lennon, who came as a garbageman; Lulu, who arrived as Shirley Temple; Derek Taylor as Adolf Hitler; Mal Evans as a Quaker; Peter Brown as King Louis XIV of France; and Judy and George Martin, who came dressed as the Queen and Prince Philip.)

20. In 1968, Jerry Perencio was an agent out of Los Angeles commissioned by the Beatles to lease "Magical Mystery Tour" to a U.S. television network.

CHAPTER 28

HARRISONGS AND STARTLING MUSIC

With each 20th anniversary observation making the songs of the Beatles the music of "the good old days" (remember the hoopla surrounding **Sgt. Pepper's** twentieth?), George and Ringo seem to be the members most over-looked by the general public. In 1983, Ringo was unable to get an American label to distribute his **Old Wave** album, but when his eldest son, Zak, presented him with a granddaughter in 1985, the press gladly ate up the news (even the 1986 Tom Hanks/Jackie Gleason film, "Nothing In Common," went out of its way to mention that Ringo was a grandfather).

George stayed out of the limelight (and the recording studio) for most of the eighties, influenced perhaps by the poor critical reception each of his solo projects received, preferring instead to man the helm of Hand-Made Films. His only solid press in 1986 was a square off with London's Fleet Street in defense of Madonna and Sean Penn, the press-scarred stars of the HandMade Film "Shanghai Surprise."

As the eighties drew to a close, however, fortune smiled again on Messrs. Harrison and Starr. George released **Cloud Nine** in 1987 to glowing reviews and impressive sales; he quickly followed that up with membership in the Traveling Wilburys. Their first album, **Volume One**, went double platinum and took the Grammy for 1989's best rock performance by a duo or group. As the nineties open, Beatle fans anxiously await the second volume, though - sadly - without the input of Roy Orbison.

Ringo, meanwhile, toured for the first half of 1989, re-energized after seeking help for his long-standing problem with alcohol. Fronting an impressive line-up of "All-Stars," Richie toured North America and Japan to enthusiastic houses. Prior to his decision to tour, Ringo hadn't been doing too badly garnering new fans from the younger set through his involvement with the PBS series "Shining Time Station."

The man who can make a guitar sing and his mate with the unshak-able backbeat are back in the nineties to claim their rightful places as respected senior statesmen of rock's legacy.

In this quiz, we'll take another look at the songs of George and Ringo.

1. What song did George try to sing when he visited the Haight-Ashbury district of San Francisco, 7 August 1967?

2. What is the name of the "Harrisong" co-copyrighted by Dratleaf Limited?

Tour program.

3.   On the night of 12 December 1969, after appearing in concert with Delaney & Bonnie & Friends at the Falkoner Theatre in Copenhagen, Denmark, what song did George begin composing after slipping away from a post-concert press conference?

4.   What exactly is Eric Idle screaming during the middle eight break on "This Song"?

5.   In a rare "Rolling Stone" interview George gave to Mick Brown in 1979, Harrison said he liked this song, from his **George Harrison** album, "...because it's so catchy; in fact, I was a bit embarrassed about it at first, but it turned out good and people seem to like it." Which song was George talking about?

6.   Name the four songs George recorded for **Somewhere In England** that Warner Bros. asked him to replace.

7.   What is the title of the Animals song that Eric Burdon dedicated to George?

8.   Which song did George say he wrote after being inspired by the Edwin Hawkins Singers' version of "Oh Happy Day"?

9.   On which of George's songs is Sir Frank Crisp credited as "Spirit"?

10.   What is the title of the song George released in which we hear him laughing intermittently?

11.   An inscription on the wall of George's Friar Park estate was the basis for what song?

12.   George has been the most prolific writer of sequels to songs he recorded while with the Beatles. Which two Beatles songs has Harrison treated to sequels, and what are the titles of those two sequels?

13.   What are the title(s) of the song(s) George has released featuring reprises later on in their respective albums?

14.   In 1987, Genesis Publications released *Songs By George Harrison*, a 2500-copy limited edition volume featuring the lyrics of over fifty of George's songs. Illustrated by artist Keith West, and signed by Harrison and West, *Songs* also included either a 7-inch EP or a 5-inch

Songs
by
George Harrison

GENESIS

Q & A #14

Genesis Publications brochure.

compact disc of Harrison material unique to this book's release. What songs are included on this EP/CD?

15. Name the artist and the title of the song he sang that Ringo cites as his first musical influence, garnered, at the age of 8, from a visit to the cinema.

16. Beginning 14 October 1968, Ringo and his family took a two-week holiday in Sardinia. While aboard a boat lent to him by a friend, an unusual luncheon fare and a conversation he had with the boat's captain inspired him to write a song later recorded by the Beatles. Can you name the song?

In the following three questions, list all the songs John, Paul, and George have given Ringo to record over the years, songs that Ringo subsequently released on his various solo albums.

17. John:

18. Paul:

19. George:

20. Who is the "Raymond" Ringo is singing about in "Sunshine Life For Me (Sail Away Raymond)"?

21. On the fade of "You're Sixteen," Ringo sings a line from what other song?

22. Which song from Polydor Super's **Scouse The Mouse** soundtrack appears in a modified version on one of Ringo's solo LP's?

23. During the Harrison-produced sessions for **Stop And Smell The Roses**, Ringo recorded an early version of this Harrison song, one which George later recorded himself after rewriting the lyrics. What is the name of this song?

24. What are the title(s) of the song(s) Ringo has released that feature reprises later on in their respective albums?

25. List all the instrumentals Ringo has released.

1.   As retold in Brown/Gaines' book *The Love You Make*, when George visited the Haight-Ashbury in 1967, he tried (unsuccessfully) to sing "Baby You're A Rich Man."

2.   Written by George and Eric (Dratleaf) Clapton, Cream featured "Badge" on their last album, **Goodbye** (RSO).

3.   That night at the Falkoner Theatre, George went to an upstairs room with his guitar and began composing "My Sweet Lord."

4.   After Harrison sings the line "This song could be 'You,' could be...," Eric Idle, in his best Monty Python elderly Scouse female voices, argues, "Could be 'Sugar Pie Honey Bunch'"; "No! Sounds more like 'Rescue Me'!"

5.   George was talking to Mick Brown about the first new tune he wrote for the **George Harrison** album, "Blow Away."

6.   The four songs rejected by Warner Bros. for inclusion on **Somewhere In England** were "Lay His Head," "Sat Singing," "Tears Of The World," and "Flying Hour."
   (These songs were replaced by "Blood From A Clone," "Teardrops," "That Which I Have Lost," and "All Those Years Ago.")

7.   Eric Burdon dedicated "Winds Of Change" to George.

8.   "Oh Happy Day" inspired George to write "My Sweet Lord."

9.   Sir Frank Crisp is credited as "Spirit" on the **Dark Horse** cut "Ding Dong, Ding Dong."

10.   George laughs all the way through "Miss O'Dell," the B-side of his single "(Give Me Love) Give Me Peace On Earth."

11.   A Sir Frank inscription above the entrance hall at Friar Park is the basis for the **Extra Texture** album cut "The Answer's At The

End."

("Scan not a friend with a microscopic glass, for you know his faults, now let his foibles pass. Life is one long enigma true my friend; read on, read on, the answer's at the end.")

12. George's sequel to "Here Comes The Sun" is "Here Comes The Moon," from the **George Harrison** album. "This Guitar (Can't Keep From Crying)," from the **Extra Texture** album, was the sequel to "While My Guitar Gently Weeps."

13. George's only song reprise is "A Bit More Of You," the reprise of "You," both off **Extra Texture**.

14. Contained in a concealed drawer underneath *Songs By George Harrison*, one will find either an EP or CD featuring three of the four songs dropped by Warner Bros. from the first submitted version of **Somewhere In England** - "Sat Singing," Lay His Head," and "Flying Hour" - plus a live version of "For You Blue" recorded at the Capitol Centre in Washington, D.C., 13 December 1974.

15. Ringo's first musical influence was Gene Autry's "South Of The Border."

16. A proffered lunch of octopus and a conversation Ringo had with his boat's captain about how octopuses build their seabed gardens were the catalysts behind the song "Octopus's Garden."

17. On the three occasions John gave Ringo songs to record, Lennon also played piano on the sessions. The songs include "I'm The Greatest," for the **Ringo** album; "(It's All Da-Da-Down To) Goodnight Vienna" (on which John also sings backing vocals), for the album of the same name; and "Cookin' (In The Kitchen Of Love)," included on **Ringo's Rotogravure**.

(One of four songs Lennon is known to have contributed to Starr's 1981 album, **Stop And Smell The Roses,** was the ironically titled "Life Begins At Forty," which Ringo opted not to include.)

18. Co-written with Linda and featuring the McCartneys on backing vocals, Paul's first song contribution to a Starr LP was "Six O'Clock," included on the **Ringo** album. For **Ringo's Rotogravure**, Paul contributed "Pure Gold," once again featuring the backing vocals of Paul and Linda. For **Stop And Smell The Roses,** Paul gave Ringo two songs,

"Private Property" and "Attention," which he also produced.

19. George has given Ringo the most help in the song contribution department. The **Ringo** album includes three Harrison compositions, "Sunshine Life For Me (Sail Away Raymond)," "Photograph" (co-written with R. Starr), and "You and Me (Babe)" (co-written with faithful roadie Mal Evans). In 1976, George gave Ringo "I'll Still Love You" for his **Rotogravure** LP. In 1981, George wrote and produced "Wrack My Brain," the most successful single released from **Stop And Smell The Roses.**

20. The "Raymond" Ringo was referring to was the lawyer appointed by Allen Klein to represent John, George, Ringo, and Apple when Paul was suing them to break up the Beatles.

21. During the sessions for "You're Sixteen," producer Richard Perry realized that this Johnny Burnette classic had the same melody as the Clarence 'Frogman' Henry tune "(I Don't Know Why I Love You) But I Do." Ringo can be heard singing this title lyric behind his fade of "All mine, all mine, all mine."

22. Ruan O'Luchlainn's song, "A Mouse Like Me," from the **Scouse The Mouse** soundtrack, later appeared as "A Man Like Me" on Ringo's 1978 LP, **Bad Boy.**

23. Ringo was the first to record "All Those Years Ago," before it became George's tribute to John. Starr decided not to include the song on his forthcoming album as he didn't feel comfortable with the original lyrics. Harrison later wrote new lyrics for the tune, and included the song on his **Somewhere In England** LP.

24. Ringo's only reprise was for the title track to his 1974 LP, **Goodnight Vienna**; it is featured as the closing cut on side two.

25. Ringo waited until his 1983 LP, **Old Wave**, to release his first instrumental tracks - "Everybody's In A Hurry But Me," and "Going Down."

CHAPTER 29

IMAGINE NO POSSESSIONS

Just for a moment, imagine you have lost all your Beatles albums. After you've recovered from the initial shock, test your memory, wrack your brain perhaps, on the following questions pertaining to album sleeve details. (Remember: No peeking!)

1. Who is the "H" in the Beatles' semaphore formation of "HELP!"?

2. How many of the Beatles are wearing their MBE medals on the **Sgt. Pepper** album sleeve?

3. Who is holding a French horn on the front cover of **Sgt. Pepper**?

4. Who is holding a trumpet on the front cover of **Sgt. Pepper**?

5. Which Beatle portrays what animal on the **Magical Mystery Tour** cover?

6. What is the number on the chest of the Butterfly Stomper on the front of the **Yellow Submarine** album sleeve?

7. Who is using a microphone on the cover of **Let It Be**?

8. On the cover of John's **Plastic Ono Band** album, is John resting his head in Yoko's lap, or is Yoko resting her head in John's lap?

9. On the cover of John and Yoko's **Some Time In New York City** album, who is Richard Nixon dancing in the nude with?

10. On what other Wings album cover can one see the statuette featured on the cover of the **Wings Greatest Hits** album?

11. What kind of pipe is Paul holding in his left hand on the **Pipes Of Peace** album cover?

12. What kind of silver dollar is George holding in his hand on the back of the **Living In The Material World** album sleeve?

13. What is printed on the sunglasses George is wearing on the

cover of his album, **33 & 1/3**?

14. In the back cover photo for Ringo's 1970 album **Beaucoups Of Blues**, what noted drummer is sitting to Starr's left?

15. What is Ringo holding in his hands on the cover of his 1977 album **Ringo The 4th**?

IMAGINE NO POSSESSIONS (ANSWERS)

---

1. George is the Beatles' semaphore "H." E = John, L = Paul, P = Ringo
    (Mark Lewisohn notes in his excellent sessionography *The Beatles: Recording Sessions*, that the letters of the Beatles' semaphore formation actually spell "NUJV," or "NVUJ" if you're examining the American copy of the album.)

2. As verified by outtake photos printed in the booklet included in Parlophone's limited edition release of the **Sgt. Pepper** CD, only two of the Beatles - George and Paul - wore their MBEs on their jackets during the album photo session.

3. John is holding the French horn.

4. Ringo is holding the trumpet.

5. On the front cover of **Magical Mystery Tour**, John is the walrus (this despite Paul's assertion on **The McCartney Interview** record that he was the walrus), Paul is the hippopotamus, George is a rabbit, and Ringo is dressed as a parrot.

6. Butterfly Stomper #23 is on the front cover of **Yellow Submarine**.
    (Butterfly Stompers, from their description in the U.S. liner notes for the **Yellow Submarine** sleeve, "...perform the tasks that any evil butterfly stomper worth their soul would perform with supreme acuity." *The Yellow Submarine Gift Book* identifies Butterfly Stomper #23 by the name of Robin.)

Q & A #3

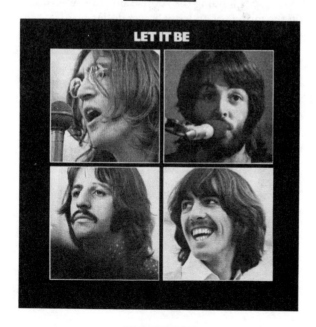

Q & A #7

7. In photographs taken by Ethan Russell for the **Let It Be** album sleeve, John and Paul are pictured using microphones.

8. On the cover of John's **Plastic Ono Band** album, John is resting his head in Yoko's lap.
(On the cover of Yoko's **Plastic Ono Band** album, Yoko is resting her head in John's lap.)

9. Through the magic of airbrushing, Richard Nixon dances nude with Chairman Mao Tse-Tung (also sans clothing).
(This doctored photo is included to illustrate Yoko's song "We're All Water," specifically the lines, "There may not be much difference/ Between Chairman Mao and Richard Nixon/If we strip them naked.")

10. The "Wings" statuette can also be seen resting on the fireplace mantel on the cover of **Back To The Egg**.
(This statuette is also included in a photograph on one side of the giveaway poster included in the **Wings Greatest Hits** album.)

11. Paul is holding a pan pipe in his left hand.

12. George is holding the reverse side (an American bald eagle landing on the moon) of an Eisenhower dollar.

13. "1776-1976" is printed on the front and sides of George's American Bicentennial souvenir sunglasses.

14. Of note for having once been the drummer for Elvis Presley, D. J. Fontana can be seen sitting to Ringo's left.

15. Ringo is holding a sword in his hands.

CHAPTER 30

THE **W**ALRUS AND

HIS **O**CEAN **C**HILD

He wrote his lyrics while sagging off from school with one of his best mates. He wrote them in the back of tour buses, while trapped in hotel rooms, while sealed inside theaters. He wrote his words alone in his private home recording studio, while making movies, and after meditating.

He drew his inspiration from myriad sources: reading newspapers and magazines, watching television commercials, commenting on good friends, hated enemies, secret lovers, and even the drawings of his young son. He wrote of his own private, restless thoughts, of the events and desires in his life, and of his hopes for the world to embrace peace and love. He wrote about Yoko. Before he died, he wrote about Sean and the joys of family life.

He disliked musical craftsmanship, preferring instead the inspiration of his muse. His songs were tender, angry, sad, thought-provoking, and timeless - just like the man himself.

John Lennon.

1. What "sometimes takes a week or two"?

2. What must a man do to earn his day of leisure?

3. Who owns a "special cup"?

4. Who "may mourn the dead"?

5. What is "in your sweaty hand"?

6. What "is measured out in miles"?

7. What "will be a daisy chain"?

8. What was "donated to the National Trust"?

9. Who has "hair of floating sky"?

10. How can one "see how the other half lives"?

11. "I feel so suicidal, just like..." who?

Postage stamp issues
honoring John Lennon.

12. Who is always "arriving late for tea"?

13. Who is "trying to save paper"?

14. How does he accomplish this?

15. What can you syndicate?

16. John sings of John Sinclair, "They gave him ten for two." Ten what for two what?

17. Who are "putting their soul power to the karmic wheel"?

18. "Uptight's all right, but if you can't stand the heat..." what should you do?

19. What's "...in the bathroom, just below the stairs"?

20. Where did Beatle fans first hear the phrase "old brown shoe"?

21. When John wrote the lines, "...friends I still can recall/ Some are dead and some are living," for "In My Life," what two people was he thinking of?

22. In the song "Girl," when John sings that "She's the kind of girl that puts you down when friends are there...," what are the other Beatles chanting?

23. For which Beatles song did John draw lyrical inspiration from an item in the "Far and Near" column in the 17 January 1967 edition of "The Daily Mail"?

24. In which song can John be heard shouting "Cut the cable, drop the cable!"?

25. Which Beatles song includes a recording of John and Pete Shotton shouting random phrases out the windows of Lennon's Kenwood attic recording studio?

26. In this Beatles song, John declares he is "happy to be that way." What way is that?

27. Where did John get "Goo goo ga joob," the famous line from "I Am The Walrus"?

28. In this Beatles song, what two things was the Queen doing and where?

29. "She wants to be married with Yeti," sings John in what unreleased Beatles song?

30. "Everybody gets well done" was a line from this song, performed in the "Let It Be" movie, but not included on the soundtrack album. What is this song's title?

31. Which song from the "Let It Be" movie soundtrack contains these lines (not included on the soundtrack album): "Are you big enough to get it? Well if you're big enough, c'mon and get it - it's free!"

32. Which Beatles song, in a working stage, contained the line "Everybody got a facelift"?

33. Which of Lennon's songs ends on the line, "I want you to make love, not war; I know you've heard it before"?

34. Which of John's post-Beatle songs begins with someone saying "nine"?

35. "Who is that, who is that, and why are they doing those strange things?" In what song does John say this?

36. Which of John's post-Beatle songs begins with several people yelling "one!"?

37. What song does John end with the announcement, "We'll take a listen"?

38. "When you come over next time, don't sell a cow," is the spoken fade from which of John's songs?

39. In Yoko's liner notes for this LP she says, "Thank you John, for a beautiful life together." Which album was this quotation taken from?

40. In which song does John sing of "putting a crack in the egg"?

In the next five questions, test your recall of the "lyrics" to "Revolution 9."

41. "Everyone of them knew that as time went by..." what would happen?

42. Portions of the (edited) fade from what other Beatles songs can be heard on "Revolution 9"?

43. "So anyroll," relates John, "he went to see the dentist instead ...." What did the dentist give him "that wasn't any good at all"?

44. Complete this "Revolution 9" wordplay between John and George:
    John: "Industrial output...financial imbalance...the watusi...the twist."
    George: ?

45. Supply the line that completes this recitation by John from "Revolution 9": "Sitting in my broken chair."

46. "Penny Lane is one I'm missing/ Up Church Rd. to the clock tower./ In the circle of the Abbey/ I have seen some happy hours." These early lyrics were later dropped by John from which of his Beatles songs?

47. In which of John's songs is cocaine mentioned?

48. "Don't come tomorrow, don't come alone" was a line from an early version of which Beatles song?

49. List three songs John released utilizing the sound of a bell.

50. John released two songs chronicling the adventures of a king in the kitchen. Do you remember their titles?

51. What was the working title for "And Your Bird Can Sing"?

52. What are the lyrics to "Tomorrow Never Knows" based upon?

53. Though officially uncredited, who co-authored most of the lyrics to the first half of "Happiness Is A Warm Gun"?

54. How does John describe Bungalow Bill?

55. The Duke was having problems in this Lennon song. What were they?

56. "When I wrote it, I went to the other three Beatles and said, 'Hey, lads, I think I've written a new single.' But they all said, 'Ummm...arrr...well,' because it was going to be my project, and so I thought, 'Bugger you, I'll put it out myself.' " What song was John referring to?

57. While "Beautiful Boy (Darling Boy)" was written for Sean, which Beatles song did John say he wrote for Julian?

58. On the Rolling Stones' **Exile On Main Street** album, Mick Jagger sings about a "Sweet Black Angel." John has also sung about this "angel." Who is she and what is the title of the song John wrote about her?

59. In which of John's post-Beatle songs does he take his "loved one to a big field" to "watch the English sky"?

60. The Maharishi Mahesh Yogi's remark, "Time is a concept by which we measure eternity," later showed up in which of John's songs?

> THE WALRUS
> AND HIS OCEAN CHILD
> (ANSWERS)

---

1. "When I want to speak to you."
   (From "Tip Of My Tongue," recorded by Tommy Quickly.)

2. "A man must break his back."
   ("Girl")

3. Doctor Robert owns a special cup.
   (Writer-director Joel Schumacher, in Jean Stein's book, *Edie*

[Sedgwick]: *An American Biography* (Knopf, 1982), remembers Doctor Charles Roberts, John's inspiration for the song, "Dr. Robert," and his "vitamin shots" laced with methedrine:

"Dr. Roberts was the perfect father image. His office, down on Forty-eighth Street on the East Side, was very reputable looking, with attractive nurses, and he himself looked like a doctor in a movie. He was always telling me of his wonderful experiments with LSD, delivering babies, curing alcoholics... and he was going to open a health farm and spa where all this was going to go on...and naturally he was stoned all the time, too. He wasn't a viper. I just think he was so crazy, he truly thought he was going to help the world."

Dr. Roberts had a part in Robert Margouleff's "verite underground" film, "Ciao! Manhattan.")

4. "Ignorance and hate..."
("Tomorrow Never Knows")

5. A "jack-knife"
("Hey Bulldog")

6. "Some kind of happiness..."
("Hey Bulldog")

7. "The clouds..."
("Dear Prudence")

8. "A soap impression of his wife..."
("Happiness Is A Warm Gun")

9. "Julia"

10. One can see how the other half lives by "looking through the bent-backed tulips."
("Glass Onion")

11. "...Dylan's Mr. Jones."
("Yer Blues")

12. The Duchess of Kirkcaldy is always arriving late for tea.
("Cry Baby Cry")

13.   "Mean Mr. Mustard"

14.   Mr. Mustard saves paper by shaving in the dark.

15.   You can syndicate "any boat you rowed."
("Dig A Pony")

16.   John Sinclair was given *ten* years in jail for selling *two* joints to an undercover agent.
(A feature film John made of the 10 December 1971 John Sinclair Freedom Rally, held in Ann Arbor, Michigan, has yet to be released in the U.S. Titled "Ten For Two," John's immigration problems at the time kept the film off American screens.)

17.   "Millions of mind guerrillas."
("Mind Games")

18.   "...get back in the shade."
("Tight A$" from **Mind Games**)

19.   In "Nobody Told Me," a cut from **Milk And Honey**, there are "Nazis" just below the stairs.

20.   On "The Beatles' Third Christmas Record" (1965), John made the suggestion that the group sing "We'll Gather Lilacs In An Old Brown Shoe."

21.   John was thinking of Pete Shotton and Stuart Sutcliffe
(See Shotton/Schaffner's book *John Lennon: In My Life.*)

22.   The other Beatles are chanting "tit."

23.   John's line in "A Day In The Life" about "Four thousand holes in Blackburn, Lancashire," was taken from a "Far and Near" column headlined "The holes in our roads."
(The item reads as follows: "There are 4,000 holes in the road in Blackburn, Lancashire, or one twenty-sixth of a hole per person, according to a council survey. If Blackburn is typical there are two million holes in Britain's roads and 300,000 in London.")

24.   "Yellow Submarine"

25. "Revolution 9" includes some of the randomly shouted thoughts of John and Pete.

26. "Tuned to a natural E..."
("Baby You're A Rich Man")

27. "Goo goo ga joob" is a line from *Finnegan's Wake*, by James Joyce.
(Humpty Dumpty, another famous eggman, said this before falling off the wall.)

28. In "Cry Baby Cry," the Queen is playing piano in the parlour, and painting pictures in the playroom.

29. "What's The New Mary Jane"

30. "Suzy Parker"

31. These lines are from the long version of "Dig It."

32. "I've Got A Feeling"

33. "Mind Games"
("Make Love Not War" was this song's working title.)

34. "You Are Here"
(From **Mind Games**)

35. "Meat City"
(Also from **Mind Games**)

36. "What You Got"
(From **Walls And Bridges**)

37. "Bless You"
(Also from **Walls And Bridges**)

38. "Dear Yoko"
(From **Double Fantasy**)

39. This quotation is from the sheet insert Yoko included in **Heart Play - Unfinished Dialogue.**

217

40. "(Forgive Me) My Little Flower Princess"
(From **Milk And Honey**)

41. "They'd get a little bit older and a little bit slower..."

42. Snippets of John's "all right" fade, edited from "Revolution 1," can be heard on "Revolution 9."

43. The dentist "gave him a pair of teeth."

44. George: "Eldorado."

45. "My wings are broken and so is my hair."

46. These lyrics were taken from an early draft of "In My Life."

47. "I Found Out"
("Don't let them fool you with dope and cocaine." From John's **Plastic Ono Band** album.)

48. In its original form, "Come Together" included this line.
("Come Together" was originally written for Timothy Leary's campaign to be elected governor of California. According to Leary's autobiography, *Flashbacks*, "Come Together" was originally titled "Come Together Join The Party" (which was also Leary's campaign slogan). Leary writes that Lennon's taped version of this original "Come Together" played for a time on California radio stations.)

49. John's three songs utilizing the sound of a bell are "Mother," "(Just Like) Starting Over," and "Beautiful Boy (Darling Boy)."

50. "Cry Baby Cry" (from the White Album)
("The King of Marigold was in the kitchen/Cooking breakfast for the Queen.")
"Clean Up Time" (from **Double Fantasy**)
("The King is in the kitchen/Making bread and honey.")

51. "You Don't Get Me"

52. The lyrics for "Tomorrow Never Knows" are based on writings from *The Tibetan Book Of The Dead.*

53. Lines such as "lizard on a window pane," "The man in the crowd with the multi-colored mirrors on his hobnail boots," and "lying with his eyes while his hands are busy working overtime," were thought up by Derek Taylor.

54. Bungalow Bill is "...the all-American, bullet-headed, Saxon mother's son."
    (From "The Continuing Story Of Bungalow Bill," off the White Album.)

55. The Duke's problems (in "Cry Baby Cry") were with a message at the local Bird and Bee.

56. As quoted in the 21 July 1970 issue of "Rolling Stone" magazine, John was referring to the song released the previous October as the A-side of the Plastic Ono Band's second single, "Cold Turkey."

57. "Good Night" was written for Julian; John gave it to Ringo to record. The song closes side four of the White Album.

58. "Angela," from the **Some Time In New York City** album, is John's song about black radical and intellectual Angela Davis.
    (Davis was charged with conspiracy, kidnapping, and murder when, in 1970, she purchased the guns used in an unsuccessful attempt to free Black Panther George Jackson and two others from California's Soledad Prison.)

59. "Well, Well, Well"
    (From **John Lennon/Plastic Ono Band**)

60. The Maharishi's remark later showed up in John's song, "God," from his **Plastic Ono Band** album.
    ("God is a concept by which we measure our pain.")

JOHN LENNON FOR PRESIDENT

DAVID PEEL & THE SUPER APPLE BAND

Q & A #7

CHAPTER 31

WITHOUT YOU, THERE'S
NO POINT TO THIS SONG

The following ladies and gentlemen of fact and fiction have been given the nod in Beatles and solo Beatle compositions over the years. Their names are listed below. All you need (besides love) is to identify the title of the song that John, Paul, George, Ringo, or Yoko included them in. "Like a rolling stone..."

1. Lear
    (Beatle-noted novelist)

2. Sexy Sadie

3. Dennis O'Dell
    (Head of Apple Films, director of Apple Publicity.)

4. Matt Busby
    (At the time this song was written, Busby was a manager for Manchester United, an English soccer club.)

5. Elmore James
    (Blues slide guitarist)

6. Bob Dylan

7. David Peel
    (New York street-musician and Apple recording artist.)

8. 666
    (The Devil, the number of the Beast of the Apocalypse, Revelation 13:18.)

9. The One-Eyed Witch Doctor

10. Don Quijote [sic]
    (Character from Miguel de Cervantes' novel, *Don Quixote de la Mancha*.)

11. Sailor Sam

12. Jet
    (Name of one of Paul's dogs.)

13. Mrs. Washington

14. The Crimson Dynamo
    (Marvel Comics character)

15. Geronimo
    (Apache Indian chief)

16. The Head Nurse, Sister Scarla

17. The Artful Dodger
    (Character from Charles Dickens' classic, *Oliver Twist.*)

18. Molly
    (Noted "stair sweeper" - not related to Desmond Jones' wife of the same name.)

19. Ben
    (A chauffeur)

20. Richie
    (Richard Starkey, a noted drummer)

WITHOUT YOU, THERE'S NO POINT TO THIS SONG (ANSWERS)

---

1. "Paperback Writer"
   ("It's based on a novel by a man named Lear.")

2. "Sexy Sadie"
   "Devil Woman"
   ("Sexy Sadie, you look like the devil to me.")
   "Simply Shady"
   ("You may think of Sexy Sadie, let her in through your front

Ringo Starr featured on a
Sun Country Cooler refund coupon.

RINGO
REFUND
$2.00
Any flavor!

(see other side for deto

Q & A #20

door." From George's **Dark Horse** LP)

3. "You Know My Name (Look Up The Number)"
("Good evening and welcome to Slagger's, featuring Dennis O'Bell [sic]." "You Know My Name" is the B-side of the "Let It Be" single. It is also available on the **Rarities** albums issued in both the U.S. and U.K.)

4. "Dig It"
("B.B. King and Doris Day. Matt Busby.")

5. "For You Blue"
(Spoken by George: "Elmore James got nothin' on this baby." From the **Let It Be** album.)

6. "Give Peace A Chance"
("Everybody's talking about John and Yoko, Timmy Leary, Rosemary, Tommy Smothers, Bobby Dylan...")
"God"
("I don't believe in Zimmerman." From John's **Plastic Ono Band** album. Bob Dylan's given name is Robert Allen Zimmerman.)

7. "New York City"
("His name was David Peel, we found that he was real." From John and Yoko's album, **Some Time In New York City.**)

8. "Bring On The Lucie (Freda People)"
("666 is your name." From John's **Mind Games** LP.)

9. "Nobody Loves You (When You're Down And Out)"
("I've seen the One-Eyed Witch Doctor leading the blind." From John's **Walls and Bridges** LP.)

10. "You're The One"
("In a moment of freedom, we were Don Quijote and Sancho." From John and Yoko's **Milk And Honey** LP.)

11. "Helen Wheels"
("Sailor Sam he came from Birmingham, but he never will be found.")
"Band On The Run"
("And the jailer man and Sailor Sam were searching everyone....")

224

In the U.S., both songs are included on the **Band On The Run** LP. In the U.K., "Helen Wheels" is only available as the A-side of a single released 26 October 1973.)

12. "Jet" and "Picasso's Last Words (Drink To Me)"
(Both songs are from the McCartney & Wings LP, **Band On The Run.**)

13. "Mrs. Vanderbilt"
("Leave me alone, Mrs. Washington." From Paul's LP **Band On The Run.**)

14. "Magneto and Titanium Man"
("But when the Crimson Dynamo finally assured me, well, I knew." From the Wings LP, **Venus And Mars.**)

15. "Spirits Of Ancient Egypt"
("You could sell an elevator to Geronimo." This song is also from **Venus And Mars.**)

16. "Girls School"
("Well head nurse is Sister Scarla..." "Girls School" is available on a double A-sided single with "Mull Of Kintyre." The song was also issued as a bonus track on the **London Town** CD.)

17. "No Values"
("The Artful Dodger says he wants to pick a pocket or two." From Paul's album, **Give My Regards To Broad Street.**)

18. "Ballad of Sir Frankie Crisp (Let It Roll)"
("Joan and Molly sweep the stairs." From George's album, **All Things Must Pass.**)

19. "Miss O'Dell"
("The record player's broken on the floor and Ben he can't restore it." Song included as the B-side of the single "Give Me Love (Give Me Peace On Earth)," released by George in 1973.)

20. "Living In The Material World"
("Though we started out quite poor, we got 'Richie' on a tour.")

Q & A #1

CHAPTER 32

ZAPPLES, RAPPLES, SCRUFFS, AND CORPS

It was called an espousement of "western communism," a "controlled weirdness," and everybody's favorite, "the longest cocktail party." A is for Apple.

The first reference to Apple was contained within the back album sleeve liner notes for **Sgt. Pepper:** "Cover by M C [Michael Cooper] Productions and The Apple." The green Granny Smith apple of Apple was designed by Gene Mahon. George has said it was Paul who wanted the apple colored green. George would have preferred it orange, while John wanted it white, and Ringo saw it tinted blue. (An interesting note: In Japanese, "ringo" [pronounced "leen-gaw"] means "apple.")

While records released today by such artists as Robert Plant, the Talking Heads, and David Lee Roth have featured the disc notes on one side of the record label (with the other side left for a picture, logo, or design), it was originally the Beatles who wanted their "whole apple" A-side left blank, with all the song titles and other pertinent production credits relegated to the "sliced apple" B-side. (Legal restrictions in the record industry at the time made this impossible.)

Perhaps Apple Corp was doomed from the start, a way to spend money the taxman would have gotten otherwise, another theory as to why the group broke up.

But when Apple was still fresh, still ripe, young and ambitious, it was very likely just as Mary Hopkin once sang, "Those were the days..."

1. How long did it take, from Gene Mahon's initial design to Alan Aldridge's final copyright lettering, to complete the Apple record label logo?

2. At various times, the Beatles' Granny Smith apple has been colored green, red, blue, orange, and white. The first green apple Beatles album was the White Album. Name a Beatles/post-Beatle record that used one of the other four colors.

3. Who was the busker in Apple's "This Man Has Talent" poster and ad campaign? Who wrote the text for this ad?

4. What was Derek Taylor's job prior to being hired back by the Beatles as Apple's press officer and publicist?

5. This woman arrived in London in the spring of 1968 from New York City trying to sell Apple her film script on the life of a street violinist she knew; she ended up on Apple's press office staff. Who is she?

6. What was Richard DiLello's official title while under Apple's employ as house hippie?

7. What is the title of the first Apple album released in the U.S.?

8. In late 1967, Grapefruit became the first group signed to Apple Music Publishing. Though they never released anything on the Apple label, the top side of their first Apple single was announced. What was the name of this song?

9. Had this Apple group listened to John, their name might have been "Prix." What name did this group finally go with?

10. Had they gone with Paul's suggestion, this Apple band might have been called "Home." Who were they?

11. Who were the most people, comprising a group, signed to Apple Records?

12. According to Jack Oliver, then head of production at Apple, how did Apple plan to distribute Brute Force's single, "King of Fuh"?

13. What is notable about the Apple albums **White Trash** by Trash, and **Accept No Substitutes** by Delaney and Bonnie?

14. What is the name of the Manhattan department store that once considered opening an Apple Boutique within its walls?

15. Of the several Apple subsidiaries that didn't get off the ground, one of the most interesting was Apple Limousines. How did John envision an Apple limousine?

16. What happened to Apple's cosmetic division?

17. Who was the first person to get free merchandise the morning the Apple Boutique started giving everything away, 30 July 1968?

18. Where was Apple's first board meeting held? How many of the Beatles attended?

19. Who sent each of the Beatles a letter in October of 1968 telling them (in short) that "Apple is a mess"?

20. Who was appointed Apple's last press officer before the office was closed in August of 1970?

21. Who is Apple's managing director today, running what remains of the company out of his London office?

22. What was "Walkabout"?

23. Who was "Mr. Policeman"?

24. What were "The Pineapple Archives"?

25. Lyrics from which Beatles song were included on Apple's Christmas/New Year's card for 1969-70?

ZAPPLES, RAPPLES,
SCRUFFS, AND CORPS
(ANSWERS)

---

1. From start to finish, it took six months to design Apple's logo.

2. Red apple: **Let It Be** (U.S. only), and Ringo's **Blast From Your Past.** Blue apple: Ringo's single "Back Off Boogaloo" b/w "Blindman." Orange apple: George's **All Things Must Pass.** White apple: **John Lennon/Plastic Ono Band, Imagine,** and the single released from it, "Imagine" b/w "It's So Hard."

3. The one-man busker band in Apple's ad campaign was Alistair Taylor. The text for this ad was written by Paul.

   (In 1988, Alistair Taylor's Beatles reminiscences, *Yesterday: The Beatles Remembered*, were published in the United Kingdom by Sidgwick

& Jackson Ltd.)

4.   When the Beatles asked Derek Taylor to come to Apple, his previous job had been at A&M Records as publicist for such acts as the Byrds, the Beach Boys, Captain Beefheart, and Paul Revere and the Raiders. He was well known to the Beatles from yet an earlier job, that of assistant to Brian Epstein.

(Taylor was also instrumental in organizing the Monterey Pop Festival. His first day at Apple Corp Ltd. was 8 April 1968 at the company's first offices in 95 Wigmore Street, London.)

5.   Francie Schwartz was the press office staffer with the dream of selling her movie script.

(Schwartz went on to write the book, *Body Count*. A chapter from the book, "Don't Cry - I'm A Cunt," details her affair with Paul McCartney.)

6.   Richard was Apple's "Client Liaison Officer."

(DiLello is the author of the screenplay for the 1982 Sean Penn film, "Bad Boys.")

7.   The first Apple album released in the U.S. was **Two Virgins** on 29 November 1968.

(**Wonderwall Music**, Apple's first U.K. album, was delayed in the U.S., and did not reach record stores until 2 December 1968.)

8.   The top side of Grapefruit's first Apple single was to have been "Elevator."

(Paul had even directed a three-minute promotional film of the group at the Albert Memorial Statue in Hyde Park, 26 May 1968. NOTE: Grapefruit's first single, "Dear Delilah"/"The Dead Boot," was not on Apple Records.)

9.   "Prix" was John's suggestion for the group from Swansea, Wales, that eventually called themselves "Badfinger."

10.   Had Badfinger listened to Paul, they would have been called "Home."

(Originally called the Iveys, the name Badfinger was thought up by Neil Aspinall.)

11.   Boasting 39 members, the most people signed to Apple Records

as a group was the Black Dyke Mills Brass Band. In a one-shot record deal, this group recorded "Thingumybob" b/w "Yellow Submarine" for Apple in 1968.

12.   Apple's plan for the single by Brute Force (a.k.a. Steven Friedland) was to distribute it by mail order.
    (An alternative distribution plan was necessary as "King Of Fuh," the story of "Fuh-King," had been rejected by EMI for distribution.)

13.   **White Trash** and **The Original Delaney & Bonnie (Accept No Substitutes)** were both albums slated for, but never released on, the Apple label.

14.   For a time, Macy's considered opening an Apple Boutique in its Manhattan store.

15.   John envisioned Apple limos customized in psychedelic fashion like his own Phantom V Rolls Royce.
    (On 29 June 1984, John's psychedelic Rolls was auctioned off by Sotheby's in New York for $2,229,000 to Canadian businessman and Expo '86 chairman Jim Pattison, making it the highest price paid (to date) for a used car. In 1986, Pattison earned himself a hefty tax deduction by giving the Roller to the Canadian provincial government. The car was displayed in front of the British pavilion during Expo '86 [held in Vancouver, British Columbia].)

16.   Apple's Cosmetics division never got off the drawing board.

17.   The first customer to get free merchandise from the Apple Boutique was actor Michael J. Pollard (C.W. Moss in the movie "Bonnie & Clyde"), who had gone in to order some shirts and jackets when he was told by the cashier to put away his wallet.

18.   Apple's first board meeting was held at London's Hilly House on Stafford Street. None of the Beatles attended.

19.   When Apple accountant Steven Maltz resigned in protest over the financial mismanagement of his employer's company, his five-page resignation letter included a warning of impending disaster.

20.   Apple's last acting press officer was Richard DiLello.

21. As of this writing, Neil Aspinall was still Apple's managing director.

22. "Walkabout" was the title of a film the Apple Films division had planned to make, but never did.

(Other Apple films that never got past the planning stages included "The Jam," "Gorgeous Accident," and a film based on Lennon's two books for which John had planned to write a screenplay.)

23. "Mr. Policeman" was George's name for the Beatles' water cooler at Apple.

24. The Pineapple Archives were Richard DiLello's system for cataloguing the press clippings relating to the Beatles and other Apple artists.

25. Several lines from "In My Life" were included as part of the text on Apple's 1969-70 Christmas/New Year's card.

CHAPTER 33

NOT GUILTY (BY ASSOCIATION)

Just ask any non-Beatlemaniac spouse about the condition of their mate - hard-core Beatle people are incurable! We'll search everywhere for that Beatle connection. Sometimes you just can't predict where that next fix will come from.

You might be reading a new book and the author describes her main male character, Jake, as looking like Paul McCartney (as Brett Singer did in her book, *The Petting Zoo*). You switch on your local public television station and there's Leo McKern starring as barrister Horace Rumpole in "Rumpole of the Bailey." Later, you decide to go over to a friend's house to watch "Under The Cherry Moon," starring Prince.

"By God," you exclaim, "that bathtub scene reminds me an awful lot of John's wash in 'A Hard Day's Night.' And that video the Purple One made with the Revolution for 'Raspberry Beret'," you note after taking a glom at it on MTV, "weren't those extras dancing just like the Blue Meanies did at the end of 'Yellow Submarine'? How about David Lee Roth's video for 'California Girls'," you persist, "wasn't it just a bit reminiscent of 'Magical Mystery Tour'?"

Esoterica, you say? Perhaps. But it's our esoterica.

1.   What was Pattie Harrison Clapton's contribution to her former husband's '85 album **Behind The Sun** (Warner Bros.)?

2.   Danceville Records' 1980 release **The Moonlight Tapes** and Cherry Red Records' compilation album **Burning Ambitions: A History Of Punk** both share something of Beatle note on their album sleeves. What is it?

3.   Who released **The Other Side Of Abbey Road**?

4.   Released by Capitol in 1983, why is Marillion's album **Script For A Jester's Tears** of note to Beatle fans?

5.   Elton John, Al Kooper, Paul, and countless others have drawn inspiration from this American group's 1966 landmark album. The voices of Banana and Louie on this album specifically influenced "Good Morning, Good Morning." Name this group and the album they released.

6. This album first brought Harry Nilsson to the attention of the Beatles. What is its title?

7. "Old Dirt Road," the Lennon/Nilsson composition that John released in 1974 on his **Walls And Bridges** album was included by Harry in 1980 on this (U.K. only) Mercury LP. What is its title?

8. Which of Billy Joel's albums did he call his tribute to the Beatles?

9. A snippet from what Beatles song was played at the start of the 58th and final episode of "The Monkees" TV show?

10. In one scene from the Monkees' 1968 film "Head," we see Peter Tork entering a restroom. What Beatles tune is he whistling?

11. In 1982, a duo billing themselves as Andy Z & Leslie released an album featuring this song, its lyrics describing a girl who's got "Jane Asher's eyes/And the bangs fall just right." What is the title of this song and the name of the album it was included on?

12. Marty Asher's 1986 novel *Shelter* (Arbor House) is the story of Billy, a man so worried about the threat of nuclear obliteration that he turns to the lyrics of this Beatles album for what he believes will be the answers to the world's nuclear nightmare - answers he believes were left for him to decode by John Lennon. Which album does Billy pore over?

13. Beginning in May of 1987, the Southland Corporation employed this Ringo Starr song in radio and television ads for their 7-11 convenience store chains. What is the title of this song?

14. On 10 September 1966, CBS-TV attempted to cash-in on the Saturday morning success of "The Beatles" cartoon series on ABC when it debuted its own animated series about a pair of rock and roll canines named Stringer and Tubby. What was this show's title?

15. In Francis Ford Coppola's 1986 film "Peggy Sue Got Married," Peggy Sue (played by Kathleen Turner) faints at her 25-year high school reunion; upon awakening, she finds herself back in the year 1960. In one scene, Peggy gives her future husband (played by Nicholas Cage) this Beatles song, which she tells him she wrote. What is the title of this song?

1. Pattie's contribution to **Behind The Sun** was her photograph of Eric inside the album's gatefold.

(Clapton has written several songs to Pattie over the years, beginning in 1970 with "Layla," which he modeled after Persian writer Nizami's "The Story Of Layla And Majnun." Other songs include "Wonderful Tonight," from Eric's 1980 LP **Just One Night**; "Pretty Girl," from the 1983 LP **Money And Cigarettes**; and "Never Make You Cry," from **Behind The Sun.**)

2. Both these album sleeves parody the front sleeve of **Sgt. Pepper**.

(On **Burning Ambitions** one can spot the faces of Andy Warhol and John Lennon. The Beatles, dressed in their Douglas Hayward-made silk suits from *their* cover of **Sgt. Pepper**, can be seen on a small TV screen in the lower left corner of the cover.)

3. Recorded in late October/early November of 1969, jazz guitarist George Benson released **The Other Side Of Abbey Road** on A&M Records.

4. On the front sleeve artwork for **Script For A Jester's Tears**, in a violin case to the left of the jester, one can spot a piece of paper upon which are written some of the lyrics to "Yesterday."

(The back cover of Marillion's 1987 Capitol release **Clutching At Straws** features a drawing of a leather-clad John Lennon (circa 1961) in attendance - along with James Dean and Jack Kerouac, among others - during a game of pool.)

5. Paul has cited the Beach Boys' **Pet Sounds** album as a major influence on **Sgt. Pepper**.

(Banana, a beagle, and Louie, a Weimaraner, were the names of Brian Wilson's dogs heard barking at the end of "Caroline, No.")

6. **Pandemonium Shadow Show**, released 23 October 1967 on RCA, first brought Harry to the Beatles' attention.

(**Pandemonium** contains "You Can't Do That," Harry's fifteen-song Beatles medley.)

FEATURING THE HIT
"FOREVER MAN"

ERIC
CLAPTON

Behind the Sun

Q & A #1

7. Harry's version of "Old Dirt Road" appears on his Mercury album **Flash Harry.**

(**Flash Harry** also features "How Long Can Disco On," which Nilsson co-wrote with Ringo.)

8. Billy Joel has referred to his 1982 Columbia album **The Nylon Curtain** as his tribute to the Beatles.

(In a "Playboy" interview published in the magazine's May 1982 issue, Joel says of the Beatles:

"I didn't start going out and buying records until the Beatles in '64. I saw them on the 'Ed Sullivan Show' and that just knocked me out. I thought, These guys don't look like Fabian. They don't look like they were manufactured in Hollywood. They look just like me and my friends. I could see this look in John Lennon's eyes that told me something. They were irreverent, they were making fun of the whole thing. It was this smirk on his face. They were a bunch of wise guys like me and my friends! That's when it all took shape. I said, 'That's what I want to do.'"

9. First aired 25 March 1968, "Mijacogeo" or "The Frodis Caper," the final episode of "The Monkees" TV series, included the opening strains of "Good Morning, Good Morning."

10. Peter Tork enters the restroom whistling "Strawberry Fields Forever."

11. Andy Zwerling and his sister Leslie released the song "She Never Married A Beatle" on the Snow Beach album **Opportunity Rocks (And Rolls).**

12. Billy turns to the lyrics in the songs from **Sgt. Pepper** for the answers to the end of the threat of nuclear war.

13. "It Don't Come Easy"

14. Lasting only one season, the final episode of "The Beagles" aired 2 September 1967.

15. Peggy Sue gave Charlie "She Loves You."

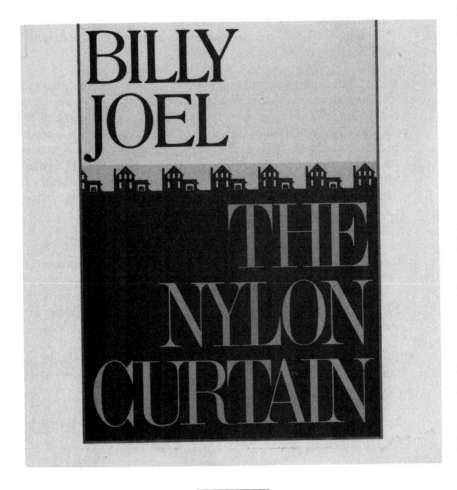

Q & A #8

CHAPTER 34

(JUST LIKE) STARTING OVER

Speaking with "Daily Express" journalist David Wigg in New York City in October of 1971, John sounded more than a bit irritated answering the oft-asked question, "Will the Beatles record together again?"

"If people need the Beatles so much," said John, "all they have to do is to buy each album...put it on tape, track by track, one of me, one of Paul, one of George, one of Ringo if they really need it that much."

Hmmm...

(The year is 1973. The following is an "entry" from the Rookman/ Podrizzle discography *Still Together? Wow!*")

NOV 2, 1973 (US) Apple SO 3145 (LP)
NOV 9, 1973 (UK) Apple PSC 7165 (LP)
Recorded: September 1973
by The Beatles
BAND ON THE RUN Prod: John Lennon, Paul McCartney and
    George Harrison (except % - produced by George Harrison
    and Ringo Starr and + - produced by John Lennon and Ringo
    Starr.)
side one
    Band On The Run - McCartney - 5:09
 % Photograph - Starkey-Harrison - 3:58
    Tight A$ - Lennon - 3:55
    Give Me Love (Give Me Peace On Earth) - Harrison - 3:32
    Bluebird - McCartney - 3:22
    Aisumasen (I'm Sorry) - Lennon - 4:41
side two
    Mind Games - Lennon - 4:10
+I'm The Greatest - Lennon - 4:41
    Jet - McCartney - 4:08
    Living In The Material World - Harrison - 5:27
    Meat City - Lennon - 2:52
    Nineteen Hundred And Eighty-Five - McCartney - 5:30

Killer lineup, eh? Sorry if I left out anybody's favorites - "You're Sixteen," "Intuition," "Helen Wheels" - not enough vinyl to squeeze 'em on, y'see. Of course songs like "Sunshine Life For Me (Sail Away Raymond)," "Let Me Roll It," and "Sue Me Sue You Blues" might never have been written if the Beatles were still together. For my next trick, I will reduce the

GIVE PEACE A CHANCE
PLASTIC ONO BAND

12" MAXI SINGLE

REMEMBER LOVE

Q & A #4

White Album from a double LP to a single! What d'yer think?

1. Which of John's solo LPs did Anthony Fawcett, John and Yoko's personal assistant through the late sixties and early seventies, call John's "Sgt. Lennon" album?

2. What instrument is Yoko credited as playing on John's **Plastic Ono Band** album?

3. What was Mal Evans' credited contribution to John's **Plastic Ono Band** album?

4. The picture cover for the German 12-inch single "Give Peace A Chance" b/w "Remember Love" reproduces a portion of which of John's album covers?

5. What were the titles on the first Lennon solo single (in either the U.S. or the U.K.) not to feature a Yoko Ono B-side?

6. Enclosed in first printing copies of the **Some Time In New York City** album were two inserts. What were they?

7. What is the connection between Edward MacLysaght's book, *Irish Families: Their Names, Arms And Origins* and John's **Walls And Bridges** album?

8. What were two working titles for John's **Rock 'N' Roll** album?

9. Which Lennon album employed the "Listen To This..." ad campaign?

10. From all the records released in the U.S. and the U.K. during John's solo years, please list the titles of those discs that included a poster.

11. What is the title of the only Yoko Ono composition whose lyrics are not copyrighted?

12. "Together" and "Hushabye" are cuts from which Beatle's solo album?

13. Which post-Beatle album did "Melody Maker" refer to as "The

People's Album"?

14. On which of Paul's records can you hear him sing "Now Hear This Song Of Mine"?

15. "On His Own" reads the headline on this full-page ad run in "Rolling Stone" to promote the release of this McCartney LP. What is this album's title?

16. "All my Best (+Three Great New Ones!) regards, Paul." This was the handwritten headline on this full-page color ad run in "Billboard." What album was Macca promoting?

17. Which of Paul's solo LPs did "Time" magazine once describe as "...McCartney's **Nashville Skyline**?

18. For what album did Paul originally plan to release the following songs: "All You Horseriders"/"Blue Sway," "Mr. H Atom" and "Bogey Wobble"?

19. What was Mal's credited contribution to George's **All Things Must Pass** album?

20. When **Living In The Material World** was released on Apple in 1973, what was the artwork used as the disc's A and B side labels?

21. What did George use for the cover art of his **Dark Horse** album?

22. What is unique about the Apple logo on George's last Apple LP, **Extra Texture**?

23. What is the subtitle of the **Extra Texture** album?

24. What does the original (rejected) cover of **Somewhere In England** look like?

25. Which of George's albums featured his eyes on side one and the eyes of his future wife, Olivia, on side two?

26. On which Beatle's solo album inner sleeve liner notes can you read a recipe for making cement?

27. Which U.K. solo Beatle LPs have utilized the White Album give-away photos of George and Ringo as their respective album covers?

28. "I've Been Through The Metaphaser," this Beatle declares on one of his solo albums. Which Beatle? Which album?

29. Originally, Rhino Records' 1989 release of **Starr Struck: Best Of Ringo Starr, Vol. 2** was to have featured this previously unissued song. What was its title?

30. What is the title of the first Beatle solo album to be released on compact disc?

```
(JUST LIKE) STARTING OVER
(ANSWERS)
```

1. Anthony Fawcett used the term "Sgt. Lennon" to describe John's **Plastic Ono Band** album, which Lennon felt was a peak in his solo career.
    (Fawcett is the author of the book *John Lennon: One Day At A Time*.)

2. Yoko is credited as playing "Wind" on John's **Plastic Ono Band** album.

3. Mal's contribution to John's **Plastic Ono Band** LP was "Tea and Sympathy."

4. The German twelve-inch single for "Give Peace A Chance" features a portion of Michael Bryan's artwork from the **Shaved Fish** album sleeve.
    (Bryan's artwork for "Give Peace" is based on a photograph from John and Yoko's Amsterdam bed-in, included on a poster in the **Wedding Album**.)

5. John's first single without a Yoko Ono B-side was "Imagine" b/w "It's So Hard," issued in the U.S. on the Apple label, 11 October 1971.

6. First-run copies of **Some Time In New York City** included a

In the belief that the stature of our nation in international opinion will be enhanced by the presence of John Lennon and Yoko Ono in America;

That the Lennons make a singular cultural contribution to our nation;

That it is in the public interest to have individuals of international artistic accomplishment residing in our country;

That the history of our nation encourages individuals capable of great contributions to our culture to live and work here and promotes the free expression of their artistry;

And in the belief that the principles of our constitution guarantee as fundamental personal rights the entitlement of John Lennon and Yoko Ono to live and work freely in our country, I wish to publicly add my name to those who oppose their impending expulsion and who support the legal and legislative steps necessary for their permanent residence in the United States.

NAME

ADDRESS

Interior of self-mailer petition included in the
first edition of Some Time In New York City (LP).

postcard of the Statue of Liberty raising a clenched fist, and a petition one was instructed to sign and return to the "Justice For John and Yoko Committee" (an aid in their fight to stay in the U.S.).

7. An excerpt from MacLysaght's book, an entry on the "O'Lennon, Linnane, Leonard" family, was reprinted on the back page of the eight-page booklet enclosed in first printing copies of **Walls And Bridges**. Of particular note is the entry's final paragraph: "No person of the name Leonard has distinguished himself in the political, military or cultural life of Ireland (or for that matter in England either.)" In reply to this statement John had written below it, "Oh Yeh?"

(When MacLysaght released his revised and enlarged fourth edition of the book in 1985, it included this entry under the "(O) Lennon" family: "...John Lennon, an outstanding member of the Beatles group, assassinated in 1980, became well known outside Ireland not only as a talented musician but also for his connection with the Peace Movement.")

8. **Oldies But Mouldies** and **Old Hat** were two working titles for the **Rock 'N' Roll** album.

9. The "Listen To This..." (Badge, Mending Packet, T-shirt, Ad, etc.) campaign was used to promote the **Walls And Bridges** album and its single release, "Whatever Gets You Through The Night" b/w "Beef Jerky."

10. These Lennon solo records have included posters: **Wedding Album** (two posters + press clippings booklet + more); **Imagine** (one poster, one of two different postcards); **Double Fantasy** (Nautilus Records' half-speed mastered "Super-Disc," released in 1982; includes one poster and lyric sheet). To date, the only non-LP poster inclusion is U.K. Polydor's seven- and twelve-inch singles for "Borrowed Time" b/w "Your Hands" (on twelve-inch only) and "Never Say Goodbye." The twelve-inch single includes one poster, while the seven-inch single features a poster picture sleeve.

11. The U.S. copyright office will not copyright a lyric consisting of a few words or short phrases. Thus, the lyrics to "Why," which consist of the word "why" continuously repeated, did not qualify for copyrighting. John and Yoko had to settle instead for a copyright on the song's melody.

(See the Pang/Edwards book, *Loving John*, page 12. "Why" is included on Yoko's **Plastic Ono Band** LP.)

12. Lennon's **Two Virgins (Unfinished Music No. 1)**

13. "The People's Album" is **Some Time In New York City.**

14. "Now Hear This Song Of Mine" was included on the promotional-only album **Brung To Ewe By Hal Smith,** a series of fifteen radio spots issued in the spring of 1971 to promote **Ram.**

15. "On His Own" was the headline to an ad promoting the **McCartney II** LP.

16. "All My Best (+Three Great New Ones!) regards, Paul" was the headline in an ad promoting the soundtrack for **Give My Regards To Broad Street.**

17. Paul's first solo LP, **McCartney,** "...could well be called McCartney's **Nashville Skyline,**" a comparison by "Time" magazine to the style of music Bob Dylan recorded for the latter album.

18. Test pressings exist for a proposed double-LP version of Paul's **McCartney II** album that was to have included the tracks mentioned.

19. On George's **All Things Must Pass** album, Mal is credited with "Tea; Sympathy; and Tambourine."

20. Side one of the **Living In The Material World** LP features a label reproducing a painting of Krishna and Arjuna. Side two's label is a photograph of a chauffeur on the grounds of George's Friar Park estate standing next to a grey stretch limousine.
   (The rendering of Krishna and Arjuna is described as follows, from the *Bhagavad-Gita As It Is*, by His Divine Grace A.C. Bhaktivedanta Swami Prabhupada: "Lord Krsna, the Supreme Personality of Godhead, drives the chariot of Arjuna, His friend and pure devotee. The scene is the Battlefield of Kuruksetra, just after Krsna enlightened Arjuna with the sublime teachings of the 'Bhagavad-Gita'.")

21. The original cover for **Dark Horse** was a section of The Liverpool Institute High School's Lower School class portrait, taken in April of 1956.
   (In other sections of this photograph, reprinted in its entirety in

Mike McCartney's book, *The Macs*, pages 44-45 and as a quadruple foldout in the $354 Genesis Publications edition of *I Me Mine*, are portraits of young Paul and Mike McCartney, George, Neil Aspinall, and Quarry Men Len Garry and Ivan Vaughan. When Capitol reissued **Dark Horse** for its budget series in 1980, the photo of George sitting on a bench that was once the back cover photo on the original album was switched to the front cover.)

22. George's **Extra Texture** "Apple" is just a core.
(Speaking of cores, the U.K. release of **Live Peace In Toronto** is numbered Apple CORE 2001.)

23. "Read All About It"

24. The rejected cover for **Somewhere In England** shows a black-and-white photo of George in profile, a satellite photo of the United Kingdom blended into his hair.

25. The eyes of the Harrisons are featured on first printings of the **Dark Horse** record labels.
(Olivia's eyes appear on the A-side of the "Ding Dong, Ding Dong" single, while George can be seen staring back at you when you play side B, "Hari's On Tour (Express)." George wasn't the first Beatle to put his wife's face on a record label; in 1971, Paul put Linda's face on side two of the **Wild Life** LP.)

26. The art of making cement (and even how to clean your cement mixer afterwards) is outlined on the inner sleeve liner notes from George's 1982 album **Gone Troppo**.

27. The Music For Pleasure (MFP) reissues of **The Best Of George Harrison** and **Blast From Your Past** feature John Kelly's "White Album" photos of George and Ringo, respectively.

28. Ringo's been through the Metaphaser, or so he says in a caption accompanying a photo of himself inside the gatefold sleeve for **Ringo's Rotogravure** LP.

29. Rhino had planned to include "Can't Fight Lightning" on its **Starr Struck** compilation.
(According to an article in "Beatlefan" (Vol.11, No.1), an aide to Ringo who had been assigned to deliver the song to Rhino deliber-

ately neglected to bring the tape, claiming - in his opinion - that the song wasn't good enough.)

30.   The first solo-Beatle CD was McCartney's **Tug Of War**. (John's first CD release was **Milk And Honey**.)

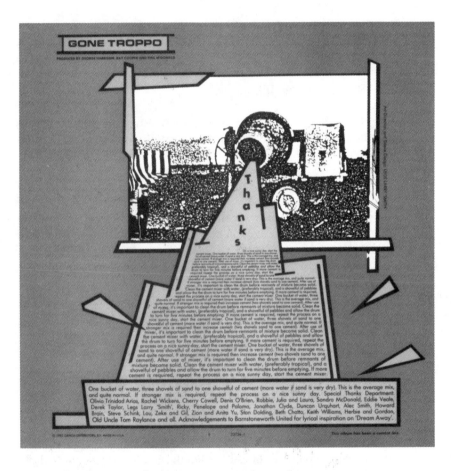

Gone Troppo (LP) inner sleeve featuring instructions on how to make cement.

Q & A #26

CHAPTER 35

WHAT THE MAN SAYS

Yes, it was John's group, but without him it couldn't have been the Beatles. Sagging off from school together, he instilled between John and himself a creative competition - what songs that competition would soon unleash upon the ears of the world!

He was there, watching the walls "sweat," hearing nothing at times but the screaming his music would inspire. Ringo may have been Billy Shears, but he was Sgt. Pepper. He believed in the Beatles even when John no longer cared to.

His songs can be light as a feather or hard as a rocking sweat. His songs can be loving and sentimental. Look again and he's got you - hooked on his incurable knack for writing pro pop.

It would be unwise to write off James Paul McCartney, even twenty-five years on from "Love Me Do." He's not finished yet.

1. In which of Lennon and McCartney's compositions can a church mean so much?

2. "If I ever see another banjo," Paul sings, what will he do?

3. Who owns an hourglass?

4. Who "feels as if she's in a play"?

5. Who has "always been my inspiration"?

6. What do "swaying daisies sing"?

7. What was "your first mistake"?

8. "It will be L7 and I'd never get to heaven if I..." do what?

9. What were you doing "when I met you at the station"?

10. In this song "up popped" who, "ready to go"?

11. When "the tension mounts, you..." do what?

12. What do rainclouds hide?

13. While writing "Eleanor Rigby," Paul has said that Father Mc-Kenzie was not his first choice for the good clergyman's name. What was?

14. What was the working title for "For No One"?

15. Paul mentions Led Zeppelin guitarist Jimmy Page in which of his songs?

16. What are the lyrics to the "Rockestra Theme"?

17. In "Ballroom Dancing," what is the first dance in the competition?

18. What phrase is uttered at the conclusion of "Tug Of Peace"?

19. How do the lyrics of "Here, There and Everywhere" differ between the version Paul released on **Revolver** and his remake on the **Give My Regards To Broad Street** album?

20. Paul has "always thought that it's a crime." What is?

21. What does Paul advise us to do "the next time you see L.A. rainclouds"?

22. "Alright, okay, it's really good to see you down in New Orleans, man..." is the spoken intro to which of Paul's songs?

23. As Paul was "walking down the sidewalk" in this song, what color was the afternoon? Later we learn Paul "was arrested by a rozzer" [policeman] wearing what?

24. Paul sings, "I saw Errol Flynn in a tiger skin." In which song?

25. In this song Paul declares, "And if you love your life everybody will love you too." What is the song's title?

26. Why did Paul include the line "Boy, I love you so bad" in his song "So Bad"?

27. In which of his songs does Paul ask, "Was that the intro I should've

been in?'"?

28. In "Sally G," Paul knows for sure that the "G" beginning Sally's last name doesn't stand for what? What did it really stand for?

29. McCartney was once quoted as saying, "It's kind of like a pornographic St. Trinian's!" Which of his songs was Paul referring to?

30. "Sticks and stones may break my bones, but names will never hurt me." This phrase opens which of Paul's songs?

WHAT THE MAN SAYS
(ANSWERS)

---

1. A church can mean so much in "That Means A Lot."
   (Recorded by P.J. Proby.)

2. "I'll go out and buy a big balloon."
   (From "Please Don't Bring Your Banjo Back," part of "The Beatles Fourth Christmas Record" [December 1966].)

3. The fireman with the clean fire engine in "Penny Lane" owns an hourglass.

4. The pretty nurse selling poppies from a tray (also on "Penny Lane") feels as if she's in a play.
   (She is anyway.)

5. Martha
   ("Martha My Dear")

6. Swaying daisies sing "a lazy song."
   ("Mother Nature's Son")

7. Your first mistake was that "you took your lucky break and broke it in two."
   ("Too Many People")

8. I'll never get to heaven if I "fill my head with glue."
   ("C-Moon")

9. "You were standing with a bootleg in your hand."
("Hi, Hi, Hi")

10. "A sea lion" popped up, ready to go.
("Junior's Farm")

11. When the tension mounts, you "score an ounce."
("Rock Show")

12. Rainclouds hide the moon in "World Without Love" (recorded by Peter and Gordon) and the sun in "Rainclouds," the B-side of "Ebony and Ivory."

13. Paul shelved Father McCartney for McKenzie (selected from the phone book over Father McVicar) because he didn't want people to think the song was about his father.

14. "Why Did It Die?" was the working title for "For No One."
    ("Why Did It Die?" included this unused chorus: "Why did it die/You'd like to know./Cry - and blame her.")

15. Jimmy Page is mentioned in "Rock Show," a track from the **Venus And Mars** LP.

16. "Why haven't I had any dinner?"

17. As announced by Peter Marshall, the first dance in the competition is "the Cha-Cha-Cha."

18. "Hey, new ending!"

19. Paul sings, "To lead a better life, I need a love of my own," on **Broad Street** rather than, "I need my love to be here," on **Revolver**.

20. Paul has always thought it was a crime to be "fussing and fighting."
    ("We Can Work It Out")

21. "Don't complain - it rains for you and me."
    ("Mamunia")

Q & A #26

WINGS

Graham Hughes

GIRLS SCHOOL

4504

Capitol

Q & A #29

22. "Listen To What The Man Says"

23. Paul walked down the sidewalk "one purple afternoon." The rozzer who arrested Paul was "wearing a pink balloon about his foot." ("London Town")

24. We hear of Errol Flynn in a tiger skin from a lyric on "Move Over Busker."

25. From "Simple As That," a featured cut on The Anti-Heroin Project's double-LP **It's A Live-In World** (EMI).

26. Because the line "Girl, I love you so bad" was directed to Paul's wife and daughters, "Boy, I love you so bad" was added so that Paul's son, James Louis, wouldn't feel left out.

27. "C-Moon"

28. The "G" in Sally G. doesn't stand for "Good." Paul doesn't know what the letter G stood for because he "never thought to ask her."

29. "A pornographic St. Trinian's" (a reference to the movie "Blue Murder At St. Trinian's") is Paul's description of "Girl's School."
    (Lyrics from "Girl's School," a double A-side single with "Mull Of Kintyre," including "Curly Haired," "School Mistress," "Kid Sister," and "Woman Trainer," are all titles from X-rated movies.)

30. "Check My Machine"
    (Side B of the "Waterfalls" single.)

CHAPTER 36

NOTHING IS BEATLEPROOF

When the Beatles broke up, I was only nine years old. Consequently, my memories of the group at its zenith are fragmentary at best. I remember Paul singing "Yesterday" on the "Ed Sullivan Show," and those first fragments of Beatle tunes coming over the car radio. My parents dismissed the band's music as simply noise not worthy of consideration until given the Arthur Fiedler/Boston Pops treatment. (I now know for a fact that me mum likes "The Long And Winding Road" whenever she hears it on the radio.)

Some of my classmates at St. Joseph's Elementary used to carry their sandwiches in Yellow Submarine lunchboxes. Once, on a family vacation in Seattle, I remember eying a model car display case in the downtown Bon Marche's toy department. The display featured a Yellow Submarine Corgi toy; I didn't buy it, of course; now they're worth $$$. My tastes in music at that time had not fully developed. The first pop record I remember listening to was my brother's copy of "Tie A Yellow Ribbon 'Round The Old Oak Tree," by Tony Orlando and Dawn. All that changed on the night of 29 October 1972 when "Yellow Submarine" had its network premiere on CBS television.

The "Eleanor Rigby" sequence was stark and surreal. "Nowhere Man" became my first Beatles single after watching animated Beatles parade to it across my television screen, leaving trails of psychedelia in their wake. When the images comprising the Sea of Holes flashed before my eyes, my young brain overloaded, unable to take it all in. By the time the "All You Need Is Love" sequence was over, I was hooked.

On the morning playground the next day, I annoyed friends no end, constantly telling them how "Yellow Submarine" had "blown my mind." That Christmas, **Yellow Submarine** became my first Beatles album. My Dad even admitted to liking George Martin's music on side two (he was still undecided about the Beatles' contributions on the flip). I certainly wasn't undecided - I will always be a fan of the Beatles.

This is a quiz on the movie that started it all for me.

1.   "Yellow Submarine" began as a two-minute pilot film giving animated life to which Beatles song?

2.   Erich Segal, one of the co-authors of the storyline of "Yellow Submarine," intended Jeremy Hillary Boob, Ph.D., to be a parody of whom?

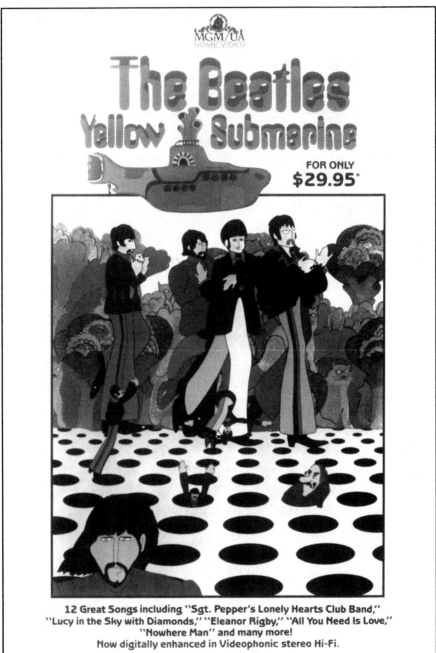

3. What kind of apples do Apple Bonkers drop on unsuspecting Pepperlanders?

4. Following the "Eleanor Rigby" sequence, a balloon pops and Ringo speaks his first line. What does he say?

5. What is the name of the building where our animated heroes live?

6. What words do the letters in the word "help" signify to Old Fred who, on bended knees, implores Ringo to come to his aid against the Blue Meanie menace?

7. When the animated version of George is introduced, what Beatles song is playing?

8. On which day of the week does Old Fred enlist the Beatles' aid?

9. While traveling through the Sea of Monsters, a button is pressed to deploy a leg and a foot, enabling the sub to stomp on the toes of two monsters preparing to attack. What were these monsters identified as being?

10. Despite Old Fred's warning, which button does Ringo press that causes him to be propelled out into a sea of monsters?

11. Who rescued Ringo from the Indians (and assorted monsters) inhabiting this hostile sea?

12. When the Yellow Sub's engine breaks down (in a nowhere land between the Sea of Monsters - sucked into oblivion by the Vacuum Flask Monster - and the Sea of Phrenology), why can't the Beatles call a road service?

13. When one of the Yellow Sub's propellers malfunctions in the Sea of Phrenology, how does Jeremy go about repairing it?

14. As Pepperland lies in colorless ruin, we see its citizenry tormented by the Meanies' sadistic minions, including the Dreadful Flying Glove, Apple Bonkers, and those cigar-smoking, chalice-drinking brutes who shoot revolvers from their shoes. By what name are these villains identified?

15. Having found their way to Pepperland via the Sea of Green, the Beatles find the Lord Mayor buried under an Apple Bonker apple barrage. Singing a "snatch of a tune" revives him. What tune do the Beatles sing a snatch of?

16. What does Ringo step on that awakens the Meanies from their golden slumber?

17. After a snippet of "Baby You're A Rich Man," what is Paul's rallying cry to the newly color-restored Pepperlanders?

18. Near the end of the film, who does the Chief Blue Meanie admit is his cousin?

19. At the end of the movie, during the *live* Beatles film segment, why does Ringo only have half a hole?

20. John has sighted "newer and bluer Meanies within the vicinity of this theater." What was John using to spot these hybrid Meanies? Also, what do the Beatles suggest is the best way to combat these newer and bluer foes?

21. George Martin's composition from the **Yellow Submarine** soundtrack, "Sea of Monsters," includes a portion of what well-known classical composition?

22. Originally, the Beatles had planned to issue their four new songs for "Yellow Submarine" ("Only A Northern Song," "All Together Now," "Hey Bulldog," "It's All Too Much," plus the version of "Across The Universe" eventually issued on the World Wildlife Fund charity LP) on an EP. What was to become of George Martin's background score?

23. Following the world premiere of "Yellow Submarine" at the Pavilion in London, 17 July 1968, where was the celebratory party held?

24. What is "A Mod Odyssey"?

25. Established in Bombay, India, in 1793, why would the "Society for International Trust and Respect" (SITAR) be of interest to the Beatles?

1. "Yellow Submarine" began as a two-minute pilot film by Bill Sewell for "Lucy In The Sky With Diamonds."

(The "Lucy" sequence was rotoscoped from old Busby Berkeley clips from the 1930s.)

2. Noted primarily for his novel *Love Story*, Segal, an expert on classical Roman comedy, created Jeremy as a parody of himself and his academic kind.

3. Apple Bonkers use Baldwin apples.

(See the liner notes from the U.S. version of the **Yellow Submarine** album. Max Wilk's 1968 Signet paperback adaptation of "Yellow Submarine" offers an additional listing of Bonker produce varieties, including Murderous McIntoshes, Deadly Delici, and the Especially Poisonous Pippins.)

4. "Woe is me."

5. The animated Beatles live at "The Pier."

6. H is for Hurry
   E is for Urgent (Ergent?)
   L is for Love me
   P is for Please

7. "Love You Too" can be heard as the animated version of George is first seen, deep in meditation.

8. Old Fred enlisted the Beatles' aid on either Thursday or Saturday. Ringo's second line after "Woe is me" was an observation that "Liverpool can be a lonely place on a Saturday night...and this is only Thursday morning." Later, back at The Pier, after Ringo and Old Fred have retrieved John, John asks Ringo, "What day is it?" Ringo replies that it's "Sitterday."

9. The two monsters in need of a good stomping are identified as a

pair of Kinky Boot Beasts.

10. Ringo is ejected from the Yellow Sub into the Sea of Monsters after pressing the panic button.

11. On the press of a button from John's boot tip, the Yellow Sub descends to the floor of the Sea of Monsters and dispenses the U.S. 7th Cavalry (or a reasonable facsimile), which promptly retrieves Ringo.

12. Old Fred and the Beatles couldn't call a road service because there weren't any roads in the Sea of Nowhere and, as Ringo pointed out, "We're not 'sub'-scribers."

13. Jeremy: "Log sin, clog sin, big thingmabob...chewing gum will do the job."

14. The Meanie villains described are known as the Hidden Persuaders.

15. "Think For Yourself"
      (This six-second excerpt of "Think" was taken from a rehearsal by John, Paul and George of the song's vocal harmonies, recorded at Abbey Road Studios, 8 November 1965.)

16. Ringo awakens the Blue Meanies (by setting off their Count Down Clown alarm) when he steps on a set of bagpipes.

17. After releasing "Sgt. Pepper's Lonely Hearts Club Band" from the confines of the anti-music missile, Paul declares, "Beatles to battle!"

18. The Chief Blue Meanie's cousin is the Bluebird of Happiness.

19. Ringo only had half a hole because he gave the rest to Jeremy.

20. John sighted his Blue Meanies with the help of a spyglass. In the Beatles' estimation, the best way to combat Blue Meanies is to "...go out singing!"

21. As used in the film, an excerpt from Bach's Air ("For The G String") from Suite No.3 is heard just before the Boxing Monster's cigar explodes.

22.   George Martin planned to release his background score, combined with voices from the film and narration, as an album.

(Erich Segal was to have assembled the LP. The project was scrapped when the Beatles decided an EP wouldn't sell in America and that they would need Martin's instrumental tracks to fill out a long-player.)

23.   The "Yellow Submarine" premiere party was held at the Royal Lancaster Hotel's "Yellow Submarine Discotheque Room."

24.   "A Mod Odyssey" (1968) is the title of a film documenting the making of the "Yellow Submarine" movie.

25.   SITAR's Submarine Insurance Department was of particular interest to the Beatles - at least to the ones in Max Wilk's paperback adaptation of "Yellow Submarine" (see page 123 for policy terms).

Cheap Trick

Q & A #2

CHAPTER 37

TRY TO SEE IT MY WAY

Record execs, take note, take heed, take one! The next time you have some spare vinyl lying around, don't make it into a Duran Duran record - there are Beatle fans waiting right now for a masterwork album of Beatles song covers to add to their record library. I know, I know, the purists among you are out there thinking, "No one can do justice to Beatles songs but Beatles!"

I hear you, mate! You've held out for so long, passing up such "blasphemies" as the **Sgt. Pooper** soundtrack and **All Miss And World War Too?** But I say unto you, true believer, that buried beneath this bastion of Beatle boredom, banality, and bullshit (boy!) are, in my slightly biased opinion, a baker's dozen of definitive Beatles song interpretations. No Hollywood Strings or Mystic Moods muzak to your ears here, just the creme de la creme!

Beginning side one of our disc will be the 1963 Stones singing "I Wanna Be Your Man," just to show the rest of the world that even your so-called "World's Greatest Rock and Roll Band" got their start covering a Beatles song. For cut two, we feature Tina Turner doing her tender ballad rendition of "Help!"

1.   Takin' up the slack on cut three is this "killer-B" cover by Heart. Which Beatles song did Heart cover, and which of their albums would you currently need to give it a spin?

2.   Cut four is a first-rate cover of this Beatles song by Cheap Trick. Name the song and the record they released it on.

Cut five features Todd Rundgren's excellent cover of "Rain," first released on his 1976 Bearsville album **Faithful**. Of course no compilation would be complete without Joe Cocker doing his raspy version of "With A Little Help From My Friends," back-to-back with Elton John's No. 1 classic "Lucy In The Sky With Diamonds."

Do you recall:

3.   Who suggested to Elton that he include a reggae break on his "Lucy"?

4.   What other Beatles songs have Elton and the boys released covers of?

5.   Opening side two is this excellent interpretation from Crack the Sky. Introduced by their lead guitarist, Rick Witkowski, which Beatles song did Crack the Sky cover in 1978? What is the title of the live album they released it on?

6.   Side two's second track was first released in 1983 by Siouxsie and the Banshees as the debut single from their then-current Geffen LP. Siouxsie and Co. even produced a very psychedelic video to promote it. Name this Beatles song classic and the title of the album it was released on.

Next up, have a listen to John Denver doing a very competent version of "Mother Nature's Son" - not bad for a country boy.

7.   Someone was thinking when they suggested to Pat Benatar that she cover this Beatles song: it's good enough to qualify as cut four on side two of our Beatles compilation album. What is this song's title and which album did Pat release it on?

Just for fun, we'll include Fats Domino, Mr. "Blueberry Hill" himself, doing "Lady Madonna." If ever a song was custom made for Antoine "Fats" Domino, it's this one.

8.   To close our disc, I'd like to include this Lennon solo song as sung by Roxy Music - a fitting tribute to its composer. What is the title of this song, which Bryan Ferry later sang at Live Aid. On which record is this song featured?

Well, what did I tell you? Only the best covers for the discriminating Beatle fan eardrum. Available in your record stores soon???

And now, in the also-ran category:

9.   Who was the first artist to release a cover of a Beatles song in England?

10.   Who sang a medley of Beatles songs titled "Sing a Song of Beatles"?

11.   What are the titles of the three Beatles songs Peter Sellers covered in fine Goon style?

12. Which Beatles song did Frank Sinatra include on his triple-LP anthology, **Trilogy**?

13. On his **Two Sides Of The Moon** album, Keith Moon covers "In My Life." Did Moonie ever cover any other Beatles songs? If you think so, name them, dear boy.

14. Who is the only performer/group to have done Beatles song remakes for both the **Sgt. Pepper** and **All This And World War II** movie soundtracks?

15. Nils Lofgren covered this Beatles song for an album he released in 1981. What is this song's title?

16. Which Beatles song did Billy Joel include as the flip side of his "Innocent Man" single?

17. The Thompson Twins covered this Beatles song at Live Aid. Name this song and the title of the studio album it later appeared on.

18. What two songs did Paul sing to London's Wembley Stadium throng at the close of the U.K. portion of Live Aid, 13 July 1985?

19. Which two Beatles songs did Paul sing at the Prince's Trust's Tenth Birthday Gala Concert, 20 June 1986, at London's Wembley Arena?

20. What is the title of the song released by Peter, Paul and Mary that mentions the Beatles?

21. What is the title of the song by the Animals that features Eric Burdon singing the opening line from "A Hard Day's Night"?

22. What is the title of the Beatles song that Bad Company refers to in the lyrics of "Shooting Star"?

23. This group originally covered Yoko's "Don't Worry" (recorded by Ms. Ono as "Don't Worry, Kyoko") for the **Every Man Has A Woman** album. Because of contractual restrictions, it could not be included. Name the group and the title of the album their version of "Don't Worry" surfaced on.

24. What is the title of the song by Ian Hunter that includes the line: "Oh look Lennon here I come - land ahoy, hoy, hoy!"

25. Which song by the Clash states that "all that phoney Beatlemania has bitten the dust"?

26. Which Beatles-related novelty song contains the line "Remember 'Twist and Shout' and 'No Reply'"?

27. What is the title of the record by the Babys that mentions "Lucy In The Sky With Diamonds"?

28. John Fogerty has recorded a song that mentions the Beatles, though not by name. What is the title of this song?

29. What is the title of the song by the Dream Academy that includes a line mentioning "John F. Kennedy and the Beatles"?

30. What is the title of the song by Def Leppard that mentions "Sgt. Pepper"?

**TRY TO SEE IT MY WAY
(ANSWERS)**

---

1. Heart's cover of "I'm Down," in medley with "Long Tall Sally," is from their Epic album, **Greatest Hits/Live.**
   (Heart's "heart," sisters Ann and Nancy Wilson, are long-time Beatle fans from childhood. It should come as no surprise then that the cut "Hit Single," from the same album, includes a woman's voice declaring, "You've just won a trip to Denver and ninety others..." This is a reference to the game show sketch the Beatles included on their 1967 Christmas message. In it, emcee John declares to contestant George, "Well, you've just won a trip to Denver and five others...")

2. Cheap Trick covered "Day Tripper" on their Epic EP **Found All The Parts.**

3. John Lennon suggested the reggae break to Elton for his version of "Lucy In The Sky With Diamonds."

4.   Elton sang "Get Back," in medley with "Burn Down The Mission" and "My Baby Left Me," on his MCA album **11/17/70**. Elton also covered "I Saw Her Standing There" with John, recorded live at Madison Square Garden on Thanksgiving Day 1975.

(Elton also released a cover of the Lennon solo tune "One Day (At A Time)" as the B-side of his "Lucy In The Sky With Diamonds" single.)

5.   Featuring Gary Lee Chappell on lead vocals, Crack the Sky did a live cover of "I Am The Walrus" for their Lifesong album **Live Sky**.

6.   Siouxsie and the Banshees released "Dear Prudence" as the first single from their **Hyaena** album.

(The Banshees have also covered "Helter Skelter," featured on their 1978 debut LP, **The Scream,** and on **Nocturne**, their double LP live set released in 1984.)

7.   Pat Benatar covered "Helter Skelter" for her 1981 Chrysalis album **Precious Time**.

8.   "Jealous Guy" is featured on Roxy Music's Warner Bros. EP **The High Road**.

9.   Kenny Lynch was the first to cover a Beatles song, "Misery," for the HMV Pop label; it was released on 22 March 1963.

("Misery" was originally intended for Helen Shapiro. John was especially adamant in his dislike for Burt Weedon's guitar playing on Lynch's cover version.)

10.   "Sing a Song of Beatles" was sung by former Beatles music publisher Dick James.

(James died 1 February 1986 at the age of 65.)

11.   Sellers' lunatic touch enhances his covers of "She Loves You" (two different versions), "A Hard Day's Night," and "Help!"

12.   Ole Blue Eyes covered "Something" for his **Trilogy** album (Reprise).

13.   Besides "In My Life," Keith also had a go with "When I'm Sixty-Four," included on the 20th Century album **All This And World War II**.

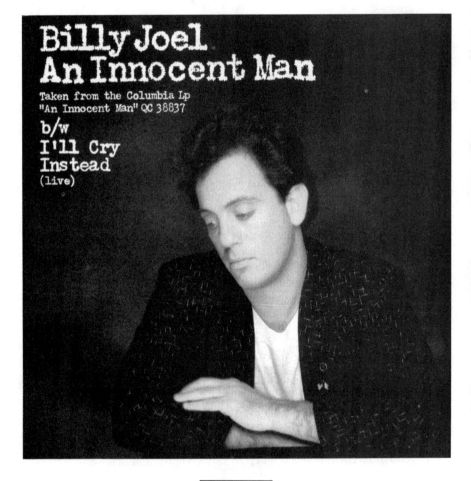

Billy Joel
An Innocent Man

Taken from the Columbia Lp
"An Innocent Man" QC 38837

b/w
I'll Cry
Instead
(live)

Q & A #16

14. The Bee Gees have the dubious distinction of being the only group to contribute Beatles-song remakes to the soundtracks of **Sgt. Pepper** and **All This And World War II**.

15. Nils Lofgren included "Anytime At All" on his Backstreet album **Night Fades Away**.

16. Joel's B-side to "Innocent Man" is a live version of "I'll Cry Instead."

(Joel included a cover of "Back In The U.S.S.R." on his 1987 Columbia album, **Billy Joel KOHUEPT** ("Billy Joel in Concert"), a double LP culled from material Joel recorded live during appearances in Moscow and Leningrad, July/August 1987.)

17. The Thompson Twins sang "Revolution" at Live Aid; it was released later in '85 on their Arista album **Here's To Future Days**.

18. Paul sang "Let It Be" and "Do They Know It's Christmas?" at Live Aid.

19. In addition to doing a Little Richard raver version of "Long Tall Sally," Paul, backed by a band dubbed "The Prince's All Stars" (including Elton John and Eric Clapton), covered "I Saw Her Standing There" and "Get Back."

20. Peter Yarrow, Paul Stookey and Mary Travers mention the Beatles on "I Dig Rock And Roll Music."

("And when the Beatles tell you/They've got a word love to sell you/They mean exactly what they say.")

21. Eric Burdon sings the opening line from "A Hard Day's Night" on "Story of Bo Diddley."

22. "Johnny was a schoolboy when he heard his first Beatles song/ 'Love Me Do' I think it was..."

(From Bad Company's Swan Song LP **Straight Shooter**.)

23. Originally slated for the **Every Man Has A Woman** album, the B-52's included "Don't Worry" on **Whammy!**, released in 1983 on the Warner Bros. label.

24. This line is from the title track of Ian Hunter's 1976 LP **All American Alien Boy.**

25. "All that phoney Beatlemania has bitten the dust" is a line from "London Calling," the title track from the Clash's 1979 Epic album.

26. This line is from the "Stars On 45"/**Stars On Long Play** Beatles medley.

27. John Waite sings of "Lucy in the Sky with Diamonds" in "White Lightning," a cut from the Babys' Chrysalis album **Head First.**

28. Fogerty mentions the Beatles in "I Saw It On T.V.," from his 1985 Warner Bros. album **Centerfield.**
   (Fogerty refers to the Beatles in this song as "...four guys from England (who) took us all by the hand.")

29. The Dream Academy mentions the Beatles in "Life in a Northern Town," the first single from their 1985 Warner Bros. album **The Dream Academy.**

30. Def Leppard's lead vocalist, Joe Elliot, sings of "Jack Flash, Rocket Man, Sgt. Pepper and the band" in a verse from "Rocket," a cut from Def Lep's 1987 Mercury LP **Hysteria.**

CHAPTER 38

AN IMAGINARY FIVE SHILLINGS TO HAMMER IN AN IMAGINARY NAIL

To no small degree, the roots of the Beatles are traceable to the world of art. While we're not talking about something like "the influence of Van Gogh over Elvis," art has played an important role in the development of the Beatles, and in the role the Beatles have had in the development of our society. It was art that brought John and Stu Sutcliffe together. The strong friendship these two men shared reaped them rewards that we, as fans, would ultimately share in as well.

For John, the additional encouragement (and recruitment) of his best friend made a dream called the Beatles seem possible. Through the group, Stu would meet his soul mate, Astrid Kirchherr. Trading his bass for a brush again, Stu was soon enjoying the opportunity of studying under Eduardo Paolozzi at the Hamburg State Art College. Stuart Sutcliffe's role in the genesis of the Beatles should never be underestimated; it seems probable that only death had the power to deny us his artistic promise.

It was art that brought John and Yoko together, playing a part in their courtship, marriage, and even their honeymoon. For us, as fans, the Beatles' music is inextricably linked to their art, specifically the photographs, drawings, and paintings gracing their album covers.

Revolver is "Eleanor Rigby," "Tomorrow Never Knows," and dozens of little black-and-white Beatles cavorting in and around Klaus Voormann's line drawings. **Sgt. Pepper** is "Lucy In The Sky With Diamonds," "A Day In The Life," the shine of silk army uniforms, and that famous bass drum logo.

Speaking of that logo, do you remember:

1.   Who painted the bass drum logo for the **Sgt. Pepper** cover?

2.   In which Beatles film can a sharp-eyed fan also spot the "Sgt. Pepper" logo?

3.   Who designed the **Sgt. Pepper** back cover sleeve?

4.   Originally, the centerspread of **Sgt. Pepper** was to have been a psychedelic rendering by The Fool. Why was a Michael Cooper photograph of the Beatles used instead?

5.   Within the **Magical Mystery Tour** booklet, cartoonist Bob

Q & A #8

Q & A #9

Gibson makes a reference to John's two books, *In His Own Write* and *A Spaniard In The Works*. Where is this reference made?

6. Where else have Bob Gibson's Beatle cartoons been featured?

7. Sixties pop artist Peter Max has often been mistakenly called the creator of the surrealistic animation for "Yellow Submarine." Who actually created the animation for this film?

8. Who did the artwork for **Ram**?

9. What is the name of the rock group sketched by Humphrey Ocean on the inner sleeve of the **Wings At The Speed Of Sound** album?

10. The panoramic painting of Wings that is the centerspread of their live album, **Wings Over America**, is the work of illustrator and painter Jeff Cummins. But it was Cummins's work on another Mc-Cartney album that led to his centerspread commission. What is the title of that album?

11. What happened during Yoko's "Cut Piece," staged at Carnegie Recital Hall, New York City, March 1965?

12. What comprised Yoko's "Half Wind Show"? What was the show's subtitle?

13. It was at John Dunbar's Indica Gallery that John met Yoko for the first time. What was the title of the show that Yoko was then holding at the gallery?

14. On 1 July 1968, John and Yoko attended the grand opening of Lennon's first art exhibition, "You Are Here," held at the Robert Fraser Gallery, Mayfair. A highlight of the exhibit was the release outside the gallery of 365 helium-filled balloons each carrying a tag which read "You Are Here" on one side, and "Write to John Lennon, c/o Robert Fraser Gallery, 69 Duke Street, London, W1" on the other. What was John's inspiration for the balloon release?

15. John and Yoko were planning to collaborate on a set of lithographs based on the symbols from what book?

The next four questions deal with the Chicago Peace Museum's exhibit,

"Give Peace A Chance," which ran in the Windy City from September 1983 through January 1984. While the peace efforts of many music artists were represented, including Pete Seeger, Joan Baez, Phil Ochs, and U2, the highlight of the exhibit had to be the John and Yoko memorabilia loaned to the exhibit by Yoko herself.

16. What was the centerpiece of the Lenono display?

17. An original Beatles song manuscript was also displayed at the exhibit. What was its title?

18. What did George donate to the exhibit?

19. What comprised the "Imagine Room" of the "Give Peace A Chance" exhibit?

20. What did New York landscape artist Bruce Kelly do for Yoko Ono in 1985?

21. Why is Vincent Van Gogh's painting "The Chair" of particular interest to Paul?

22. Why is Mark Boyle's painting "Holland Park Avenue Study" (1967) of importance to George?

23. When Paul was living with Jane Asher and her parents, the walls of his attic bedroom were decorated with several of the Beatles' gold records and two drawings by what artist?

24. What do New York artist Richard Lindner, Los Angeles artist Wallace Berman, and Victorian-era artist Aubrey Beardsley have in common with the Beatles?

25. Who paid £65 for one of Stuart Sutcliffe's canvases, on exhibit at the time at Liverpool's Walker Art Gallery, thus giving Stu the funds to buy his Beatle bass guitar?

26. What have Arthur Dooley, Tommy Steele, and John Doubleday all done in Liverpool relating to both art and the Beatles?

27. Peter Max and "Glass Onion"; Rudolf Hausner and "Fool On The Hill"; Ethan Russell and "Got To Get You Into My Life." What

do these artists have in common with these noted Beatles songs?

28. Who did the artwork for the jacket of Geoffrey Stokes's coffee table-sized book *The Beatles* (Rolling Stone Press/Times Books, 1980)?

29. What is the title of the picture Humphrey Ocean painted that won him the 1982 Imperial Tobacco Portrait Award and the chance to paint a well-known figure as part of the prize?
    (In this instance, Ocean chose a sitting with Paul McCartney.)

30. Who drew the cartoon of Paul and Michael Jackson that illustrates the song "The Girl Is Mine" on the inner sleeve of Michael's **Thriller** album.

**AN IMAGINARY FIVE SHILLINGS
TO HAMMER IN
AN IMAGINARY NAIL
(ANSWERS)**

---

1. Australian fairground artist Joe Ephgrave painted the bass drum logo for **Sgt. Pepper.**
    (Ephgrave actually painted two versions of the Pepper logo. The unused alternate version belongs to Paul, the other to John's estate.)

2. An animated bass drum with the **Sgt. Pepper** logo appeared in "Yellow Submarine."

3. The back cover sleeve for **Sgt. Pepper** was designed by Gene Mahon.

4. The Fool's design for **Sgt. Pepper's** centerspread had not been executed to album scale; with the deadline for the album's release approaching, a Michael Cooper photograph was used instead.
    (The Fool had also submitted a design for the **Pepper** cover which Robert Fraser, the co-ordinator of the album's artwork, nixed in favor of Peter Blake's design. The Fool eventually contributed the design used for the LP's inner sleeve.)

5. On page 11, top row, second frame, Bob Gibson has included a series of Lennon doodlings seated around the lunch table.

Q & A #10

(From left to right, the following Lennon doodlings are seen gathered around a banquet table at "The Magic Piper" restaurant: the dog and two people from the crowd are from "The Wrestling Dog" (from *In His Own Write*); the first gentleman (wearing glasses) seated at the table is from "Unhappy Frank" (*IHOW*). The gentleman with the bug eyes and long goatee is, one might assume, Alec, from the poem "Alec Speaking" (*IHOW*). Behind Alec is the pirate and parrot (drawn here in reverse) from "Treasure Ivan" (*IHOW*). Seated at the end of the table wearing a very posh hat is the gent who was featured on horseback in the poem "Deaf Ted, Danoota, (and me)" (*IHOW*). Finally, walking away from the table and looking very green is the two-handed head first seen on a leash accompanying the poem "The Faulty Bagnose" (from *A Spaniard In The Works*).)

6.   In addition to the **Magical Mystery Tour** booklet, Bob has also drawn Beatle cartoons for issues of "The Beatles Book." In 1963, Gibson's drawings also appeared in Billy Shepherd's book *The True Story Of The Beatles*.

7.   Design for "Yellow Submarine" is credited to German poster artist Heinz Edelmann.
   ("Yellow Submarine" was directed by George Dunning. The over 5 million separate sketches comprising what has been called a pop version of "Fantasia" were created by TVC (Television Cartoons) under John Coates.)

8.   Paul created the collage for **Ram's** cover with help from Linda, who took the photographs.

9.   Ian and the Kilburns
   (Humphrey Ocean probably based the name of his group sketch after Kilburn and the High Roads, the name of the London-based art school band he played in during the early seventies.)

10.   Jeff Cummins did the artwork for the front and back covers of Percy "Thrills" Thrillington's (alias Paul McCartney's) **Thrillington** album, an instrumental interpretation of the **Ram** LP.

11.   During the "Cut Piece," members of the audience were instructed to cut off pieces of Yoko's clothes.
   (This "event" was recreated for the NBC-TV movie, "John and Yoko: A Love Story.")

The "Imagine" mosaic in New York City's
Central Park "Strawberry Fields" garden,
as reproduced on a Granola Dipps cardboard record.

Q & A #20

12. The "Half Wind Show," which opened at London's Lisson Gallery, 11 October 1967, featured a bed, a radio, mirrors, chairs, pillows, wash basins, and other everyday objects, all cut in half.

(The subtitle of this show was "Yoko Plus Me." "Me" was a reference to John who, at the time of the show, preferred that his financial contribution remain anonymous.)

13. "Unfinished Paintings and Objects by Yoko Ono"

14. John's idea for the balloon release was drawn from the memory of a tagged balloon from Australia that he found when he was a child.

15. John and Yoko's collaborative lithos were to be based on symbols from the *I Ching* ("Book of Changes").

(Though John later lost interest in the project, at least one proof exists from the Lennon's collaboration of the fourteenth hexagram, Ta Yu (Great Possessions): he who possesses much - supreme success.)

16. The centerpiece of the Lenono display was the acoustic guitar (a Gibson J160E six-string) John played while recording "Give Peace A Chance" in his room at the Queen Elizabeth Hotel in Montreal, 1 June 1969.

17. The original Beatles song manuscript on display at the Peace Museum's exhibit was the "The Word."

18. George's contribution to the Peace Museum exhibit was a signed, leather-bound copy of his autobiography, *I Me Mine.*

19. The walls of the "Imagine Room" featured photographs sent in by visitors, which were interspersed with mirrors. The function of the "Imagine Room" was to illustrate the lines from one of John's most famous songs: "You may say I'm a dreamer, but I'm not the only one. I hope someday you'll join us, and the world will be as one."

20. Kelly designed Strawberry Fields, the tear-shaped garden memorial to John in New York's Central Park.

21. Van Gogh's "The Chair" was reprinted as part of the artwork for the **Pipes Of Peace** album.

22. George is posed against "Holland Park Avenue Study" on the (revised) cover for **Somewhere In England.**

23. Paul's attic room at the Asher's home once displayed two drawings from Jean Cocteau's "Opium" series.

24. Lindner, Berman, and Beardsley are all pictured on the cover of **Sgt. Pepper.**

25. John Moore, who had sponsored the Walker Art Gallery exhibition Stu's canvases were featured in, purchased one of Sutcliffe's painting for £65.

26. Dooley, Steele, and Doubleday have all created original sculptures as tributes to the Beatles.
    (Dooley's work, located on Mathew Street across from the original Cavern, features a plaque that reads, "Four Lads Who Shook The World." Steele's bronze sculpture, titled "Eleanor Rigby," is located on Stanley Street, while Doubleday's controversial bronze sculpture of the four Beatles (many claim the work does not look enough like the group) is located on the actual Mathew Street site of the original Cavern club.)

27. Max, Hausner, and Russell illustrated their respective Beatles songs for Alan Aldridge's book, *The Beatles' Illustrated Lyrics.*

28. Andy Warhol's silk-screen print, over four Dezo Hoffman portraits of the Beatles, graces the cover of Geoffrey Stokes's book, *The Beatles.*
    (An Andy Warhol silkscreen of John graces the cover of Capitol's 1986 Lennon outtakes LP, **Menlove Avenue.**)

29. Humphrey Ocean's winning portrait was titled "Lord Volvo and His Estate."

30. "The Girl Is Mine" cartoon, featuring Paul and Michael pulling on the arms of a hapless (lucky?) girl, is the work of Michael Jackson.

CHAPTER 39

LIVING IN THE MATERIAL WORLD

"Well, I must admit, this all looks very nice, very nice indeed. Algernon, can you give us a quick rundown of what we have here?" "Straight away, sir. We begin with the bass guitar Stuart Sutcliffe played while a member of said Beatles. Next up, we have John Lennon's 64-foot yacht (be careful with that, it's still wet on the bottom!). A bit more compact, but still quite stylish, is this blue satin jacket once worn by Michael Jackson (NOTE: No sequined glove in pocket).

"Oooh, now this is nice - a red Gibson Les Paul guitar once used by George Harrison (a gift from God). For good measure, I've thrown in a few assorted elf statues from Crackerbox Palace, a mint copy of Milton (key to fun and learning) Bradley's Flip Your Wig game, and last - but certainly not least - a Revell model of Paul McCartney that doesn't even know what airplane glue smells like!"

"Wonderful, Algernon! With memorabilia like this - dare I say it - I could rule the world!"

("Wait a minute!" the voice of reason interjects, "What is this, a page from the upcoming Sotheby's rock 'n' roll auction catalogue?")

Why *non, monsieur*, it's just a few of the *objects d'material* pertinent to our next quiz:

1. One of Paul McCartney's rarest Beatle acquisitions is the only copy of the first recording John, Paul, and George ever made. What are the titles of the two songs on this priceless shellac? Also, name the person from whom McCartney bought the record.

2. During the Beatles' Hamburg days, what brand of bass guitar did Stu Sutcliffe play?

3. What are Bedford and Commer?

4. In 1964, Revell was given a license by NEMS Enterprises to manufacture plastic model kits of the Beatles. Accompanying the cover painting on the box of each Beatle kit was an identifying slogan; Paul's slogan read: "The Great McCartney." What were the slogans for the other three?

5. How does one win the Flip Your Wig game?

6. What game(s) did the Beatles and Elvis play the night they met at Elvis' Perugia Way home (in Bel Air), 27 August 1965? (Hint: It wasn't Flip Your Wig.)

7. Who owned the portable TV seen on the cover of **Sgt. Pepper**?

8. Who donated the "WMPS Good Guys Welcome The Rolling Stones" pullover worn by the Shirley Temple doll on the cover of **Sgt. Pepper**?

9. What brand of bass guitar does Paul play in the Beatles' "Hello Goodbye" promotional film?

10. An old brewery in Camden Town next to Regent's Park Canal had been the planned location of a recording studio that the Beatles and the Rolling Stones had discussed the possibility of jointly investing in. What was to have been the name of this company? Also, who was to have run this company's management office?

11. Where did Mick Jagger first hear the Beatles' forthcoming single "Hey Jude" b/w "Revolution"?

12. In August 1968, the Beatles gave something to the Queen Mother, the Queen, Princess Margaret and Lord Snowdon, and Prime Minister Harold Wilson. What did they all receive and who delivered it to them on behalf of the group?

13. In August of 1968, Eric Clapton gave George a red Gibson Les Paul guitar. What did George nickname this guitar?

14. Why are Mackintosh's "Good News" chocolates of particular importance to George?

15. Where did Beatle fans see these posters displayed?
    "Grow Your Hair"
    "Hair Peace"
    "Remember Love"
    "Bagism - Love and Peace"
    "L'amour et La Pait"

16. What brand of drum kit did Ringo play before he joined the Beatles and switched to Ludwig?

Q & A #20

Michael Jackson/Paul McCartney
"The Girl Is Mine"

Taken from the Epic Lp "Thriller" (TE 38112)

Q & A #24

17. What did John Lennon give to Eric Clapton in lieu of payment for playing in the Plastic Ono Band at the "Toronto Rock 'n' Roll Revival" at Varsity Stadium, 13 September 1969?

18. What did John once do in London that allegedly violated Section 54(12) of the Metropolitan Police Act, 1839, and the third schedule of the Criminal Justice Act, 1967?

19. On the cover of **All Things Must Pass**, George sits on a stool surrounded by gnome sculptures. Where else can a sharp-eyed Harrisonophile see the quiet one posing with these gnomes?

20. What brand of motorcycle is Paul posing with on the cover of **Red Rose Speedway**?

21. What celebrity's bar had inspired John to create the "Club Dakota"?

22. What is the name of John's 64-foot yacht?

23. The name of another Lennon sailboat was taken from a Beatles song title. What is the name of this boat?

24. What is significant about the blue satin jacket Michael Jackson is wearing in Linda McCartney's picture sleeve photograph for his duet with Paul, "The Girl Is Mine"?

25. What is the year, make, and model of the custom hot rod Paul drove in "Give My Regards To Broad Street"?

LIVING IN THE MATERIAL WORLD
(ANSWERS)

---

1. Recorded in mid-1958, John, Paul, and George's first record together (along with Colin Hanton and John Lowe) features "That'll Be The Day" b/w "In Spite Of All The Danger," the latter song a McCartney composition. In July 1981, McCartney purchased the disc from former Quarry Men pianist John Lowe.

(Paul played a portion of the Quarry Men's cover of "That'll Be

The Day" (which he cites as his favorite Holly song) for "The Real Buddy Holly Story," a joint MPL Communications/BBC-TV production on the life of Holly. The special first aired in the U.S. on Cinemax in September 1986.)

2.   Stu played a Hofner President 500/5 bass guitar.
(On 27 August 1987, a string from this bass was sold at the Phillip's auction house in London for $360. The entire bass was sold at that same auction for $15,675. The bass had been put up for sale by Astrid Kirchherr.)

3.   Bedford and Commer are the makes of two vans Neil Aspinall used to drive the Beatles to concerts, radio shows, and other early personal appearances.

4.   John: "Kookiest Of Them All!"
George: "Lead Guitar - Loud And Strong"
Ringo: "Wildest Skins In Town"
(Oddly enough, when Revell first issued these models, only the John and George kits were released in the U.K., while Paul and Ringo were the only models available in the U.S.)

5.   After each player is designated as one of the Beatles, the winner of Flip Your Wig is the first player to collect (through movement around the board, determined by the roll of a die) his or her respective instrument card, signature card, and picture card, plus a hit record card.

6.   One of the most colorful rumors of the Beatles' meeting with "The King" was that they played Monopoly - using real money. However, according to Albert Goldman's book *Elvis*, the Beatles and Elvis shot pool. Colonel Parker is said to have opened a game of roulette, the wheel for said diversion having been built inside a cocktail table.

7.   When Peter Blake encouraged the Beatles to bring their favorite objects for the cover of **Sgt. Pepper**, John brought his portable television.

8.   Shirley Temple's pullover was donated by Michael Cooper's son Adam.

9.   Paul is playing a Rickenbacker 4001S bass guitar in the "Hello Goodbye" film promos.

10.   Shortly after Brian Epstein's death, Paul and Mick Jagger discussed the possibility of their two bands investing jointly in a company to be dubbed Mother Earth. This company's plans included a management office to be run by Peter Brown.

11.   Mick first heard "Hey Jude" at Tony Sanchez's "Vesuvio Club," on the occasion of Mick's twenty-sixth birthday, 26 July 1968.
     (Paul slipped the disc to Tony, who played it following Jagger's debut to the party crowd of the Stones' new album, **Beggar's Banquet**.)

12.   The Beatles gave the Royal Family and the PM a special presentation box containing "Our First Four," Apple's first four singles. The delivery of these boxes was entrusted to Apple's house hippie Richard DiLello.

13.   George nicknamed his Gibson gift from Eric "Lucy."
     (Clapton used "Lucy" for all the lead work he did on "While My Guitar Gently Weeps." George used "Lucy" for the first time while recording a version of "Not Guilty," at one time considered for release on the White Album. "Not Guilty" was also scheduled for inclusion on the aborted **Sessions** album.)

14.   George's description of the various chocolates in a box of "Good News" was the basis for the song "Savoy Truffle."
     (The chap who was originally eating those chockys from which Harrison drew his inspiration was Eric Clapton.)

15.   These posters covered the walls of Suite 1742, John and Yoko's room at the Queen Elizabeth Hotel during their Bed-In in Montreal, Canada, 26 May - 2 June, 1969.

16.   Ringo's first "professional" drum set was a black pearl kit made by Ajax.

17.   For his "guitartistry" at the Toronto Rock 'n' Roll Revival, John gave Eric Clapton five drawings executed by him on Apple Records stationery.

John Lennon/bag one

John Lennon

"Bag One" exhibit catalog.

18. John's alleged violation of English law entailed the displaying of his "Bag One" lithographs at the London Arts Gallery, beginning 15 January 1970. Scotland Yard confiscated eight of these lithos following complaints of indecency. John was later found innocent of these charges, and his lithos were returned.

19. George, his father, Harold, and the aforementioned gnomes appear in a photograph inside **33 1/3**'s gatefold sleeve.

20. Rose in mouth, Paul is posed next to a Harley-Davidson motorcycle.

21. The "Club Dakota" was inspired by Dan Aykroyd and John Belushi's "Blues Bar."
    (The short-lived "Club Dakota" had but three members, John, Yoko, and Elliot Mintz.)

22. John's 64-foot yacht is called "The Isis."
    (Isis is the ancient Egyptian goddess of fertility.)

23. The Lennon sailboat named after a Beatles song is the "Strawberry Fields Forever."

24. The blue satin jacket Michael Jackson is wearing was from McCartney's aborted 1980 Japanese tour.

25. Paul's "Broad Street" hot rod was a 1955 Ford Popular.

CHAPTER 40

THE BALLAD OF RINGO KLAUS
AND ROSIE PETROFSKY

Ringo Starr did not like "I Wanna Hold Your Hand," the 1978 Universal film comedy that includes among its credits noted director Steven Spielberg as executive producer. In an interview with Brant Mewborn published in the 30 April 1981 issue of "Rolling Stone," Mewborn noted that Ringo refused to view "Beatle-related entertainments" like "Beatlemania" and "I Wanna Hold Your Hand," labeling them "rip-offs."

"It always amazed me that Steven Spielberg got involved with that movie," said Starr, "though I know from one meeting with him that he was a Beatles freak."

The fact that Mewborn's interview came so soon after Lennon's death (and the ensuing merchandising, a la Elvis, that it inspired) may explain some of Ringo's vehemence on the subject. Regardless, "I Wanna Hold Your Hand" is an amusing examination not so much of the Beatles, but of Beatlemania in all its frantic, frenzied, materialistic manifestations during the group's initial invasion of America's shores.

While the characters in the movie resort to various acts of violence, theft, deception, vandalism, and (very nearly) prostitution in order to be closer to their idols, a comparison of actual Beatlemania (circa 1964) with that depicted in "I Wanna Hold Your Hand" might show that Hollywood, well known for taking creative license in the name of entertainment, was probably just toeing the line in this case.

1.   Following the film's opening credits, run over footage of the Beatles' arrival at New York's Kennedy Airport on 7 February 1964, "I Wanna Hold Your Hand" opens in a record shop in Maplewood, New Jersey. Which two Beatles albums appear to comprise the store's entire stock?

2.   What noted Beatles-related personality played himself in "I Wanna Hold Your Hand"?

3.   What is nerdish Beatle fan, Richard "Ringo" Klaus (Eddie Deezen) doing when first confronted by Rosie Petrofsky (Wendie Jo Sperber)?

4.   A short time later in Klaus's commandeered Plaza Hotel room, what does Rosie watch him put on his face?

5.   Described by himself as his "masterpiece," what is Klaus' most prized Beatle possession?

6.   Grace Corrigan (Theresa Saldana) and Larry Dubois (Marc McClure) incur the wrath of an all-girl street gang when gang members discover that they've been sold bogus Beatle bed sheet squares. What was the name of the gang?

7.   What is notable about the "Playboy" magazine Tony Smerko (Bobby DiCicco) is reading in a shoeshine stall prior to the scene where Peter Plimpton (Christian Juttner) almost loses his Beatle haircut?

8.   What Beatles trivia question does Rosie correctly answer? What prize does this correct answer entitle her to?

9.   During the course of the movie, three other Beatles questions were asked. Can you think of one of them?

10.   What does "I Wanna Hold Your Hand" have in common with the 1983 Universal film "Back To The Future"?

> ### THE BALLAD OF RINGO KLAUS
> ### AND ROSIE PETROFSKY
> ### (ANSWERS)

1.   The record store in the opening scene of "I Wanna Hold Your Hand" appears to have a limitless supply of Vee-Jay's **Introducing The Beatles** and Capitol's **Meet The Beatles** albums.

2.   Murray the K starred as himself in "I Wanna Hold Your Hand."
     (Murray Kaufman died in Los Angeles of cancer, 21 February 1982.)

3.   When Rosie first encounters Klaus, he is trying to rip up the carpet in front of the Beatles' hotel suite (1232).
     (The Beatles and their entourage actually occupied suites 1209-1216 when they stayed at the Plaza in February 1964.)

Q & A #1

4. Klaus applies a liberal dose of Beatles Talcum Powder (made by Margo of Mayfair, no doubt) to his face.

5. Klaus's most prized Beatles possession is a "clump of grass that Paul stepped on."

6. While trying to raise the fifty dollars necessary to bribe the CBS security guard into letting her into that evening's "Ed Sullivan Show," Grace is forced to cheerfully refund the money paid her by the Flatbush FeLions.

7. Dated February 1965 (so much for continuity), the "Playboy" Tony Smerko was reading features Jean Shepherd's interview with the Beatles.

8. Rosie won a pair of tickets to the Beatles' first appearance on the "Ed Sullivan Show," 9 February 1964, by correctly answering the question: "Which particular Beatle is at the same time the oldest and youngest member of the group?"
(Ringo is the oldest Beatle in terms of age, having been born 7 July 1940, more than three months before the next oldest Beatle, John, born on 9 October. Starr is also the youngest Beatle as he was the last to join the group following the dismissal of Pete Best. Ringo officially joined the Beatles on 18 August 1962.)

9. The three other Beatles trivia questions that Murray the K asked his 1010 WINS radio audience were:

"What is Ringo Starr's real name?"
"Which Beatle is left-handed?"
"Who is the youngest Beatle?"
(The answers are: Richard Starkey; Paul and Ringo; George.)

10. "I Wanna Hold Your Hand" and "Back To The Future" were both directed by Robert Zemeckis. The screenplays for both films were written by Zemeckis and Bob Gale. Wendie Jo Sperber, who played Rosie in "Hand," plays Marty McFly's older sister, Linda, in "Future."

CHAPTER 41

A CROWD OF PEOPLE
STOOD AND STARED

While the films "A Hard Day's Night" and "Help!" are considered classics within the Beatles community, one could easily draw the conclusion from interviews that John, Paul, George, and Ringo gave in later years that they never held their group film appearances in very high regard. From their standpoint, these early reels could be seen as mostly exploitive - a means of marketing a line of products with the word "Beatles" on them. "Let It Be," their final film, was released merely to fulfill a contractual obligation with United Artists. Despite its bright moments (the rooftop concert, for example), "Let It Be" could easily have been retitled "Let It Be Over."

In the ensuing years, however, films and filmmaking have continued to fascinate the solo Fabs. Director Richard Lester felt that John could have been the most successful thespian of the four. While Lennon never accepted another solo film role after the Lester-directed "How I Won The War," the art films made by John and Yoko between 1968 and 1971, though not readily accessible (yet!), are well-known among Lennonophiles.

In 1984, Paul released "Give My Regards To Broad Street," Macca's first big screen role since "Help!" in '65. While the results weren't as well received as Paul and his fans might've hoped, one certainly can't fault McCartney for not putting his heart (and a lot of his own money) into the project.

George's film projects are mostly conducted behind the camera. As executive producer and staunch supporter of the highly successful Hand-Made Films production company, Harrison has had a hand in such noted hits as Monty Python's "Life Of Brian," "Time Bandits," "The Missionary," and "A Private Function."

Then there's Ringo - alias Emmanuel the Gardener, Youngman Grand, Frank Zappa, Candy, Merlin, The Pope, Atouk, and even Ringo! (Nuff said?)

While the "Broad Street" film has merited its own chapter elsewhere in this volume, this quiz still has plenty of other ground to cover; with assorted cameo appearances, "rockumentaries," and other Beatle-related film releases, it's easy to see why the Beatles are one of the most cinematically documented rock groups ever.

1.   In what movie did Jane Asher make her film debut?

2. Filmmakers Albert and David Maysles are perhaps best known for their movie about the Rolling Stones, "Gimme Shelter," which includes footage from the infamous concert at Altamont, 6 December 1969. Several years earlier, the Maysles brothers filmed the Beatles. What is the title of this film?

3. What is the title of Joe Orton's screenplay, rejected by the Beatles as the script for their third movie?

4. In Dick Lester's 1967 film "How I Won The War," what color were the ghost soldiers from the Alamein campaign painted?

5. If John's character, Musketeer Gripweed, had appeared after his battlefield death as a ghost soldier, what color would he have been painted?

6. Besides John, name the only other actor to appear in both "A Hard Day's Night" and "How I Won The War." While we're at it, name the only other actor besides John to appear in both "Help!" and "How I Won The War."

7. Who did John approach at one point to direct the Beatles in an adaptation of J.R.R. Tolkien's *The Lord Of The Rings*?

8. What is the subject of Yoko's "Film No. 1"?

9. Yoko's film subtitled "No. 4" went by what other title?

10. By what other title was "Film No. 5" known? When "No. 5" had its world premiere at the Chicago Film Festival in November 1968, what were members of the audience encouraged to do?

11. What was John's only spoken line in "Film No. 5"?

12. John and Yoko's first joint filmmaking venture was subtitled "Film No. 6." What was the film's other title?

13. What is the title of John and Yoko's film of John's penis?

14. This film by John and Yoko went by the subtitle "Balloon." What is this film's main title?

15. Name the actress who allowed flies to walk on her nude body for Yoko's film "Fly."

16. When John and Yoko attended a preview of George's "Concert For Bangla Desh," what segment of the film was playing when they walked out of the theater?

17. HandMade Films was initially created in 1978 to finance Monty Python's film "Life Of Brian." What was this film's original title?

18. What film features George's song "Only A Dream Away"?

19. Besides Ringo, name two other actors who appeared in both "Help!" and "The Magic Christian."

20. Name four films (TV movies accepted) that Ringo and Barbara Bach have acted in together.

21. What were the names of the characters played by Barbara Bach and Shelley Long in "Caveman"?

22. Who wrote the storyline for "Rupert and the Frog Song"? Who was the voice of Rupert Bear?

23. What is the title of the "frog song" McCartney composed for this twelve-minute featurette?

24. Released in January 1985, this HandMade film, starring Michael Caine and Valerie Perrine, featured cameo appearances by George and Ringo. What is the title of this film?

25. Paul McCartney composed and sang the title theme for this film, released in November 1985 and starring Gene Hackman and Ann-Margret. What is the title of this film?

1.   At the age of five, Jane played a deaf mute in "Mandy."

2.   The Maysles' Beatles film, documenting the Beatles' first visit to New York City in February 1964, is titled "What's Happening: The Beatles In The U.S.A."
(Granada Television first broadcast the Maysles' film on 12 February 1964 under the title "Yeah, Yeah, Yeah - The Beatles In New York.")

3.   Orton's rejected script was titled "Up Against It" (1967).
(According to *Prick Up Your Ears*, John Lahr's biography of the playwright, Orton's favorite Beatles song at the time of his death (9 August 1967, aged 34) was "A Day In The Life." A tape recording of the Beatles' version of this song was played at Orton's funeral, 18 August 1967. Lahr notes in his book that the recording was played as Orton's coffin was brought up the aisle, but that "the psychedelic references had been spliced out, and the sound was barely audible." Among the people brought in following Orton's death to try and salvage his screenplay was Scaffolder Roger McGough.)

4.   Alamein's ghost soldiers were colored pink.
(Neil Aspinall appears as a ghost soldier from this campaign. Other campaign colors include green for Dunkirk, orange for Dieppe, and blue for Arnem.)

5.   Musketeer Gripweed was killed during the Arnem campaign. Had he returned as a ghost soldier, he would have been painted blue.

6.   Listed in the credits as a "Large Child," John Junkin, who played Shake in "A Hard Day's Night," had a small part in "How I Won The War" as an overgrown lad asking his father for his reminiscences of the second battle of Alamein.
Roy Kinnear played Victor Spinetti's bumbling assistant, Algernon, in "Help!" and fought alongside John as Musketeer Clapper in "How I Won The War."
(Two actresses who had small parts in both "Help!" and "How I

JOE ORTON

UP AGAINST IT

$4.95

E-736

A SCREENPLAY FOR THE BEATLES

With an Introduction by John Lahr

Won The War" were Dandy Nichols and Gretchen Franklin. Early on in "Help!" these women are seen waving at the Beatles, while commenting to each other on how success has yet to change the boys. In "War," they are shown in a theater viewing and commenting upon Musketeer Spool's breakdown from lack of water at Alamein.)

7.   Lennon wanted Stanley ("2001") Kubrick to direct the Beatles' adaptation of *The Lord Of The Rings*.

8.   Yoko's "Film No. 1" is a superslow-motion shot of a match striking.

9.   "Film No. 4" is also known as "Bottoms."
(The feature-length version of "Bottoms," filmed in the spring of 1967, starred 365 bare buttocks.)

10.   "Film No. 5" is also known as "Smile." During "Smile," the Chicago Film Festival audience was encouraged to bring their own musical instruments to supplement the soundtrack.

11.   John's only line in "Smile" is "Don't worry, love."

12.   "Film No. 6" is also known as "Rape."
("Rape" (1969) features twenty-one year-old Hungarian actress Eva Majlata as the woman relentlessly pursued by cameraman Nick Knowland and his sound assistant.)

13.   "Self-Portrait"

14.   Made in 1969-70, "Balloon" is also known by the title "Apotheosis."
(An "apotheosis" is the act of elevating someone to the rank of a god.)

15.   The actress in "Fly" was Virginia Lust.

16.   John and Yoko got up and left the "Concert For Bangla Desh" film during Bob Dylan's segment.

17.   Originally, "Life Of Brian" was to have been titled "Jesus Christ - Lust for Glory."
(Another working title for this film was "Brian of Nazareth.")

Barbara Bach and Ringo Starr
in a "Broad Street" publicity still.

Q & A #20

18.   George sings "Only A Dream Away" on the "Time Bandits" soundtrack.

19.   Patrick Cargill played the auctioneer in Sotheby's in "The Magic Christian" and Superintendent Gluck of Scotland Yard in "Help!" Jeremy Lloyd had a small part in "Help!" as a customer of the "Rajahama" who remarks to his dining companion about what a "jolly place" it is as Clang's thugs systematically replace the restaurant's staff. In "The Magic Christian," Lloyd plays Lord Hampton, one of the "boardroom tycoons" from whom Sir Guy Grand solicits an advertising slogan for his "Zeus" automobile.

20.   Ringo and Barbara have acted together in "Caveman" (feature film, 1981); "The Cooler" (film short, 1982); "Princess Daisy" (TV mini-series, 1983), and "Give My Regards To Broad Street" (feature film, 1984).
    (Bach also starred in Ringo's "Wrack My Brain" promotional video.)

21.   Barbara Bach played Lana and Shelley Long played Tala in "Caveman."

22.   The "Rupert Bear" featurette was written by Paul and Linda McCartney and Geoff Dunbar. Paul was the voice of Rupert.
    (June Whitfield and Windsor Davis handled all the other speaking parts.)

23.   Paul's frog song is titled "We All Stand Together."

24.   Also featuring a cameo by Eric Clapton, George and Ringo can be seen briefly in the HandMade film "Water."

25.   Paul wrote and sang the title theme for the film "Twice In A Lifetime."

CHAPTER 42

You Have Always Been My Inspiration

Their songs seem timeless. It's hard to imagine that by 1990 all the music they created together will have aged twenty years. For me, perhaps, their songs seem so sundered from time because I am only a second generation fan. I didn't receive these songs when they first came out - I can never truly associate them in my mind with the era in which they were written, recorded, and first released. Instead, I celebrate the images, emotions, and energies I feel when I hear each of the Beatles' songs.

The "complete picture" was known to me as a second generation fan; I missed watching these men grow and mature. I've studied many books, listened to hours of recorded conversations and images captured on film and video tape. I know these men as well as any fan can. I've never met them, but I love them all the same. Yet, far from being content with just my own impressions of the Beatles' music, I enjoy hearing how John, Paul, and George came to write each of their children. Not every song holds a memory, but many of their lyrics reflect their feelings of people and places during a moment in their lives.

This quiz is about some of the people who have inspired a Beatle's song.

1.   What is the title of the song George wrote for Juan Mascaro, the Sanskrit teacher at Cambridge University?

2.   In the spring of 1986, Julian Lennon was reunited with the Lucy that inspired a drawing he made as a four-year-old student at Heath House nursery school. That drawing, in turn, had inspired John to write "Lucy in the Sky with Diamonds." What is Lucy's surname?

3.   "Paul is dead" rumors aside, who was John really singing about in "A Day in the Life"?

4.   Which Beatles song, written by John, was inspired by Sleepy John Estes?

5.   On which unreleased Beatles song did Paul sing about British political leader Enoch Powell?

6. This unreleased Beatles song, available on **Let It Be** session bootlegs, features John singing about music publisher Dick James. What is this song's title?

7. Which song from **All Things Must Pass** did George write about Bob Dylan?

8. What is the title of the song George wrote about his mother, Louise, the year she was dying of cancer?

9. Which of the songs on **Walls and Bridges** did John write for Yoko?

10. Which of the songs on **Walls and Bridges** did John write for May Pang?

11. George has written one song and dedicated another to Smokey Robinson. What are the titles of these songs?

12. George dedicated this song to a circus. Name the song and the circus he was referring to.

13. What is the title of the instrumental Elton John intended to release as a tribute to John Lennon before Bernie Taupin showed him his lyrics for "Empty Garden (Hey Hey Johnny)"?

14. What is the title of Paul Simon's tribute to John?

15. What is the title of Billy Squier's tribute to John?

**YOU HAVE ALWAYS
BEEN MY INSPIRATION
(ANSWERS)**

---

1. George wrote "The Inner Light" for Juan Mascaro.
   (Mascaro sent George a copy of the book *Lamps Of Fire*, with the suggestion that he put to music the words from the Tao Te Ching.)

2. Julian was reunited with Lucy O'Donnell backstage at the Royal Albert Hall in the spring of 1986.

3.   In "A Day in the Life," John was singing about Guinness fortune heir Tara Brown and himself.

(Brown was killed 18 December 1966 in a car accident in Redcliffe Gardens, Kensington. John is the one who "blew his mind out in a car," driving under the influence of LSD one night, according to an account by Peter Brown in his book *The Love You Make*.)

4.   Sleepy John Estes was John's inspiration for "Yer Blues."

5.   Paul sang about Enoch Powell in "Commonwealth."

(In particular, Paul was addressing Powell's controversial belief that non-white immigration to the U.K. should be halted.)

6.   John sings about Dick James in "Shakin' in the Sixties."

7.   George wrote about Bob Dylan in "Behind That Locked Door."

8.   George wrote "Deep Blue" (the B-side of the "Bangla Desh" single) "during the year my mother was very ill, and dying, and after going in the hospitals over and over again...."

9.   John wrote "Bless You" for Yoko, according to May Pang's book *Loving John*.

10.   May Pang also says that "Surprise, Surprise (Sweet Bird of Paradox)" was written for her.

(There may also be a reference to Yoko in "Surprise," at least in the song's title. "Paradox" is the name of a restaurant Yoko worked for during her Greenwich Village days before meeting John.)

11.   George dedicated "Ooh Baby (You Know That I Love You)" (from the **Extra Texture** LP) to Smokey Robinson. The song "Pure Smokey" (from Harrison's **33 1/3** album) was written about Mr. Robinson.

12.   "Faster" is dedicated to the Formula One (Racing) Circus.

("Faster" derives its title from Jackie Stewart's book of the same name.)

13.   Elton intended to release an instrumental tribute to John titled "The Man Who Never Died," until Bernie Taupin showed him his

Q & A #13

Q & A #14

lyrics to "Empty Garden."

("Empty Garden" was included on Elton's 1982 Geffen album **Jump Up!** "The Man Who Never Died" was eventually released in 1985 as the B-side of the singles "Wrap Her Up" (in the U.S.) and "Nikita" (in the U.K.).)

14. Paul Simon's tribute to John is "The Late Great Johnny Ace," included on his 1983 Columbia LP **Hearts and Bones.**

(Simon first performed this song in New York's Central Park, 19 September 1981, during his reunion concert with Art Garfunkel.)

15. Billy Squier's tribute song to John is "Nobody Knows," from his Capitol album **Don't Say No.**

Promotional wall poster.

CHAPTER 43

IT'S A THOUSAND PAGES
(GIVE OR TAKE A FEW)

Carol Terry's incredibly exhaustive Beatles bibliography, *Here, There & Everywhere* (Popular Culture, Ink.; originally Pierian Press, 1985), lists over 600 Beatles book titles published worldwide. Let's face it, even Bungalow Bill would have to admit it's a jungle out there! Even if you discount the listings for reprints and foreign translations, you'd still need to plan on getting a few extra bookshelves to accomodate them all!

If you're new to the Beatles, there's no better basic "textbook" than Nicholas Schaffner's first book, *The Beatles Forever* (Cameron House, 1977). When you're up for a good Beatles bio, try the one-two punch of Philip Norman's *Shout! The Beatles In Their Generation* (Fireside, 1981), and the book many fans have compared to Albert Goldman's *Elvis* (fair warning), *The Love You Make: An Insider's Story Of The Beatles* (McGraw-Hill, 1983), by Peter Brown and Steven Gaines.

For reference "bibles," there are none better than the Popular Culture, Ink. (originally published by Pierian Press) discographic trilogy by Wally Podrazik and Harry Castleman: *All Together Now* (1975), *The Beatles Again* (1977), and *The End Of The Beatles* (1985). For a day-to-day look at the Beatles' lives from 1960 to 1970, go no further than Tom Schultheiss's *A Day In The Life* (Popular Culture, Ink.; originally Pierian Press, 1981). Mark Lewisohn's *The Beatles Live!* (Henry Holt, 1986) is positively indispensable in its coverage of the Beatles' live performances, while his history of the group's recording sessions, *The Beatles: Recording Sessions* (Harmony Books, 1988) can well and truly be called "the bible" on the subject.

There have been a lot of books written in the last few years about John; two of the best are *John Lennon: In My Life* (Stein and Day, 1983), a loving remembrance by Pete Shotton with Nicholas Schaffner, and Ray Coleman's enormous tome, titled simply *Lennon* (McGraw-Hill, 1984). For Lennon photographs, Nishi F. Saimaru's photos in *John Lennon: A Family Album* (FLY Communications, 1982) make it a Beatle fan's heirloom.

The best book about Paul was written by brother Michael: *The Macs: Mike McCartney's Family Album* (Delilah, 1981). Sorry, no strong recommendations for George or Ringo (and I haven't forgotten George's *I Me Mine*, either!) Finally, if you're dying to visit Liverpool and London, but just haven't got the pounds to spare, the next best thing is David Bacon and Norman Maslov's photo guide to Beatle shrines, *The Beatles' England*.

The above recommendations are by no means complete or definitive.

Don't think, for example, that having all the above titles means you're excused from reading *In His Own Write*, *A Spaniard In The Works*, and *Skywriting By Word Of Mouth*. Also, don't think reading this whole intro excuses you from taking the following quiz on Beatles and Beatles-related books:

1. "If you liked this, come again next week. It'll be even better." This line concluded a serial story from a book John wrote at the age of seven. What is the title of this unpublished work?

2. What is the title of John's unreleased book written in 1968?

3. What does Yoko want you to do with her book *Grapefruit* after you've read it?

4. The first printing of *Grapefruit* consisted of a 500-copy limited edition. What was the name of the press that first published her book?

5. Who wrote the introduction added to later editions of *Grapefruit*?

6. What is the title of Paul's unreleased 20,000-word manuscript chronicling his January 1980 Tokyo pot bust?

7. What are the titles of Linda McCartney's three books of photographs?

8. Featuring a contribution from Linda, what is the title of Alvin Stardust's collection of horse stories?

9. What has George said was once contemplated as the title of his 1980 autobiography, *I Me Mine* (Genesis/Simon and Schuster)?

10. To whom did George dedicate *I Me Mine*?

11. What is the title of Mike McCartney's first book?

12. Why wasn't Mike's first book published in the U.S.?

13. What are the two titles Mike's autobiography has been published under?

14. Brian Epstein's author's note at the end of his autobiograhy, *A*

Cellarful Of Noise, acknowledges Derek Taylor, "for whose invaluable help with the preparation of this book and his professional experience I am greatly indebted." What was the extent of Taylor's help in the preparation of *Cellarful*?

15. What is the title of the book Shake is reading on the train in "A Hard Day's Night"?

16. Where can one read of the adventures of Jesus El Pifco?

17. Who thought up *In His Own Write* as the title for John's first book?

18. In 1964, John and Gerry (Pacemakers) Marsden planned to release a book together; Ringo was also planning to release a book at about this time as well. Neither book got out. What was to have been the subject matter of these two books?

19. In 1967, the Beatles expressed interest in adapting J.R.R. Tolkien's classic *The Lord Of The Rings*. Each Beatle had even gone so far as to select the character they would portray. Who wanted to play what in the Fab version of *Rings*?

20. Signet Books' release of the paperback version of *Yellow Submarine* was cause for the publisher to boast of this paperback being the first to feature something. What did Signet's Sub feature?

21. What are the titles of the Reverend David Noebel's anti-Beatle books?

22. What is the title of the McCartney sheet music book illustrated with the composer's drawings?

23. Which Beatles song does horror author Stephen King quote two lines from in his 1983 novel *Christine*?

24. Which of Paul's songs was based on characters created for a children's book written by Raymond Briggs? What is the title of Briggs' book?

25. What is Paul's favorite book, according to the answer given on BBC radio's "Desert Island Discs" show?

26. When George met Henry Kissinger in 1976, he gave the secretary of state a copy of what book?

27. In J. Marks' book *Rock And Other Four-Letter Words* (Bantam, 1968), the music and lyrics to which Beatles song are reprinted?

28. This novel was originally titled *The Shine*, after the chorus from John's song "Instant Karma": "Well we all shine on, like the moon and the stars and the sun...." This well-known author changed his novel's title when he discovered that "shine" might be construed as a degrogatory remark against black people. Who is this author and what eventually became the title of his book?

29. Originally printed in the 5 March 1981 issue of "Rolling Stone," what is the title of Ken Kesey's essay on the passing of John Lennon, later reprinted in his book *The Demon Box* (Viking, 1986)?

30. What are the titles of Dezo Hoffman's four books of Beatles photography?

31. David Bacon and Norman Maslov, the authors of *The Beatles' England* (1982), adopted a Beatles song as the name of their production company. Name this Beatles song and the authors' company.

32. John wrote the introduction for a book by Jay Thompson. What is the book's title?

33. According to Robert Graham and Keith Barry's fictional biography of the King, *Elvis - The Novel* (Panther (U.K.), 1984), what is the title of the Beatles' follow-up to **Revolver**?

34. What was the working title of May Pang's book *Loving John: The Untold Story* (Warner Books, 1983)?

35. Jon Wiener's book chronicling John's political activities, *Come Together: John Lennon In His Time* (Random House, 1984), was originally to be published under what other title?

36. "The authoress, already a firm favourite of mine, scores with her first outing in print." The quotation above was Paul's "review" for what book, published in 1976?

37. Paul said of this book: "Looking through it myself I've found out things I didn't know went on...." What book was Macca talking about?

38. Humphrey Ocean's "Macc(art)" work can be viewed in between the covers of what book?

39. Paul's reaction to *The Love You Make* was, to say the least, unfavorable. When Peter Brown sent them a copy of the book, what did Paul and Linda do with it?

40. What is the title of producer George Martin's autobiography?

41. In his book *Making Music* (Quill, 1983), George Martin included the original arrangements to which two Beatles songs?

42. Whose Beatle book was touted on its cover as being "The Magical Memory Tour"?

43. Which Beatles album is mentioned in Richard Brautigan's novel *The Abortion: An Historical Romance 1966* (Simon and Schuster, 1971)?

44. "The Beatles are the creature's head. The teeny freaks are the body." According to Tom Wolfe's counterculture classic *The Electric Kool-Aid Acid Test* (Bantam, 1968), the preceding quotation is Ken Kesey's definition of what?

45. Which Beatles song does George Orr acquire from an antique shop in Ursula LeGuin's novel *The Lathe Of Heaven* (Avon, 1971)?

46. Which Beatles record does Paul Bentley listen to in Walter Tevis' novel *Mockingbird* (Doubleday, 1980)?

47. What is the psychological test relating to the Beatles that Tom Robbins details in his novel *Still Life With Woodpecker* (Bantam, 1980)?

48. Which of the Beatles' associates wrote the book *The Making of Raiders Of The Lost Ark* (Ballantine, 1981)?

49. Why is the third book in Douglas Adams' "Hitchhiker's" trilogy, *Life, The Universe And Everything* (Harmony Books, 1982), of particular note to Beatle fans?

50. Featured in Vol. XIV of *The Year's Best Horror Stories* (Daw, 1986), what is the title of the short story by Christopher Burns that tells of a visit by John Lennon to Liverpool - following his assassination?

**IT'S A THOUSAND PAGES
(GIVE OR TAKE A FEW)
(ANSWERS)**

---

1. This line was from a book John titled *Sport And Speed Illustrated*.

2. Written in 1968, John's unreleased book is titled *Diary Of A Working Man*.

3. "Burn this book after you've read it" - Yoko.

4. Wunternaum Press of Tokyo first published *Grapefruit* in 1964.

5. John would later add an introduction to *Grapefruit*.
    (John's introduction, in its entirety, reads: "Hi! My name is John Lennon. I'd like you to meet Yoko Ono.")

6. *Japanese Jailbird* is the title of Paul's 20,000-word manuscript chronicling his arrest (16 January 1980) at Tokyo International Airport for possession of marijuana, and his subsequent nine-day imprisonment.

7. Linda McCartney's three books of photos are titled *Linda's Pictures* (Knopf/Ballantine, 1976), *Photographs* (MPL Communications, 1982), and Linda McCartney's *Sun Prints* (Salem House, 1989).

8. Linda's horse story, recounting her purchase of an Appaloosa, appears in Alvin Stardust's book *Tales From The Saddle* (Stanley Paul (U.K.), 1984).
    (Stardust was once married to Iris Caldwell, Rory Storm's sister.)

9. *The Big Leather Job* was once contemplated by George as the title of *I Me Mine*.

10. *I Me Mine* is "dedicated to gardeners everywhere."

11. Mike McCartney's first book is titled *Roger Bear*.

12. According to Mike, the cover artwork for *Roger Bear* (an illustration of Roger holding a black child's hand) was deemed unacceptable to potential American publishers.

13. *Thank U Very Much: Mike McCartney's Family Album* (Arthur Baker/Weidenfield - Granada (U.K.), 1981,82)
    The Macs: Mike McCartney's Family Album (Delilah (U.S.), 1981)

14. Derek Taylor ghost-wrote *A Cellarful Of Noise* for Epstein.

15. During the train scene in "A Hard Day's Night," Shake (John Junkin) is seen reading a copy of William M. Gaines's *Son Of Mad*.

16. Jesus El Pifco is a character in John's short story "A Spaniard in the Works."

17. The title *In His Own Write* was thought up by Paul.
    (A rejected title for this book was *In His Own Write And Draw*.)

18. John and Gerry's book (which Brian Epstein quickly nixed) was to have been a collection of jokes.
    Ringo's book, according to an article in "Mersey Beat," was to have been a collection of photographs, mostly of the Beatles.

19. The Hobbit, Frodo Baggins - Paul
    Frodo's retainer, Sam - Ringo
    The wizard, Gandalf - George
    Gollum - John

20. Signet's *Yellow Submarine* was touted as the first all-color paperback ever published.

21. *Communism, Hypnotism And The Beatles* (Summit Ministries, 1965)
    The Beatles: A Study In Sex, Drugs And Revolution (Christian Crusade, 1969)
    John Lennon: Charming Or Harming A Generation? (Thomas Nel-

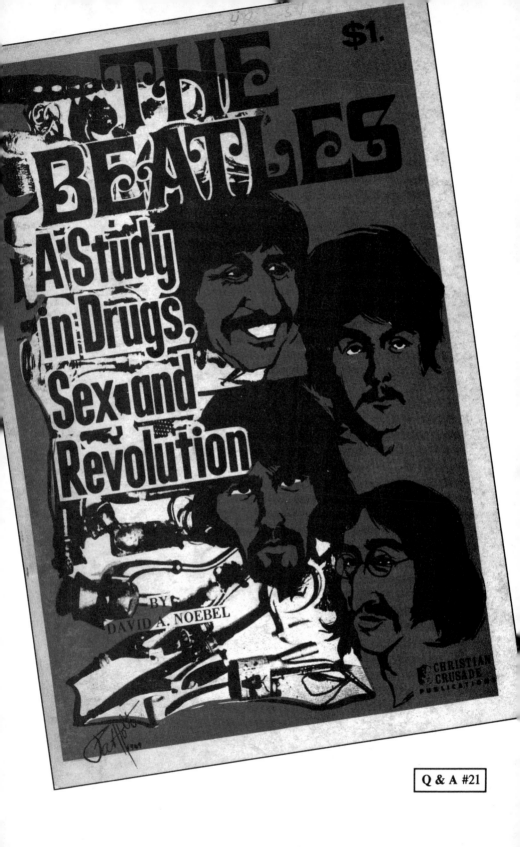

THE BEATLES

A Study in Drugs, Sex and Revolution

BY
DAVID A. NOEBEL

$1.

CHRISTIAN CRUSADE PUBLICATION

Q & A #21

son, 1982)

(Noebel also refers to the Beatles in *The Marxist Minstrels - A Handbook On Communist Subversion Of Music* (American Christian Press, 1974.)

22. Described by Paul as "...a book of untrained songs and drawings," Simon and Schuster released *Paul McCartney Composer/Artist* in 1981.

23. "LeBay Passes," the tenth chapter of *Christine* (Viking, 1983), opens with two lines from "Drive My Car."

24. "Bogey Music," featured on **McCartney II**, is based on characters from Raymond Briggs' book *Fungus The Bogeyman* (Random House, 1979).

25. Not surprisingly, Paul's favorite book is *Linda's Pictures*.

26. George gave Henry Kissinger a copy of Paramahansa Yogananda's book, *Autobiography Of A Yogi*.
(In addition to being one of George's choices for the cover of **Sgt. Pepper**, Harrison dedicated the songs "Dear One" and "See Yourself" (from the **33 1/3** album) to Yogananda. George also offered special thanks to the Yogi on the inner sleeve liner notes from **Somewhere In England**.)

27. "I Am The Walrus"
(Marks' book also features photographs by one Linda Eastman.)

28. Stephen King originally called his work in progress *The Shine* before finally settling on *The Shining*.

29. Ken Kesey's essay is titled "Now We Know How Many Holes It Takes To Fill The Albert Hall."

30. Dezo's Beatle photography books include *Beatle Photos* (Shinko Music Publishing (Japan only), 1973); *With The Beatles (The Historic Photographs Of Dezo Hoffman* (Omnibus Press, 1982); *The Beatles Conquer America (The Photographic Record Of Their First Tour)* (Avon, 1984); and *The Faces Of John Lennon* (McGraw-Hill, 1986).
(Hoffman died in 1986 at the age of 73.)

31.   Bacon and Maslov's production company, "910 Press," is based on the Beatles song "One After 909."

("Natural E" (from "Baby You're A Rich Man") and "Thoughts Meander" ("Across The Universe") were among the authors' discarded choices for their company's name.)

32.   John wrote the introduction for Jay Thompson's book *I Am Also A You.*

33.   The Beatles' follow-up to **Revolver,** according to *Elvis - The Novel,* was a country rock LP titled **Another Place.**

34.   "Was It Just A Dream?" (a line from "No. 9 Dream") was the working title for *Loving John.*

35.   Jon Wiener's book was originally titled *Give Me Some Truth: John Lennon And The Sixties.*

36.   Paul's "review" was written for and featured in *Linda's Pictures.*

37.   Paul's quotation is from his introduction for David Gelly's book, *Facts About A Pop Group Featuring Wings* (G. Whizzard, 1976).

38.   Humphrey Ocean's "Macc(art)" is featured in *The Ocean View* (MPL Communications, 1982).

39.   According to an interview published in the December 1984 issue of "Playboy," Paul ceremoniously burned his copy of *The Love You Make* while Linda took pictures.

40.   George Martin's autobiography is titled *All You Need Is Ears* (St. Martin's, 1979).

41.   *Making Music* includes the original arrangements for "Eleanor Rigby" and "I Am The Walrus."

(*Making Music* also includes reproductions of the original score sheets to "Tug Of War.")

42.   *The Beatles, Lennon And Me* (Stein and Day, 1984), the mass market (paperback) edition of Pete Shotton's book, *John Lennon: In My Life* was touted on the front cover as "The Magical Memory Tour."

43. Brautigan mentioned **Rubber Soul** in *The Abortion*.

("Vida put a record on the phonograph. It was the Beatles' album **Rubber Soul**. I had never heard the Beatles before. That's how long I was in the library.")

44. "But the head has lost control of the body and the body rebels and goes amok and that is what *cancer* is."

45. George Orr acquired a copy of "With A Little Help From My Friends."

("It [an alien named Tiua'k Ennbe Ennbe] stood still for half a minute, then went to the front window and with precise, stiff, careful movements picked out one of the antique disk-records displayed there, and brought it to Orr. It was a Beatles record: 'With A Little Help From My Friends.'"

In a postcard written to the author in 1984, LeGuin writes of *Lathe* that "'With A Little Help From My Friends' & 'Let It Be' were kind of basic to that novel.")

46. Paul Bentley listens to the **Sgt. Pepper** album in *Mockingbird*.

("I stopped the bus on the road for long enough to play the Mozart Jupiter Symphony and a part of 'Sergeant Pepper's Lonely Heart's Club Band.' That was much better.")

47. In *Still Life With Woodpecker*, Tom Robbins' character Bernard Mickey Wrangle had developed a unique psychological test. "To administer the test, merely ask the subject to name his or her favorite Beatle. If you are at all familiar with the distinct separate public images of the four Beatles, then you'll recognize that the one chosen - John, Paul, George, or Ringo - reveals as much about the subject's personality as most of us will ever hope to know."

48. *The Making Of Raiders Of The Lost Ark* was written by Derek Taylor.

49. Paul and Linda McCartney are mentioned in *Life, The Universe And Everything*.

("Arthur could almost imagine Paul McCartney sitting with his feet up by the fire one evening, humming it [an ancient song from the planet Krikkit] to Linda and wondering what to buy with the proceeds, and thinking, probably, Essex.")

50. Originally printed in the Winter 1984/85 issue of the avant-garde fantasy magazine "Interzone," Christopher Burns's short story is titled "John's Return To Liverpool."

CHAPTER 44

You Became a Legend
of the Silver Screen

As the first generation fans who grew up with the Beatles become the new affluent market for Hollywood and Madison Avenue, so, too, will the use of the Beatles' songs and the songs of other sixties artists increase. While the use of Beatles music in commercials has drawn a strong negative reaction in the Beatles community, their use in movie soundtracks has been accepted for years.

In my opinion, the best use of a Beatles song in a movie soundtrack to date was the inclusion of the Beatles' version of "Strawberry Fields Forever" in the 1978 United Artists film "Coming Home." In the specific scene it is featured in, Sally Hyde (Jane Fonda) and Luke Martin (Jon Voight) are seen spending some time together. John's thoughts of isolation and hopelessness complement perfectly the unspoken thoughts of the lovers - thoughts the filmmakers convey to the audience, with a minimum of dialogue, that this moment of contentment will not last.

This quiz touches on films that have featured Beatles recordings in their soundtracks, as well as films that either cover a Beatles song, make reference to, or have a definite link with the group.

1.   Why was the 1938 film "Algiers," starring Charles Boyer and Hedy Lamarr, of importance to Pete Best's mother, Mona?

2.   Promotional pins released for **Goodnight Vienna** feature Ringo, dressed as Klaatu, emerging from his saucer. Above his head are the words, "Don't Forget: Klaatu Barada Nikto." In 20th Century Fox's 1951 film "The Day The Earth Stood Still," why was this phrase important?

3.   On the evening of 18 February 1964, the Beatles, in Miami at the time, attended their first drive-in movie. What film did they see?

4.   What is the title of the D.A. Pennebaker film that includes John, Yoko, and the Plastic Ono Band performing at the Toronto Rock 'n' Roll Revival, 13 September 1969?
(Pennebaker's film was also released under a different title without the Plastic Ono Band footage. What was that film's title?)

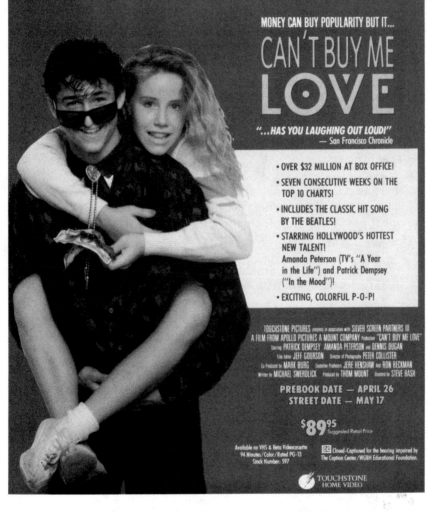

Wholesale soliciation sheet for "Can't Buy Me Love."

5.   A party scene from Columbia's 1975 film "Shampoo" features excerpts from two Beatles songs. What are their titles?

6.   Starring Robin Williams, Glenn Close, and John Lithgow, Warner Bros.' 1982 film "The World According to Garp" plays which Beatles song over its opening and closing credits?

7.   Starring Cher, Sam Elliott, and Eric Stoltz as Rocky Dennis, Universal's 1985 film "Mask" features what two Beatles songs on its soundtrack?

8.   The Beatles' version of "Can't Buy Me Love" was played over the opening and closing credits of this 1987 Touchstone comedy of the same name. What was to have been this film's original title?

9.   The Beatles' version of "While My Guitar Gently Weeps" is included on which HandMade Film, released in 1987?

10.   Which of John's songs was featured in Paramount's 1980 comedy "Little Darlings"?

11.   In one scene from 20th Century Fox's 1978 film "An Unmarried Woman," Erica (Jill Clayburgh) and her daughter (Lisa Lucas) accompany themselves on piano as they sing which of Paul's post-Beatle compositions?

12.   In one scene from Universal's 1984 comedy "Sixteen Candles," Michael Anthony Hall sings the opening lines from which two Beatles songs to Molly Ringwald?

13.   Which Beatles song is heard in the 1983 Paramount film "Testament," starring Jane Alexander and William Devane?

14.   In one scene from MGM's 1986 horror film "Poltergeist II: The Other Side," Steven Freeling (Craig T. Nelson) and his wife, Diane (Jo Beth Williams), sing a verse and a chorus from which Beatles song?

15.   More than twenty years after the Beatles' initial release of "Twist and Shout," this song's inclusion in the parade float scene from Paramount's 1986 comedy "Ferris Bueller's Day Off" put the Fabs back on the Top 40 charts again. Earlier in the film, during a monologue to

the audience, Ferris (Matthew Broderick) quotes a line from which of John Lennon's solo songs?

1. Mona named her basement club "The Casbah" after the phrase, "Come with me to the Casbah," a line attributed to, but not actually spoken by Charles Boyer in "Algiers."

(The Quarry Men were the first band to play The Casbah when it opened its doors, 29 August 1959.)

2. Klaatu (Michael Rennie) gave Helen Benson (Patricia Neal) the phrase "Klaatu Barada Nikto" to repeat to the robot Gort (Lock Martin) in the event that Klaatu was killed. Without this command, Gort would have destroyed the Earth.

3. The Beatles' first drive-in movie was Elvis Presley's 1963 romp with Ursula Andress, "Fun In Acapulco" (Paramount).

4. "Sweet Toronto" includes footage of the Plastic Ono Band at the Toronto Rock 'n' Roll Revival. Donn Pennebaker's film without the Plastic Ono Band footage was retitled "Keep On Rockin'."

(Pennebaker's legs were one of the 331 pair featured in John and Yoko's 1971 film "Up Your Legs Forever.")

5. The "Shampoo" party scene soundtrack includes excerpts from the Beatles' versions of "Sgt. Pepper's Lonely Hearts Club Band" and "Lucy in the Sky with Diamonds."

(The "Shampoo" soundtrack also features an instrumental version of "Yesterday.")

6. "When I'm Sixty-Four" is played over the opening and closing credits of "The World According To Garp."

7. The closing bars of "I Want To Hold Your Hand" and the opening bars of "Girl" were featured in "Mask" during a summer camp dance party scene.

8. "Boy Rents Girl" was the original title of the Touchstone teen comedy eventually retitled "Can't Buy Me Love."

9. "While My Guitar Gently Weeps" is included on the soundtrack of the HandMade comedy "Withnail and I."

10. "Love" (from John's **Plastic Ono Band** LP) is featured in "Little Darlings" during a canoeing scene.

11. Clayburgh and Lucas sing "Maybe I'm Amazed."

12. Michael Anthony Hall sings the opening lines from "Birthday" and "Hey Jude."

13. "All My Loving," sung by Mitch Weissman, is heard over a portable cassette player in a scene from "Testament."

14. Williams and Nelson sing part of "If I Fell."

15. During a speech to the audience on not believing in "isms," Matthew Broderick quotes Lennon from his song "God": "I don't believe in Beatles. I just believe in me."

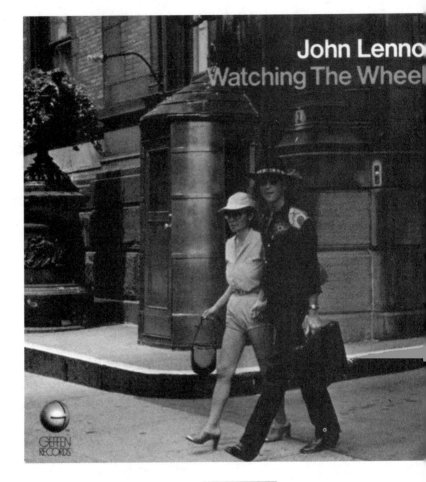

John Lenno
Watching The Wheel

GEFFEN
RECORDS

Q & A #5

CHAPTER 45

ALL I'VE GOT IS A PHOTOGRAPH

In this quiz, we take our lens caps off to the men and women who have captured the Beatles for us on film. You may not remember their names, but you're sure to recall their work.

Look this way, please...smile!

1. What Beatles photograph is Liverpool wedding photographer Albert Marrion best noted for?

2. Where did Dezo Hoffman photograph the Beatles' famous 1963 beach and go-kart antics?

3. Where and in what year did Linda McCartney first photograph the Beatles?

4. Which Beatles album sleeve did Robert Bauman photograph?

5. Paul Goresh is the photographer who took the photo of John and Yoko walking out of the Dakota used on the picture sleeve for "Watching The Wheels" b/w "(Yes) I'm Your Angel." Goresh is also noted for what other Lennon photographs?

6. It was EMI staff photographer Angus McBean who photographed the Beatles for the cover of their first album, **Please Please Me.** Originally, another photographer's work was considered for the cover. What was his name?

7. What other Beatles album covers feature photos by Angus McBean?

8. Where did the pictures of the Beatles, hidden among the psychedelia on the cover of the Rolling Stones' 1967 Decca album **Their Satanic Majesties Request,** previously appear?

9. Besides being an exchange of kudos between the Beatles and the Stones, what do the album covers for **Sgt. Pepper** and **Their Satanic Majesties Request** have in common?

10. Besides Ethan Russell, who else was given a chance to display

his photographic talents in the *Get Back* book?

11. Where were the front and back photos for the **Hey Jude/The Beatles Again** album sleeve photographed?

12. Who took the photo on the back cover of the Beatles' 1969 Christmas Fan Club message?

13. Who photographed George for the inner sleeve of his **Wonderwall Music** LP?

14. Who photographed the Beatles as they appear in the foldout of Capitol/EMI's double LP compilation **Love Songs**?

15. Who photographed John's **Walls and Bridges** LP sleeve?

16. What is the title of the first Beatle-related album sleeve to feature a photo of Sean Lennon?

17. What brand of 35mm camera is Ringo using during his solo scene in "A Hard Day's Night"?

18. When Linda McCartney's photo exhibit toured the U.S. in late 1982-early 1983, thirty-one prints were included. Seventeen of these prints featured the Beatles or were Beatle-related. One of the few color prints displayed was a 23-1/2" x 19" portrait of Paul with artist Willem de Kooning. Besides being the joint subject of Linda's picture, what else do these two gentlemen have in common?

19. What of Beatle album note happened in a photobooth somewhere in Northern England?

20. Who is generally credited as being the first person to take a color photograph of the Beatles?

```
ALL I'VE GOT  IS A PHOTOGRAPH
(ANSWERS)
```

1. A photo of the Beatles (with Pete Best) taken in December 1961 by Liverpool wedding photographer Albert Marrion appears on the front page of the January 4-18, 1962, issue of "Mersey Beat," part of the paper's story about the group's topping of its music poll.

(This photo has since appeared on numerous Beatles/Tony Sheridan reissue albums.)

2. Dezo photographed (and filmed) the Beatles cavorting at Weston-super-Mare, 27 July 1963.

(A picture of Ringo in his bathing suit from that beach shoot can be seen on the cover of **Revolver**.)

3. In 1965, Linda first photographed the Beatles in Austria, during the filming of "Help!"

(Linda's introduction to photography was a short course given by Hazel Archer at Tucson Art Center in Arizona.)

4. Robert Bauman photographed the sleeve for **The Beatles' Christmas Album**.

5. Goresh took the last two photos of John alive the night of 8 December 1980.

6. Dezo Hoffman's photo of the Beatles on the steps of Abbey Road studios was once considered for the cover of **Please Please Me**.

7. Angus McBean photographs grace the covers of Vee-Jay's first Beatles LP **Introducing The Beatles**, and Apple's 1973 double-LP compilations **1962-1966** and **1967-1970**.

(McBean's **1967-1970** photo was originally intended for the cover of the unreleased **Get Back** album. It was John's idea, by the way, to have the Beatles reconvene at the EMI House balcony for the updated group portrait.)

8. The Beatles' faces on **Satanic Majesties** first appeared inside **Sgt. Pepper's** gatefold photograph.

Side 1
MY MAN
NEVER SAY GOODBYE
SPEC OF DUST
LONELINESS
TOMORROW MAY NEVER COME

Side 2
IT'S ALRIGHT
WAKE UP
LET THE TEARS DRY
DREAM LOVE
I SEE RAINBOWS

9. Both **Sgt. Pepper** and **Satanic Majesties** were photographed by Michael Cooper.

10. Mal Evans also took photographs of the Beatles for their *Get Back* book.

11. The **Hey Jude** sleeve was photographed by Mal Evans at John's Tittenhurst Park estate.
(**Hey Jude's** front sleeve photo shows the Beatles posed in front of Tittenhurst's carriage house. While his photos were not considered for the album sleeve, Ethan Russell was also photographing the group that day. The **Hey Jude** cover sessions were the Beatles' last official photo session.)

12. Ringo's son, Zak, took the back cover sleeve photo for the Beatles' 1969 Christmas Fan Club message.
(Ringo took the photo used on the front of the sleeve.)

13. Astrid Kirchherr took the photo of George on **Wonderwall Music's** inner sleeve.

14. A Richard Avedon photograph adorns the centerspread of the **Love Songs** album.
(Avedon's photo first appeared in the 1 January 1969 issue of "LOOK" magazine.)

15. Bob Gruen, best known for his Lennon "New York City" tee-shirt photograph, did the photography for **Walls and Bridges**.
(The best of Gruen's photos of John and Yoko have been collected in *Listen To These Pictures: Photographs Of John Lennon* (Morrow, 1985). The book includes a foreword written by Yoko Ono.)

16. Sean and Yoko are photographed standing in New York's Central Park on the back cover of Yoko's album **It's Alright**.
(Two black-and-white photos of Sean appear in Andy Warhol's 1985 book *America*.)

17. Ringo is using a Pentax camera in "A Hard Day's Night."
(In the scene where Ringo is at the edge of the river trying to take his own picture - with the pressing of the time mechanism's injector sending the camera into the water - the body of an Arriflex camera and a fake lens were used.)

18. Both McCartney and de Kooning are clients of Lee Eastman, Paul's father-in-law.

(Photographs taken by Linda of de Kooning and two studies of his paint pots are included in Cross Rivers Press's 1983 book *Willem de Kooning*, by Harry F. Gaugh. A photograph of de Kooning is also featured on page 98 of *Linda's Pictures*.)

19. The picture of Ringo that graces the cover of his **Old Wave** album was taken in a Northern England photobooth.

20. Mike McCartney is generally credited as the first person to take a color photograph of the Beatles.

(Mike's photo shows a young John, Paul, and George - taken, in the photographer's own estimation, "during the Elvis era" - practicing in Auntie Gin McCartney's Dinah Lane back room as a friend (identified as Dennis) looks on.)

CHAPTER 46

THERE WILL BE A SHOW TONIGHT

Once upon a time, Quarry Men ears strained to hear their "religion" - fading, static-ridden gospels by Elvis, Little Richard, Chuck Berry, and others, broadcast nightly on Radio Luxembourg. Later, moving up on a solid foundation of Liverpudlian support and Hamburg apprenticeships, the Beatles' radio appearances on "The Beeb" made for a healthy supplement to their constant touring throughout the Britain of 1963.

While American radio did more than its share to promote this group with the funny name and "those haircuts," America well and truly "fell" to the Beatles the night of 9 February 1964. Perfectly postured and positioned, John, Paul, George and, Ringo got more out of their appearance on the "Ed Sullivan Show" that night than the mere $3,500 Ed was paying them.

Radio and television nurtured the young Beatles. Once they found fame, they left their marks upon the mediums, making each the better for having known their talent. Twenty years later, the Beatles are still the subjects of frequent radio retrospectives and specials. Television still loves interviewing a Beatle, running his promo videos, rerunning his movies....

1. The Beatles recorded their first appearance on BBC radio, 7 March 1962, for what program?

2. When the Beatles passed their audition with this producer, 12 February 1962, he booked them for their first BBC radio appearance in March. What is this man's name?

3. Who is Marsha Albert Thompson and what is her connection to the history of Beatles radioplay in the U.S., circa 1963?

4. Who dubbed Murray the K the "Fifth Beatle"?

5. Amidst the furor caused by "Datebook" magazine's misquotation of Lennon's "We're more popular than Jesus now" statement on Christianity, this Southern radio station held a Beatles record burning on Friday, 13 August 1966. The next day lightning struck the station's transmitter, knocking it off the air. What were the call letters of this station?

6. On 12 May 1967 this radio station claimed to be the first with a finished copy of the **Sgt. Pepper** LP, which it played tracks from that

day as a "Beatles World Exclusive." What was the name of this radio station?

7. What did John want Ronan O'Rahilly, the founder of pirate station Radio Caroline, to do for the Beatles?

8. A highlight of the BBC's first broadcast of its "Beatles At The Beeb" radio special, 7 March 1982, was the Beatles' version of this Lennon/McCartney composition, as yet unavailable commercially. What is the title of this song?

9. First broadcast beginning 4 June 1983, what was the title of Ringo's 26-week Beatle retrospective radio series?

10. What were the call letters of Houston's short-lived, all-Beatles radio station?

11. What was the name of the first television program the Beatles appeared on?

12. When the Beatles sang "Shout!" on their "Around The Beatles" TV special, aired 6 May 1964, who sang lead?

13. Name the character each Beatle played in their version of "A Midsummer Night's Dream," from Jack Good's "Around The Beatles" TV special, filmed 28 April 1964 at the Associated-Rediffusion studios, Wembley.

14. Prior to his appearance as John McCartney, Wilfred Brambell, Paul's grandfather in "A Hard Day's Night," was familiar to British viewers of what TV show?

15. Prior to his appearance as Norm, the Beatles' road manager in "A Hard Day's Night," Norman Rossington was familiar to Britishers who watched what TV show?

16. On 6 February 1968, Ringo sang "Act Naturally" with Cilla Black on her BBC TV show. Originally, another song was to have been their duet, one suggested by Paul's father, Jim. What song did the elder Mac suggest?

17. When the Beatles appeared (on film) on David Frost's "Frost

On Sunday" program, 8 September 1968, how did he introduce them?

18. What was Yoko dressed as for her appearance with John in the Rolling Stones' (unreleased) BBC Television special, "Rock 'N' Roll Circus"?

19. Who comprises the Supergroup backing John on "Yer Blues," one of the highlights of the "Rolling Stones' Rock 'N' Roll Circus," filmed 11 December 1968 at London's Wembley Studios?

20. On 30 December 1969, ITV aired the three-part film "Man Of The Decade." One twenty-minute segment was an interview with John. Who were the other two men examined in the film?

21. What songs did John sing with his hero, Chuck Berry, on the 16 February 1972 edition of the "Mike Douglas Show"?

22. Which Beatle was the only one to make a cameo appearance on "Monty Python's Flying Circus"?

23. During an April 1976 broadcast of "Saturday Night," producer Lorne Michaels came on camera to offer the Beatles something. What did he offer them?

24. What is the title of the album that appears in record store windows in Starr's 26 April 1978 NBC-TV special, "Ringo"?

25. Which of Paul's songs was written in large part from inspiration drawn from Alexis Korner's TV series on blues musicians?

26. On what show did Yoko debut John's "Woman" promotional video in the U.S.?

27. The producers of the mini-series "Princess Daisy" considered two other celebrity couples before going with Ringo and Barbara Bach. Who were those other couples?

28. What does the British TV show "Three Of A Kind" have in common with "Give My Regards To Broad Street"?

29. During his 23 October 1984 appearance on the "Tonight Show," what two songs did Paul informally perform?

30. Before McCartney's appearance on the "Tonight Show," who was the last Beatle to appear as Johnny's guest?

31. When Ringo became the first Beatle to host "Saturday Night Live," 8 December 1984, Starr was joined onstage during his opening monologue by this man; immediately they launched into a comic medley consisting of many of Ringo's Beatles/solo-Beatle hits. Who did Richie sing with? Later in the show, Starr acted in a sketch parodying what movie?

32. On an episode of "Gilligan's Island," a Beatles parody group called the Mosquitoes arrive on the uncharted island for a little peace and quiet. Later, the castaways are treated to a private concert by the group. What are the titles of the two songs the Mosquitoes sing? Also, name the members of the group.

33. In April of 1977, Neil Innes appeared on this U.S. TV show dressed suspiciously like Lennon (Ron Nasty?) circa 1975, to play the Rutles song "Cheese And Onions." What was the name of the show Innes appeared on?

34. Who is the fifth Rutle?

35. Which Beatles sound-alike group lent its vocals to Dick Clark's "Birth Of The Beatles" TV special? Who served as a consultant on "Birth"?

36. On an episode of the ABC-TV sit-com "Joanie Loves Chachi," the cast confront a man they believe to be Paul McCartney (Mitch Weissman). Weissman's character denies he is Macca, but says that he is - whom?

37. For the Carson Productions three-hour TV movie "John and Yoko: A Love Story," over 100 actors were auditioned before deciding on British actor Mark Lindsay for the role of John. An announcement was made of Lindsay's selection on 25 June 1985. The very next day an announcement was released that Lindsay had been fired and replaced shortly thereafter by Mark McGann. Why?

38. "Make It Jamaica" was the title of the song featured in a commercial aired in the U.S. to promote Jamaican tourism. "Jamaica" is

sung to the tune of which Lennon/Ono composition?

39. Built around a scavenger hunt for sixties memorabilia (including granny glasses), which Beatles song was used in this Lincoln-Mercury car commercial, first aired in March of 1985?

40. Built around a father/daughter fishing trip, which Beatles song was used in this Lincoln-Mercury commercial for its Mercury Topaz, first aired during the 15 November 1985 episode of "Miami Vice."

> ## THERE WILL BE A SHOW TONIGHT
> ## (ANSWERS)

---

1. With Pete Best behind the drums, the Beatles performed "Dream Baby," "Memphis, Tennessee," and "Please Mr. Postman" at the Playhouse Theatre, Manchester, for "Teenager's Turn (Here We Go)," transmitted 8 March 1962, the first of 52 radio shows the group recorded for BBC radio between 1962 and 1965.

2. The producer of "Here We Go," Peter Pilbeam, oversaw the audition the Beatles passed for the BBC.

3. A fan letter written by Marsha (then 15) to Carroll James, then a deejay on WWDC in Washington, D.C., asking if he would play some Beatles music on his show, prompted James to import a copy of the Parlophone single "I Want To Hold Your Hand," via a stewardess working for BOAC. James is generally credited with being the first deejay to play what would become the Beatles' first U.S. No. 1 song, beginning 17 December 1963.

   (James eventually gave the historic single to Ms. Thompson, who admitted in a 1984 radio interview that in the ensuing years the record was lost and "...probably got thrown away.")

4. Following Murray Kaufman's domination of the Beatles' first New York press conference, 7 February 1964, the K began traveling with the Fabs. When Kaufman appeared with the group in Washington, D.C., a reporter there purportedly asked, "What the fuck is Murray the K doing here?" "Murray's the fifth Beatle," was George's response.

5.   Longview, Texas, radio station KLUE was struck by lightning on 14 August 1966. This followed in the wake of an anti-Beatles record burning the station had sponsored the previous day.

6.   At 5:00 p.m. on 12 May 1967, pirate station Radio London began broadcasting cuts from the **Sgt. Pepper** LP.

7.   In August 1968, John wanted O'Rahilly to become Apple Corps' new business manager.
     (While the other Beatles nixed this idea, O'Rahilly did serve for a time as one of Apple's business advisers.)

8.   "The Beatles At The Beeb" featured the Fabs' version of the Lennon/McCartney composition "I'll Be On My Way," subsequently recorded by Billy J. Kramer and the Dakotas.

9.   Starr's 26-week syndicated radio series was titled "Ringo's Yellow Submarine: A Voyage Through Beatles Magic."

10.   Formerly KYST-AM 920, K-BTL (or "Beatle radio No. 9") debuted on Houston's airwaves 9 May 1984; it was replaced several months later by a Spanish-language format.

11.   The Beatles performed "Love Me Do" and "Ooh! My Soul" live on their first television appearance, Granada's "People and Places" show, 17 October 1962.

12.   All four Beatles took turns singing the lead on "Shout!"
     (Paul leads off, followed by George, Ringo, and John. "Shout" and the other numbers the Beatles performed during the concert segment of their "Around The Beatles" TV special were released in 1985 by Sony Video as "The Beatles Live.")

13.   In the Beatles' version of "A Midsummer Night's Dream," John played Thisbe, Paul played Pyramus, George played Moonshine, and Ringo was the lion.
     (This segment from "Around The Beatles" was released in 1986 by Goodtimes Home Video as part of a Beatles newsreel compilation titled "Fun With The Fab Four.")

14.   Prior to his appearance in "A Hard Day's Night," Brambell starred in "Steptoe and Son."

(Brambell died 18 January 1985 at the age of 72.)

15. Prior to his appearance in "A Hard Day's Night," Rossington starred in "The Army Game."

16. Jim McCartney suggested Ringo and Cilla duet with "Do You Like Me Just A Little Bit?"

17. David Frost introduced the Beatles as "The greatest tea room orchestra in the world."
    (Before the Beatles received Frost's glowing introduction, they did a rousing rendition of David Frost's new signature tune, "By George, It's The David Frost Theme," composed by none other than George Martin.)

18. Yoko came dressed for the "Rock 'N' Roll Circus" as a black witch.

19. The musicians comprising John's supergroup, "A.N. Other," were Eric Clapton (lead guitar), Keith Richards (bass), and Mitch Mitchell (drums).

20. "Man Of The Decade" also featured segments on Mao Tse-Tung and John F. Kennedy.

21. Backed by Elephant's Memory, John and Chuck Berry sang "Johnny B. Goode" and "Memphis, Tennessee" on the 16 February 1972 broadcast of the "Mike Douglas Show."

22. In an episode from 1972 also noted for its famous "fish slapping dance," Ringo appeared with Lulu on "Monty Python's Flying Circus" in a short sketch featuring Michael Palin (as the old man in the tattered suit) hosting a talk show called "It's!"

23. Lorne Michaels offered the Beatles a check for $3,000 if they would reunite to sing three Beatles songs on "Saturday Night." The amount was later upped to $3,200.
    (Lorne, a long-time Beatles fan, wrote the sketch "Beatles Offer" hoping the Beatles might actually play along with the joke and make an appearance. On page 74 of Avon Books' *Saturday Night Live* scrapbook (1977), there is a reproduction of NBC Certified Check #129868. Dated 4/24/76, the check for $3,000 is made out to "The

Tracey Ullman and Paul McCartney
in a "Broad Street" publicity still.

Beatles.")

24. **Ognir Rrats Greatest Hits**
(Some enterprising bootleggers later used the artwork from this fictitious album as the sleeve for a bootleg compilation of Starr rarities.)

25. Alexis Korner's blues musicians TV series inspired Paul to compose "Nobody Knows" and "On The Way," both included on his 1980 album **McCartney II.**

26. Introduced by Barbara Walters, "Woman" was broadcast for the first time in the U.S. on ABC-TV's news magazine "20/20."
(The scenes of John and Yoko walking through Central Park in this video were directed by Ethan Russell.)

27. Rod and Alana Stewart and Mick and Bianca Jagger were both under consideration for the roles of the bisexual dress designer and his scheming wife in "Princess Daisy," first aired on NBC-TV 6-7 November 1983.

28. "Three Of A Kind" and "Give My Regards To Broad Street" both featured the acting talents of Tracey Ullman.

29. Near the conclusion of his 23 October 1984 appearance on the "Tonight Show," Paul did brief, comic renditions of "Yesterday" and "You Are My Sunshine."

30. Prior to Paul's appearance, the last Beatle to appear on the "Tonight Show" was Ringo with Barbara Bach, who visited Johnny and Ed in May of 1981 to promote their latest film, "Caveman."
(A clip from "Caveman" was shown during their segment.)

31. When Ringo hosted "Saturday Night Live" he was joined during his opening monologue by Billy Crystal doing his excellent impersonation of Sammy Davis, Jr. The Ringo/Sammy medley (in order) featured "With A Little Help From My Friends"/"What Kind Of Fool Am I"/"Act Naturally"/"I Gotta Be Me"/"Octopus's Garden"/"Photograph"/"Yellow Submarine," ending with a reprise of "With A Little Help From My Friends." Later in the show, Ringo acted in a sketch parodying the movie "Bridge Over The River Kwai."

32. At the castaways' concert, the Mosquitoes - Bingo (drums), Bango (guitar), Bongo (guitar), and Irving (bass) - sang "Don't Bug Me" and "He's A Loser."

(Later in the episode, Gilligan (Bob Denver) identifies one of the songs the group is rehearsing as "I Wanna Go Back To Pago-Pago, Yeah, Yeah, Yeah, With You.")

33. Innes sang "Cheese And Onions" on "Saturday Night Live."

(Innes was parodying John's appearance on the 1975 "Salute To Lew Grade" TV special.)

34. The fifth Rutle - who knew how to have a good time in Hamburg - was named Leppo (played by Ollie Halsall).

35. The sound-alike group "Rain" sang the Beatles songs used on the soundtrack of Dick Clark's TV movie "Birth Of The Beatles." Acting as a consultant on the film was Pete Best.

(The European theatrical version of this film contains an additional school scene and some shots of bare breasts.)

36. Mitch Weissman (of "Beatlemania" fame) played a musician named Marvin O. Pizika.

37. Mark Lindsay's real name is Mark Chapman. Upon discovering this, the producers deemed it inappropriate to have an actor with the same name as Lennon's murderer playing John.

(Mark Lindsay (middle name) Chapman had a small part in "Time Bandits.")

38. "Make It Jamaica" is sung to the tune of "Happy Xmas (War Is Over)."

39. Lincoln-Mercury paid ATV Music Corp. $100,000 for the rights to use "Help!" in their sixties scavenger hunt car ad.

40. Lincoln-Mercury's Topaz commercial features a sound-alike group doing a cover of "Good Day Sunshine."

(While many Beatle fans may lament the commercialization of the Beatles' songs, it is interesting to note that in July 1987 Buick began using the MPL-controlled Buddy Holly song "Oh Boy!" in its commercials. The new lyrics were titled "Oh Buick!")

CHAPTER 47

WHERE'S HARRY?

There doesn't seem to be much doubt that "Give My Regards To Broad Street" is a Beatle fan's movie. The critics and the general public both gave "Broad Street" such a swift dismissal that for many of us our first viewing of this fictional day in Macca's life had to come from a home video purchase or rental. That's really a shame because "Broad Street" has many nice moments.

Who could forget the scene near the start of the film where Paul, driving his custom hot rod along a quiet English country road, startles the odd sox off two unsuspecting elderly ladies when he passes them, en route to the office, at nearly the speed of sound. Near the end of the film there's a touching scene between Paul and the late Sir Ralph Richardson. Richardson's character, Jim, could easily remind one of another Jim - one who had a hand in raising a fine pair of lads named Mike and Paul. Finally, one shouldn't overlook the many rehearsal scenes, notably for "Not Such A Bad Boy," "No Values," and "For No One."

Perhaps "Broad Street" would have been better served by a cable television premiere, a network showing later, and then on to home video. Such speculation, merely hindsight on my part, is academic at best. "Broad Street" deserved better than across the board dismissal as a McCartney flop. Granted, parts of this movie are a bit uneven and certain scenes (most notably, the "Eleanor Rigby" sequence) run too long. But if you're any kind of Beatle/McCartney fan at all and you've not yet seen "Give My Regards To Broad Street," well then, what's up with you? SEE IT! Of course after you've seen it you'll be ready for this "Broad Street" quiz:

1. Liverpool playwright Willy Russell produced a script for Paul which McCartney subsequently shelved in favor of his own "Broad Street" script. What is the title of Russell's rejected script?

2. What real life incident did Paul base his script upon?

3. When "Broad Street" was first being cast, what role did Ringo want to play?

4. How did Tracey Ullman audition for her role as Harry's girl-friend, Sandra?

5. What other film was being shot at Elstree Studios at the same

time as many of the interior scenes for "Broad Street"?

6. In the film's opening scene, what song is Paul writing down the lyrics to in the back of his limo?

7. What were the respective license plates of Paul's custom hot rod and limosine?

8. You may find yourself behind the eight ball if you can't answer this one: What is the number of the billiard ball used as the knob on the stick shift of Paul's custom hot rod?

9. What distinct sound can one hear in several scenes immediately preceding the entrance of William Rath (John Bennett), the head of Rathbone Industries?

10. Before the "Ballroom Dancing" rehearsal begins, Ringo spots a gorgeous journalist played by Barbara Bach. When questioned by our intrepid drummer, Barbara replies that she is writing a magazine article. What is her article about?

11. From what noted rock group did Paul recruit two members for the band in the "Silly Love Songs" sequence?

12. What is the name of the group that accompanies Paul in the sequences for "For No One" and "Eleanor Rigby"?

13. Where does Jim (Sir Ralph Richardson) live?

14. Please supply the next line (sing it if you'd like): "Give my regards to Broad Street...."

15. What song does Paul sing while imagining he is a busker outside the Leicester Square tube station?

16. Name the four non-Lennon and/or McCartney tunes included in the "Broad Street" soundtrack.

17. Movie posters for "Yellow Submarine" featured the phrase "Nothing Is Real" as the film's subtitle. What was "Broad Street's" subtitle?

18. In conjunction with the release of "Broad Street," MTV spon-

sored a contest. What was the grand prize to be won in this contest?

19. What do the films "Greystoke: The Legend of Tarzan" (Warner Bros., 1983) and "Give My Regards To Broad Street" have in common?

20. In Argus Press Software's computer game version of "Give My Regards To Broad Street," the player searches for the ten missing notes to "No More Lonely Nights." If the player fails to retrieve all ten notes by midnight, a busker version of Paul pops up playing what tune?

WHERE'S HARRY?
(ANSWERS)

1. Willy Russell's rejected script was titled "Band On The Run."

2. Paul based his script for "Broad Street" on the time an assistant to producer Chris Thomas left the master tapes to the Sex Pistols' first album, **Never Mind The Bollocks,** on a rain-soaked station platform.

3. Originally, Ringo wanted to portray the villain, Rath.

4. Ullman auditioned for McCartney by sending him one of her music videos.

5. Steven Spielberg's film "Indiana Jones And The Temple Of Doom" was being filmed at Elstree at the same time as "Broad Street."

6. Paul was seen writing out the lyrics to "Not Such A Bad Boy."

7. Paul's Limo - MUS 1C
Paul's Hot Rod - PM1
(Shades of LMW 28 1F!)

8. The stick shift knob on Paul's customized Ford Popular is a seven ball.

9. Rath's entrances in "Broad Street" were frequently highlighted

Still from the "Broad Street" press kit.

Special screening invitation card
to "Give My Regards To Broad Street."

by the sound of a rattlesnake rattle.

10. Barbara was researching a magazine article about "...the relative value of popular music as a therapeutic tool for social services."

11. Paul's "Silly Love Songs" band featured two members of the rock group Toto: Steve Lukather, playing guitar, and Jeff Porcaro on drums.

12. Paul was accompanied on "For No One" and "Eleanor Rigby" by the Gabrielli String Quartet.
(This quartet also played on the **Tug Of War** album.)

13. Jim lives above the Old Justice pub.

14. "Remember me to Leicester Square...."

15. Busker Paul sings a profitable version of "Yesterday."
(Paul donated the three or four pounds he made during the filming of this sequence to the Seaman's Mission.)

16. The four non-Lennon and/or McCartney tunes included on the "Broad Street" soundtrack are:

"Give My Regards To Broadway"

"Zip A Dee Doo Dah"
(Sung by Paul and Bryan Brown)

"Bless 'Em All"
(Sung by Paul and Ian Hastings)

"Sleepy Lagoon"

17. "Broad Street's" subtitle was "When the music stops, the mystery begins."

18. The grand prize winner of MTV's "Broad Street" contest received the $50,000 custom 1955 Ford Popular Paul drove in the movie.

19. "Greystoke" and "Broad Street" both feature the acting talents of Sir Ralph Richardson.

("Broad Street" was Richardson's last role before his death at age 81.)

20. Failure to retrieve the missing notes and mix them into "No More Lonely Nights" by midnight subjects the player to a busker version of Paul who pops up playing an out-of-tune version of "Band On The Run."

CHAPTER 48

ALL THESE PLACES
HAD THEIR MOMENTS

To an Elvis fan, "Mecca" would be a pilgrimage to Tupelo, Mississippi, to visit the King's tiny two-room birthplace, followed by a tour of the luxurious contrast of Graceland, in Memphis, Tennessee. For a Beatle fan, all roads lead to Liverpool, with stops in London and Hamburg, thank you. Don't be shy, take off your shoes when you cross Abbey Road and make sure you have your picture taken in front of Strawberry Field.

Let yourself be taken down, if you ever get the chance. Grab yourself a passport and some pounds and visit the Beatles' England - for a hardcore fan like yourself, it's this side of Pepperland. Perhaps you'll be visiting some of the places coming up in this quiz:

1. Which Beatle(s) attended Saint Silas Infants' School?

2. Which Beatle(s) attended Prescot Grammar School?

3. Which Beatle(s) attended Dovedale Primary School?

4. What is the name of the university Yoko attended prior to moving to Scarsdale, New York, to attend Sarah Lawrence?

5. Name the man who opened the Cavern.

6. What historic event took place in 1957 at the Conservation Club's New Clubmoor Hall, Liverpool?

7. What historic event took place in 1958 at a Quarry Men gig at Wilson Hall in Garston?

8. Why is Liverpool's "Razamataz Club," 108 Seel Street, of importance to Beatle fans?

9. What name does "The Kaiserkeller," 36 Grosse Freiheit, Hamburg, go by today?

10. What is "The Grapes"?

Entrance to Friar Park.
Previously unpublished photos
by Joyce Sanderson.

Q & A #22

11. On the night of 1 February 1962, the Beatles played an engagement at the "Thistle Cafe" in West Kirby, ten miles from Liverpool. What is so important about this particular gig?

12. For a time following the recording of their first single, George Martin considered recording some of the tracks for the Beatles' first album *live*. Where was Martin thinking of recording them?

13. What noted movie actor was staying in Paris at the hotel George V at the same time as the Beatles (14 January - 5 February, 1964)?

14. Name the town in Austria where the snow scenes for "Help!" were filmed.

15. What is "The Flying Cow"?

16. What was the name of George and Pattie's house on Claremont Estate, Esher?

17. What Beatle landmark did John call a "mock Tudor shithouse"?

18. According to John, what place is "...beyond the blue horizon, far above the clouds, in a land that no one knows."

19. In 1968, Peter Frank, a dental surgeon, had an office located at 94 Baker Street, London. Why would this information be of any interest to Beatle fans?

20. Who were John and Yoko's nearest neighbors when they lived at Tittenhurst?

21. At what site did John and Yoko plan to stage their Toronto Peace Festival?

22. Who built Friar Park and what is the title of the song George wrote for the builder?

23. Who is the estate manager of George's Friar Park home?

24. According to John and Yoko, what has no land, no boundaries, no passports, only people?

25. Who lived in John and Yoko's first Dakota apartment before them?

26. Sharing connecting kitchen doors, who is Yoko's next-door neighbor at the Dakota?

27. What is "Kuppuqulua"?

28. An exact replica of EMI Studio #2, the studio where the Beatles recorded most of their music, was built in the basement of Paul's MPL Communications headquarters, 1 Soho Square, London. What is the name of this recording studio?

29. Name the four streets in Liverpool named after the Beatles.

30. During what year and in what city did Mark Lapidos's first "Beatlefest" take place? ·

**ALL THESE PLACES
HAD THEIR MOMENTS
(ANSWERS)**

1. Richard Starkey attended St. Silas.
    (Another noted graduate of St. Silas was Billy Fury.)

2. Stuart Fergusson Victor Sutcliffe attended Prescot Grammar.

3. John and George both attended Dovedale Primary.

4. In 1952, Yoko attended the Gakushuin University in Tokyo before going on to Sarah Lawrence.

5. Alan Sytner opened the Cavern as a jazz club on 16 January 1957; Ray McFall took over the club 3 October 1959.
    (The Cavern takes its name from a jazz cellar in Paris, "Le Caveau Francais Jazz Club." In his book *The Beatles Live!*, Mark Lewisohn proves that, contrary to popular belief, the Beatles only played at the Cavern a total of 274 times, not the widely reprinted 292 times.)

6. On the night of 18 October 1957, Paul McCartney made his

The Grapes pub, Liverpool.
Previously unpublished photo
by Joyce Sanderson.

public debut with the Quarry Men at the New Clubmoor Hall.

7.   On the night of 6 February 1958, fourteen year-old George Harrison first met the Quarry Men.

8.   On 10 May 1960, the Silver Beetles auditioned for Larry Parnes at the Wyvern Social Club, an audition that led to their first tour of Scotland backing Johnny Gentle. Later that year, this Seel Street venue, on which now stands the Razamataz Club, would be reopened by Allan Williams as the Blue Angel.

9.   The building once known as the Kaiserkeller is now called the Colibri.
     (The Beatles played 58 nights at the Kaiserkeller from 4 October to 30 November 1960.)

10.   The Grapes was the Beatles' favorite Mathew Street pub; many ales were tipped back there by Liverpool groups between shows at the Cavern.

11.   The West Kirby "Thistle Cafe" gig was the Beatles' first contracted engagement under Brian Epstein's management and from which he took a commission.

12.   George Martin considered recording some of the material that would become the **Please Please Me** LP at the Cavern.
     (The poor acoustics of the Cavern, which Martin once described as "literally like a dungeon," ruled out any possibility of recording there.)

13.   Burt Lancaster was staying at the hotel George V at the same time as the Beatles.

14.   The snow scenes in "Help!" were filmed in Obertauern, Austria.
     (Summer scenes for "Help!" were filmed in Nassau, the capital city of the Bahama Islands.)

15.   "The Flying Cow" was the name of the bar at "Sunny Heights," Ringo's former home in Weybridge, Surrey.

16.   George and Pattie's estate in Esher was named "Kinfauns."

17. John called "Kenwood," his "stockbroker belt" home on Cavendish Road, Weybridge, a "mock Tudor shithouse."

18. In his voice-over narration for the soundtrack to the "Magical Mystery Tour" TV special, John invites us to "...that secret place where the eyes of men have never set foot."
   (In this secret place there "...live four or five magicians who spend their days casting wonderful spells.")

19. In 1968, 94 Baker Street also housed the ill-fated Apple Boutique.

20. John and Yoko's nearest Tittenhurst neighbour was dress designer (to the Queen, among others) Norman Hartnell.

21. John and Yoko's Peace Festival was to have been held at Mosport Park.
   (Toronto's Peace Festival never came off due to a disagreement between the festival's producers and John and Yoko; the Lennons ultimately demanded that the event be completely free.)

22. Sir Francis Crisp built Friar Park in the 1870's. This Victorian-era lawyer was the subject of the Harrisong "Ballad of Sir Frankie Crisp (Let It Roll)," which George included on his 1970 Apple album **All Things Must Pass**.

23. George's brother, Harold, is Friar Park's estate manager.
   (George's elder brother, Peter, is in charge of the botanist and ten full-time gardeners tending to the grounds of this forty-acre estate.)

24. John and Yoko's land of no boundaries or passports is their conceptual country "Nutopia."
   (Nutopia is described in liner notes printed on the inner sleeve accompanying the **Mind Games** LP.)

25. John and Yoko's first Dakota apartment was once home to actor Robert Ryan.

26. Yoko's next-door neighbour at the Dakota is Roberta Flack.
   (Flack covered "Goodbye Sadness" for Yoko's **Every Man Has A Woman** album. On 30 August 1972, Roberta (among others) joined

John and Yoko onstage to sing "Give Peace A Chance" at the "One to One" concert.)

27. "Kuppuqulua" is the name of George's home on the Hawaiian island of Maui.

28. Paul's recording facility in the basement of his MPL headquarters is called "Replica Studio."

29. John Lennon Drive
     Paul McCartney Way
     George Harrison Close
     Ringo Starr Close

30. Mark Lapidos's first Beatlefest was held at the Hotel Commodore in New York City, 8-9 September 1974.
     (Beatlefest's emcee at that first convention was Murray the K.)

CHAPTER 49

BEATLEGGED!

Several years back, Kustom Rekords released a pirate disc of original Beatles recordings titled **Judy**. Why this deceptive disc is worth noting at all is the interesting method these bootleggers employed in their attempts to pass off these studio cuts as a collection of outtakes/unreleased material. Of the twelve tracks listed on the back cover liner notes, eleven feature reworded title variations. "Baby You're A Rich Man" became "I'm An Opulent Man"; "Penny Lane" turned into "Copper Path"; "Strawberry Fields Forever" sprouted into "Raspberry Gardens."

While it's very likely this unscrupulous variation of bootlegging fooled very many people, the author does offer a tip of his hat to Kustom for giving him the necessary inspiration to create the next quiz. Below are the "alternate" titles to twenty-five Beatles songs. Many of these new titles are actually lines garnered from the respective song's lyrics, while others are tricky title variations. Were you to spot a "Beatleg" with these bogus boot cuts, could you reveal their true I.D.?

1. "Another Kind Of Mind"

2. "Dream Sweet Dreams"

3. "Ebony Avian"

4. "Girl, I Like Your Face"

5. "A Girl In A Million"

6. "I Get High (Dylan's Mistake)"

7. "I Won't Be Late Again"

8. "I'm Changing My Scene"

9. "In Love For The First Time"

10. "(It's So Hard) Loving You"

11. "(I've Imagined) I'm In Love With You"

1. "Got To Get You Into My Life"
("Another road where maybe I can see another kind of mind there.")

2. "Goodnight"
("Dream sweet dreams for me.")

3. "Blackbird"

4. "Ob-la-di, Ob-la-da"
("Desmond says to Molly - girl I like your face.")

5. "I'm A Loser"
("She was a girl in a million, my friend.")

6. "I Want To Hold Your Hand"
(The title, "I Get High (Dylan's Mistake)," is a reference to the Beatles' second meeting with Bob Dylan, 28 August 1964 at New York's Delmonico Hotel. During their visit (reportedly the occasion the Beatles were introduced to marijuana), Dylan mistakenly interpreted the line in "I Want To Hold Your Hand" that ends with "I can't hide, I can't hide, I can't hide" as "I get high, I get high, I get high.")

7. "I've Got A Feeling"
("And if you leave me, I won't be late again.")

8. "Getting Better"
("Man I was mean, but I'm changing my scene.")

9. "Don't Let Me Down"
("I'm in love for the first time.")

10. "It's Only Love"
("But it's so hard loving you.")

11. "I'll Get You"

("I've imagined I'm in love with you, many, many, many times before.")

12. "Misery"
("I've lost her now for sure, I won't see her no more.")

13. "I'm Only Sleeping"

14. "It's All Too Much"
("Floating down the stream of time, from life to life with me.")

15. "Sun King"

16. "Ask Me Why"
("Now you're mine, my happiness still makes me cry.")

17. "The Fool On The Hill"
(The title "Posthuma's Atop The Mound" is a reference to Simon Posthuma, a member of "The Fool," the artists/clothes designers most noted among Beatle fans for their association with the Apple Boutique. According to Pete Shotton, in his book *John Lennon: In My Life*, Posthuma took offense at "The Fool On The Hill." According to a biography statement printed in 1969, "The Fool" "...symbolizes the truth, spiritual memory, and the circle, which expresses the universal circumference in which gravitates all things.")

18. "The Night Before"

19. "For You Blue"
("Because you're sweet and lovely girl, it's true.")

20. "There's A Place"

21. "If I Fell"
("And that she will cry when she learns we are two.")

22. "All You Need Is Love"
("Nothing you can say but you can learn how to play the game.")

23. "Strawberry Fields Forever"
("That is, you know you can't tune in but it's all right.")

24. "I'll Cry Instead"
   ("And when I do you better hide all the girls.")

25. "Honey Pie"
   ("Come and show me the magic of your Hollywood song.")

Q & A #1

CHAPTER 50

TELL ME WHAT YOU SEE

To quote a certain Mr. McCartney before he spread his Wings into "Spin It On": "This is it." Our tantalizing trivia tour concludes with a puzzling picture quiz.

I've always enjoyed being challenged by Beatles trivia, whether it be Bill King's annual trivia quiz in "Beatlefan" (dey's tuff!), or Beatlefest's "Beatletrivia Quiz." I have fond memories of the latter quizzes, filling up my free moments back in my hotel room long after midnight. The following day, between special guests or films in the main ballroom, I'd be haunting the flea market stalls, consulting books and records for those last elusive answers.

I hope you've found your excursion into Beatles trivia to be both entertaining and informative. My aim was to make this book a quality "fix" for hardcore and first-time fans alike, and not just some quick cash-in on the Beatles.

Thanks again for buying me book, it was very handy. From one Nutopian ambassador to another (all rise for the white flag), here's hoping you'll find your butcher sleeve under a steamer trunk copy of **"Yesterday"...and Today** for 99 cents.

John Lennon Lives On!

Mike Hockinson
Vancouver, WA

1. ◀ This picture of the Beatles, from the Melvin Records bootleg pictured on page 18 (top), previously appeared on what legitimate Beatles record release?

2. I say! This chap first showed up on which Beatles album sleeve?

3. On which Beatles solo album has this rather clownish looking chap been previously noted?

4. This rather graphic scene was taken from which Beatle solo album?

5. This photo compilation was used as the back of the picture sleeve for the Beatles' first single of 1967, "Strawberry Fields Forever" b/w "Penny Lane." Which Beatle is which in these cute baby snaps?

1 2

3 4

6. What is the significance of this symbol to a sharp-eyed John and Yoko fan?

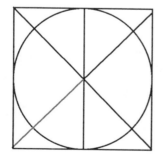

7.   Sponsored by radio station WAYX, this was the scene in Waycross, Georgia, one night in August 1966 following John's infamous (and misquoted) "We're more popular than Jesus" remark. In a slightly modified form, this photograph became the album sleeve for one of this noted rock group's LP's. Name this group, whose leader John once referred to as "Sodd Runtlestuntle," and give the title of the album that made use of this picture.

8. How many Beatles records, issued in both the U.S. and the U.K., have used this autumnal set photograph of the Beatles as part of the sleeve's artwork?

9. What is John wearing around his neck?

In the next ten questions, you will see some well-known "Beatles" logos. To correctly answer each query, you must identify the place of origin for each logo.

10.

Beatles

11.

Beatles

12.

13.

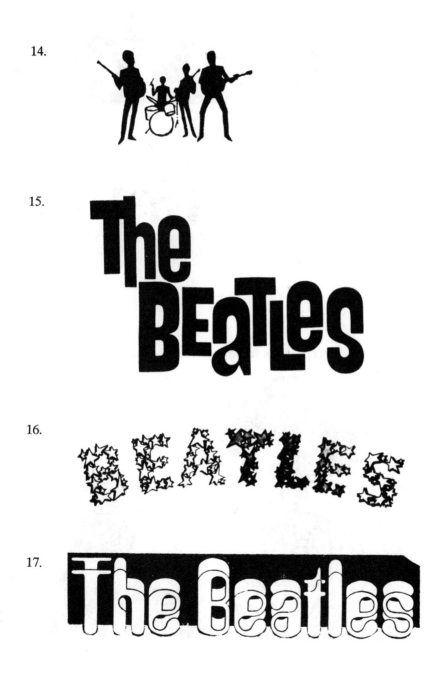

14.

15.

16.

17.

18.

19.

20. Where can the stone busts for this lovely couple be found?

21. What can you make of this star-dominated logo, Beatle people?

TM

22. **While the gentlemen in the picture below bear a striking resem-**blance to Bob Dylan, Jeff Lynne, Tom Petty, Roy Orbison and George Harrison, these are in fact merely aliases covering the true identities of the Traveling Wilburys. Can you assign the correct name that each of the Wilbury brothers goes by?

23. ▶ Ooh, what a giveaway! The top drawing of George on this picture sleeve (see page 370) was obviously borrowed from Klaus Voormann's cover for **Revolver** (note the "ER"), but who drew the updated portrait of Mr. Harrison below it?

24. What is the significance of this Beatle-related symbol?

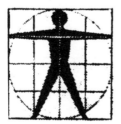

GEORGE HARRISON

ER

WHEN
WE
WAS
FAB

Q & A #23

25. Where did early Beatle fans first spot this primitive-looking gentleman?

26. Frequently photographed adorning the hats and lapels of Beatles in 1967, where did this yellow submarine button originate?

27. Aside from the **Ringo** LP, on what other post-Beatle album sleeve can one spot Ringo's short, moustachioed angel friend?

28.   What is the significance of this guitar-playing monk?

29.   Where did this tasty pastry first appear?

30.   Where is this picture of our heroes, outstanding in their field, more readily recognizable?

```
┌─────────────────────────────┐
│   TELL ME WHAT YOU SEE      │
│       (ANSWERS)             │
└─────────────────────────────┘
```

1.   Melvin's fisheye lens photograph of the Beatles, taken during their Miami Beach press conference, 13 February 1964, had earlier showed up on the cover of **Revolver.**

(An uncropped version of this photo, which also pictures Beatles press officer Brian Sommerville, originally accompanied an article by Al Aronowitz printed in the 21 March 1964 issue of "The Saturday Evening Post.")

2.   The moustachioed gentlemen in question can be seen on first pressing copies of Vee-Jay's "copulation" **Jolly What! The Beatles And Frank Ifield On Stage.**

3.   This is a detail from the painting by George Harrison used for the cover of his Zapple release **Electronic Sounds.**

4.   This drawing was used on the cover of John and Yoko's **Some Time In New York City** album to illustrate the lyrics to "Woman Is The Nigger Of The World."

5.   1. John
      2. George
      3. Paul
      4. Ringo

6.   This symbol (circa 1971) was Yoko's logo as it appeared on a plastic box containing rubber stamps of animal footprints and human handprints.

7.   The photograph of the Waycross, Georgia, Beatle-record burners graces the front of Utopia's 1982 Bearsville album **Swing To The Right.**

8.   This Robert Freeman photo of the Beatles at London's Hyde Park graces the back cover of the U.K. LP **Beatles For Sale.** In the U.S., this photo was used as the front cover photograph for Capitol's album **The Early Beatles,** as well as on the picture sleeve for the single "Nowhere Man" b/w "What Goes On."

Q & A #3

Q & A #4

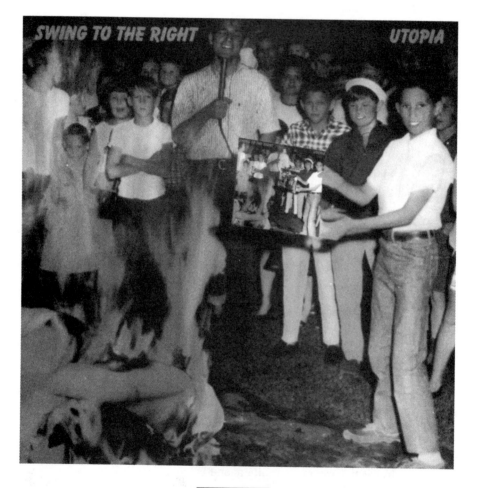

Q & A #7

(A collection of Freeman's Beatle photographs was published in 1983 by Holt, Rinehart and Winston under the title *Yesterday - The Beatles, 1963-1965.*)

9.   John is wearing a mandala around his neck in this **Two Virgins** cover shot.
(The circles comprising a mandala represent the cosmos, or all that is of order. Each of these circles is representative of a deity or of a characteristic attributed to that deity.)

10.   This "Beatles" logo was originally part of the headline "Beatles Top Poll!," featured on the 4-18 January 1962 issue of Bill Harry's "Mersey Beat" newspaper.

11.   This "Beatles" "B" antennae logo was the group's bass drum logo, circa 1962.
(Designed by Terry "Tex" O'Hara, this logo was later adopted for use by the Official Beatles Fan Club.)

12.   This logo was the Beatles' bass drum logo, circa 1963.

13.   The cover of "The Beatles Book" is the source for this Beatles logo.

14.   The four Beatles in silhouette was first used by the Official Beatles Fan Club as a part of their letterhead.
(A feature of the stationery currently in use by the Japanese Beatles Fan Club, this logo also graced the early covers of "Beatlefan" magazine.)

15.   The U.S. version of the movie soundtrack album for "A Hard Day's Night" features this "Beatles" logo on the sleeve's back cover. This logo was also used on posters and as a part of ads promoting the film.

16.   The starred "Beatles" logo was first seen on the front sleeve of the **Magical Mystery Tour** album and EP.

17.   This computer-style "Beatles" logo is taken from the front sleeve for the **Yellow Submarine** album.

18.   This "Beatles" logo is from the back cover of the **Abbey Road** album.

(To those who follow the Paul is dead rumor, the crack in the "S" in "Beatles" is a death clue; the crack signified that the group was no longer perfect.)

19.   This "Beatles" logo was created by Capitol for their 1987 releases of the Beatles' digitally remastered British albums on CD. This logo appears on the front of all Capitol CD long boxes save the White Album.

20.   The antique stone bust on the right is taken from the cover of **Sgt. Pepper,** while the hatted bust on the left is from the cover of the **Hey Jude/The Beatles Again** album.
(John provided Peter Blake and Jann Haworth with the bust used on the cover of "Pepper." This bust was the basis for Blake's portrait of Sgt. Pepper seen on the album's insert sheet of cut-outs.)

21.   The white star on a field of red and blue was the logo for Lenono Music.
(Lenono Music albums include **Double Fantasy** and **The John Lennon Collection.** After John's death, this logo was used for Ono Music albums, including **Milk and Honey, Every Man Has A Woman,** and **Starpeace.**)

22.   The Traveling Wilburys are: Lucky (Bob Dylan), Otis (Jeff Lynne), Charlie T. Jnr. (Tom Petty), Lefty (Roy Orbison), and Nelson (George Harrison).

23.   The updated drawing of George on the "When We Was Fab" picture sleeve is also credited to Klaus O.W. Voormann.

24.   This symbol was the logo for the "Our World" television special, broadcast 25 June 1967.

25.   This caveman appeared, not in advertisements for Ringo's "Caveman" movie, but in newspaper ad copy and on posters advertising the Cavern club.

26.   The "Workshop of Non-Violence," headquartered in New York, gave the Beatles their yellow submarine buttons.

27.   Ringo's angel friend can also be seen on the first U.K. issue of **The Best of George Harrison** album.
(George is wearing a tee-shirt on which this angel is displayed.)

28. This guitar-playing monk, included in the artwork on several of George's albums, is the logo for his Friar Park Studio, Henley-On-Thames (F.P.S.H.O.T.).

29. This sandwich - contents unknown - appears on issues of Paul's newsletter "Club Sandwich."

30. This picture of the Beatles on the grounds of Tittenhurst is from the front sleeve of the **Hey Jude/The Beatles Again** album.

Q & A #30

Song & Record Title Index

391

PERSONAL & GROUP NAME INDEX

417

Wings
52, 55, 58, 91, 113, 124, 126, 141,
143, 146, 148, 167, 168, 170, 171,
172, 205, 208, 225, 273, 361
Winkler, Henry
127, 131
Winnie
115, 117
Witkowski, Rick
264
Wittaker, Roger
48
Wolfe, Tom
194, 311
Wom, Barry
25
Wonder, Stevie
58, 68, 152, 155
Wood, Georgie
6
Wooler, Bob
103, 110, 176
Wrangle, Bernard Mickey
317
Wycherley, Ronald
57

The Yardbirds
48
Yarrow, Peter
269
Yogananda, Paramahansa
187, 315
Yoni, Okay
115, 117
Young, Roy
107
Zappa, Frank
89, 293
Zeffirelli, Franco
125
Zemeckis, Robert
292
Zimmerman, Robert Allen
see also
Dylan, Bob
Zimmerman, Robert Allen
224
Zwerling, Andy
234, 237
Zwerling, Leslie
234, 237

PLACES & THINGS

INDEX

426

430

Date
Index

"And that was a
Magical Mystery Tour.
I told ya.
Goodbye."

ABOUT THE AWFUL

I was bored on the 26th of Octuduleiber 1960, in Vancouver, Washing-tongue. I was razed for the most particle in Wenatchee, Washaton, where varicose schools passed befour mine eyes befive granulation.

Afflicted with second (talkin' bout my) degeneration Beatlessmania since the year of our Ford, 1972 (which Nickleless Shatner's nose is incurareable), I'm curly a cordespondent for "Beatlefan" magazion with freelunching on the slide.

I'm back in Vancooter after Some Time In Attalanta, GEE-AYE, where moist of this boot was wrotten.